THE RICH AND THE POOR
Jewish Philanthropy and Social Control in
Nineteenth-Century London

In Memory
of my Parents
Hava *née* Kohn
and Joseph Rozin

The Rich and the Poor

*Jewish Philanthropy and Social Control
in Nineteenth-Century London*

Mordechai Rozin

sussex
ACADEMIC
PRESS

Brighton • Portland

2 4 6 8 10 9 7 5 3

First published 1999 in Great Britain by
SUSSEX ACADEMIC PRESS
Box 2950
Brighton BN2 5SP

and in the United States of America by
SUSSEX ACADEMIC PRESS
5804 N.E. Hassalo St.
Portland, Oregon 97213-3644

British Library Cataloguing in Publication Data
A CIP catalogue record for this book is available from the British Library.

Library of Congress Cataloging-in-Publication Data
Rozin, Mordechaj.
The rich and the poor : Jewish philanthropy and social control in nineteenth-century London / Mordechai Rozin.
p.   cm.
Includes bibliographical references and index.
ISBN 1–898723 79 6 (h/c : alk. paper)
1. Jewish Board of Guardians (London, England) —History—19th century.   2. Jews—England—London—Charities—History—19th century   3. Working class Jews—Services for—England—London—History—19th century.   4. Immigrants—Services for—England—London—History—19th century.   5. Elite (Social sciences)—England—London—History—19th century.   6. Social control—England—London—History—19th century.   7. London (England) —Emigration and immigration—Social aspects.   I. Title.
HV3193.G7R69   1999
361.7'089'924—dc21   98-43070
CIP

Printed by Biddles Ltd, Guildford and King's Lynn
This book is printed on acid-free paper

Contents

Foreword

This promises to be a pathbreaking study in two key respects. First, it can help inform an international Jewish audience as to more of the nature and contradictions of Jewish philanthropy with reference to nineteenth-century London (over a period when that city was crucial to the movement of Jewish migrants from eastern Europe to 'better places else'), than has hitherto been demonstrated to comparable authoritative, scholarly effect. Second, it should add significantly to the understanding of the nature and dynamics of philanthropy per se, not least for the benefit of audiences schooled in conventional accounts of the Victorian origins of the British welfare state.

Much has been written about the reception afforded to the *New Jews* arriving in Britain *en masse* from eastern Europe, from the 1870s onwards; just as there has been much written about the eventual reception of some of the onward migrants (along with others who had sailed there direct) in New York. Most such accounts have had something 'modestly critical' to say about the manner and extent to which respective local Jewish élites responded to the arrival of such needy Jewish strangers in their midst; given the pronounced sensitivity of such élites to the effect continuing influxes of 'primitive' co-religionists might have on their own hard-won positions and prospects as *established* minorities poised for integration into the body social as well as politic.

Mordechai Rozin's account reaches way beyond and beneath such conventional wisdoms. By his reckoning, the behaviours of Jewish co-religionists in London had more to do with divisions of class than solidarities of religion - which were themselves divided in any case between former predominantly *Sephardic* and latterday *Ashkenazic* spheres of influence. Significantly, his account of Jewish charitable endeavour (and repeated 'missed-endeavour') starts from well before the onset of mass late-nineteenth-century 'New Jewish' immigration into London's East End. He thus sets the charitable scene, to an extent

---

no other study has done, into which the latterday newcomers were to be received. It is not an altogether nice story. But then what honest account of charitable/philanthopric endeavour and its multiple motives ever is? Conceivably the greatest service Mordechai Rozin will have performed in retrospect, for the record, is to have demonstrated to relevant Jewish and (in this case) other relevant British audiences, just how much they have had in common.

Some of this commonality of thinking and involvement was explicit and acknowledged at the time by leading exponents of both 'English' and Jewish charitable/philanthropic endeavour, as Rozin's account makes clear. Much less in evidence - and less to be expected - was any sign of common thinking let alone action openly linking the Jewish with the English poor in their protests. (Even the Irish poor - devoid as they were of any local intermediary élite - seemed better at forging such base-level native alliances; a subject worth further research in itself.)

This is not the book to end all discussion about the nature of altruism or solidarity or philanthropy, interesting though the author's observations are in this regard. Rather, this is the book to make hitherto 'innocents' and/or actual policy makers think again about how real people might be driven to react, at both ends - the rich and the poor - of a doubly unequal situation. But it is also, above all, the book for people who simply want to know how it was for poor Jews in nineteenth-century London.

Catherine Jones Finer
Reader in Comparative Social Policy
University of Birmingham

Preface and Acknowledgements

The purpose of this historical research is to discover new facts by tracing the development of the theory, practice and institutionalization of the social control and paternalizing mechanisms as had been intended in different schemes or implemented by the Jewish élite through its phil-anthropic institutions in regard to the poor and working class immigrants, mostly from eastern Europe, during the whole of the nineteenth century.

As reflected in Jewish history, helping the poor was and remained one of the most appealing and cherished values based on the assumption that such help had generally functioned satisfactorily.

The humanitarian implications of philanthropy are here discussed and tested in the light of the contrasting class interests of the rapidly acculturated Ashkenazic Anglo-Jewish élite which, in its pursuit of wealth, social status and political power in the host community, severely neglected the poor.

There was a conspicuous disparity between the rich, characterized by extreme, exclusive élitism and anti-democratic aristocracy, and the large number of poor who eked out their precarious living in the over-crowded and unsanitary Jewish East End.

Aloof from the poor and encouraged by its achievements, the Jewish élite had embraced Benthamism, Smilesianism, Social Darwinism and economic theories associated with laissez-faire as a basis for the policy of its philanthropic institutions.

The narrowness of these doctrines and the influence of the harsh Poor Law of 1834 and of the COS, which emphasized personal responsibility of the individual for his economic situation, are particularly reflected in the activities of the London Jewish Board of Guardians – the key insti-tution of the élite for controlling and regulating the poor.

The encounter between the more conscious Jewish working class and the élite and the survival of the Jewish Board of Guardians through incrementalism and gradualism, as well as the avoidance of a more radical communal split, have been analysed.

I would like to thank the Research Authority and the Schwartz Foundation, Faculty of Social Sciences of the Bar-Ilan University, Ramat Gan, Israel for their support. I should also like to thank a number of people who have given me help and assistance with this work. First I wish to acknowledge my debt and gratitude to Mr Stewart Miller for his wise counsel and support. I would like to thank the Jewish Welfare Board for permitting me to use archival material. Many thanks are due to my typist, Mrs Rosemary Tomlin of Swan Secretarial Services, for her devoted work and to Miss Christine Swan for her kindness and help. I could never have completed this study without the encouragement and tolerance of my wife, Gila.

The author and publisher gratefully acknowledge the following for permission to reproduce copyright material:

Yale University Press, New Haven and London, for permission to reproduce chapters VII, IX and X from *The Code of Maimonides, Book 7: The Book of Agriculture*, translated from the Hebrew by Isaac Klein, Rabbi Emeritus, first published 1979; *The Illustrated London News*, for permission to reproduce pictures of Baron Rothschild's New Mansion, Piccadilly, and The Sunday Trading Question – a sketch in Petticot Lane; and the Chief Librarian, Leeds University Library, for permission to reproduce MS Roth 243 – part of the text of a 'Plan for ameliorating the conditions and improving the habits of the lower order of the Jews in London', Joshua van Oven, London 1802.

The publishers apologize for any errors or omissions in the above list and would be grateful to be notified of any corrections that should be incoporated in the next edition or reprint of this book.

Abbreviations

————

The following abbreviations are used throughout the text:

BGAR   London Jewish Board of Guardians' Annual Report.
BGHYR   London Jewish Board of Guardians' Half Yearly Report.
BGMBEC   London Jewish Board of Guardians' Minutes Book of Executive Committee.
BGMSC   London Jewish Board of Guardians' Minutes of Sanitary Committee, 1885–1911.
BGMB   London Jewish Board of Guardians' Minutes Book.
BGLB   London Jewish Board of Guardians' Letter Box.
COS   Charity Organisation Society.
Encycl. Jud.   Encyclopaedia Judaica, Jerusalem, Keter, 1971-2.
JC   *Jewish Chronicle.*
JHSE   Jewish Historical Society of England.
JJS   *Jewish Journal of Sociology.*
JSS   Jewish Social Studies.
SPCJ   Society for Promoting Christianity among the Jews.
TJHSE   Transactions of the Jewish Historical Society of England.
VJ   *Voice of Jacob.*

Plan for ameliorating the condition[s] [and]
improving the habits of the lower [order]
of the Jews in London

That part of the Jewish Nation who are at pres[ent]
resident in England comprise a Body of considerable Ma[gnitude]
within the last fifty Years their numbers have considera[bly]
increased; and among these there is a very great pro[portion]
who are in very indigent circumstances.

While it is admitted that the laws of t[he]
Realm are in most instances sufficient for regulating
general economy in common with the other subjects [of]
His Majesty, it has been long felt as an Evil of great
Magnitude by the respectable part of the Jews that
the poor of this community have an equal Right with
other Classes, to parochial relief while in distress, yet
peculiar Circumstances of their religious Rites a[nd]
diet effectually shut them out of all Workhouses a[nd]
the same cause not only deprives them of the benefit
availing themselves of medical Aid as it is admin[istered]
in Hospitals when in sickness, but also precludes
Children of Jews from being bound out to Mechanic[al]
and other Employments by which they might be
enabled to become useful Members of the State [as]
Artisans and Handicrafts.

Under these peculiar Circumstances
has become a desideratum on the part of the hig[her]
Classes, that part of the Jewish Nation who ha[ve]

MS Roth 243 – part of the text of a 'Plan for ameliorating the conditions and improving the habits of the lower order of the Jews in London', Joshua van Oven, London 1802.

Introduction

During the nineteenth century the London Jewish Ashkenazic congregations, like many other Jewish communities in the Diaspora, were dominated by an autocratic oligarchic élite – one of the wealthiest and most powerful in the world. This cohesive élite, known as the Cousinhood, moved gradually from the East End to the West End then out to homes in the country, leaving the poor behind.

Throughout this period there was no governmental administration regulating the entry of aliens into Great Britain. The Ashkenazic élite was faced with elements of the westward migration of destitute East European Jews, in spite of a variety of 'voluntary' efforts to prevent, stop or divert it. Between fifteen and seventeen thousand Jews lived in London in 1800. This number grew gradually to over sixty thousand by 1880 and dramatically to one hundred and eighty-six thousand by 1914, due primarily to waves of immigration following severe persecution in Eastern Europe.

The large-scale immigration, concentrated in the East End, broadly coincided with the growth of an impoverished Jewish proletariat working in 'sweated' conditions in the consumer goods industry. Strange in their appearance, the newcomers were perceived by the native élite as backward, unenlightened and amoral – an endless stream of inferior Jews who imposed themselves on the resources of the native élite. Feeling that as a minority it would be judged by its lowest representatives, the élite feared that the immigrants would jeopardize its economic and social position in the host community.

The purpose of this book is to present an analysis of Jewish philanthropy in London during the nineteenth century in its larger socioeconomic, political, ideological and religious context, and to assess the adequacy of the philanthropic policy and activity of the Jewish élite in handling the extensive social problems created by continuous immigration.

The conceptual framework adopted is related to the broader class interests of the élite rather than merely to unified ethnic Jewish collective experience or religious and cultural identities. This is based on the proposition that philanthropic activities concealed motives rooted in class conflict and class aspirations. This framework is also related to the meanings given by the élite to its interests, and the ways in which the interests of the poor were perceived by the élite.

An attempt is made to identify the different forms and aspects of social control and patronage exercised through the Jewish Board of Guardians (hereinafter known as the "Board") and other institutions established by the Jewish élite over the poor Jewish class, and initiatives of that class to create alternative social organizations of its own. Such controlling mechanisms were an organic part of the function of the élite's philanthropic institutions and were designed and continuously directed to enforce upper-class interests throughout the nineteenth century.

The development of these institutions did not evolve in a cause/effect process resulting in a beneficial sequence but were rather the result of complex interactive class interests, individual influence, events, conflicts and policy decisions. What stands out is the adoption of individualistic and laissez-faire ideologies by the élite so that it could implement and justify its policy of social control.

The aim of this book is to present historical evidence of those often conflicting interactions in their overt, subtle and intricate forms, to analyze and explain them. It is also important to identify the functions of philanthropy, defined as collective action involving the donation of possessions for the sake of the combined interests of the élite as a group, regardless of the personal contributions of its individual members. Those functions included amongst others: the manipulation of moral arguments, consideration of economy, discouraging immigration and the subsequent drain on the Board's resources by deterring measures, instilling discipline and the regulation of the labour market by the temporary provision of absolutely minimal assistance. The undertaking of these regulatory obligations by the élite was necessitated by the limitation of laissez-faire, as a dogma that could never be fully implemented in practice.

Vivian Lipman's 1959 study, *A Century of Social Service: The Jewish Board of Guardians, 1859–1959*, was published at the centenary anniversary of the Board as an official history on behalf of the Jewish Welfare Board. Much attention was paid by Lipman to technical details in the development of the Board which are significant, and as such, are thankfully acknowledged. Having already been presented, they will not be repeated here.

Adopting a consensual approach, Lipman portrayed the relationship between the wealthy and powerful élite who led the Board and the poor Jewish immigrants as largely free of conflict. Although Lipman generally recognizes the adoption of Victorian models by the Board, minimal consideration is given in his account to the content of the Board's social philosophies and the distress caused by them to the Jewish poor. The successes of philanthropy were seen as self-justification for the Board, while its failures were denied.

This book tells the other side of the story – the growth of bitter social divisions within the Jewish community in London. Instances of disputes and grievances are discussed in terms of the precise nature of the problems, and what was done, or was planned in order to resolve them. The conflicts hidden behind the rhetoric of nobility and apparent harmony attributed to the voluntaristic and philanthropic enterprises, and the split between them are addressed in terms of the social reality of the period. The book is concerned with how class conflicts affected philanthropy and how they became embedded in the institutions vital to the welfare of the Jewish poor. Such evidence of class antagonisms is analyzed historically. Special emphasis is placed on the continuous effort of the élite to control the immigration of the Jewish poor and to prevent the establishment of alternative social services by the immigrants themselves.

The Jewish élite had a number of concerns:

• They were preoccupied with accumulating wealth and political power in the host community.
• They feared the Jewish poor would undermine the conditions under which their economic and social activities could continue undisturbed.
• They sought a physical separation from the concentration of Jewish poor in the East End.
• They wished to promote political conservatism, fearing radical social change.
• They feared collectivism, democracy and collaboration with the Jewish poor, immigrants and the working class.

For the Jewish élite, the non-Jewish environment and the models of non-Jewish philanthropy and social welfare became increasingly important, as reflected in different schemes designed to control and reform the Jewish poor. Only by the mid-nineteenth century did Jewish philanthropy, led by the Jewish élite, emerge from its separate existence, in the establishment of the Jewish Board of Guardians in 1859.

The optional and voluntary nature of Jewish philanthropy in England during the nineteenth century generally served the élite's best interests. Mandatory taxation of the Jewish wealthy and middle classes, intended to overcome the inherent limitations in providing the funds needed for assisting the Jewish poor at the beginning of the nineteenth century, was proposed by Patrick Colquhoun and Joshua van Oven on behalf of the Ashkenazic élite. The initiative for this scheme followed severe social disorganization and consequent criticism in the host community. However, the élite did not have sufficient motivation to finalize the implementation of the scheme, nor was such a proposal presented again. In the final analysis the élite was basically interested in financing Jewish philanthropy on a voluntary basis, without accepting legal obligations and the corollary accountability to the state. Rather, the Jewish élite preferred to provide for the Jewish poor and control them in a quasi-official framework. This arrangement permitted the Anglo-Jewish élite to develop elaborate checks and balances in order to control its expenditure and involvement according to its vital interests. It was also intended to deter continuous immigration. Such a framework represented the deliberate choice of a middle way between selective philanthropic concern on the one hand and laissez-faire and indifference on the other.

The deliberate use of the built-in free-market mechanism of 'destructive filtration' can be regarded as contradictory to the Jewish traditional *tzedakah*. The controlling and regulating mechanism used by the London Jewish élite during the nineteenth century was generally a secularized form of philanthropy, strongly influenced by laissez-faire and individualistic doctrines. In spite of the overwhelming prosperity of the Jewish élite and the well-to-do bourgeois class, fears were continuously expressed that an influx of needy immigrants would pauperize the community.

During the great immigration and polarization of the East End versus the West End, a period in which the voices of the poor were heard with increased regularity, the philanthropy of the Jewish élite was continuously denounced as parsimonious and bureaucratic as reflected in the inadequate relief given to the mass of Jewish poor during periods of unemployment, sickness, etc. An exception to this were some limited categories of poor considered deserving, who then received more adequate assistance.

The élite used various checks and balances to reduce its expenses for the Jewish poor, which resulted in the elementary needs of the poor remaining unfulfilled until the state developed a more pro-active role in the socioeconomic sphere and extended its embrace to include the well-being of the élite's poorer co-religionists. As the state assumed more collectivist responsibilities, the Jewish élite, through the Board, attempted to extend the mandatory responsibilities of the government and municipalities to the Jewish poor and to immigrants. The Jewish élite embarked on a prolonged dialogue with the statutory authorities to enshrine in law the rights of Jews to mandatory support and in this way to shift a significant part of its own financial burden to the public supported systems and the poor rates. Intensive efforts were made by the Board to adapt one or more of the unions' workhouses to Jewish religious requirements for those who were defined by them as 'incorrigible cases' and also serve as a deterrent for certain groups of immigrants. Later we shall explore the consequences of these processes on the poor.

Another issue considered is the political challenge presented to the Jewish élite by the poor working class, greatly enlarged by constant immigration, and concentrated in the East End. A significant influence stemmed from the doctrines of class conflict propagated by the socialist and anarchist movements, largely imported from eastern Europe. In spite of the internal divergences amongst them, they unanimously claimed that the Jewish poor were deliberately held in ignorance. Not having the required resources to establish significant alternatives to the services created by the Board over a quarter of a century, the Jewish working class increasingly agitated to become involved in the decision-making process of the Board.

The endurance of the Board under the domination of the élite is explained by the fact that the poor lacked the resources needed to establish an alternative to the Board, and the abilities of the wealthy members of the élite to subsidize some semi-independent organization of the working class in the East End. Mediation of the Jewish upper–middle class and the pragmatic incremental approach of the Jewish élite were instrumental in the avoidance of a more divisive split between the rich and the poor.

The first seventy years of the nineteenth century have been largely neglected by scholars. Poverty and other severe social problems were common throughout the century among the native, as well as the immigrant Jewish community in London, which had the largest population in Britain and absorbed most of the immigrants. Moreover, immigration was a continuous, though fluctuating, feature of this period.

There was a recurrent spiral pattern in the approach of the Jewish élite towards the poor. The processes, which manifested themselves fully after the beginning of mass immigration, were an intensification of the substantive problems that were evident in the first half of the nineteenth century and continued on a more deliberate and official basis after the establishment of the Jewish Board of Guardians in 1859.

The restrictionist approach of the Jewish élite with regard to immigration during a period when British society was generally apathetic about this problem will be discussed. The test imposed by the poor immigrants upon the élite is considered in light of their voluntary demographic concentration in the East End and the traditional ways of life created there for generations. As well, their separateness from the wealthy class, was continuously reinforced by the traditions brought over by new waves of immigrants.

OUTLINE OF THE BOOK

Chapter 1 discusses certain treatises of social theorists relevant to some Jewish philanthropic and solidarity ideologies, as well as some attempts to test such expositions in the historical context of the practical decisions taken by Jewish individuals and groups in a distinctive Jewish traditional community. This chapter includes a critical review of material related to philanthropy by historians of the Jews in England during the period under discussion, and introduces the social structure of the Anglo-Jewish London community at the end of the eighteenth century and the first part of the nineteenth century. It illustrates the patterns of poverty, its causes, the importance of social structure and contemporary models of philanthropy and welfare in determining attitudes towards the poor and their problems.

Chapter 2 deals with the Colquhoun–van Oven Scheme for a Jewish communal poor law, presented in 1802 and based on the detailed, critical accounts of Patrick Colquhoun, a metropolitan magistrate, on what was presented as widespread Jewish criminality. His work was published in 1797 as *A Treatise on the Police of the Metropolis*. This ambitious scheme for social and police control over the poor was intended to be introduced to Parliament as a bill, but never passed beyond its incipient stage.

The scheme reflects the direct involvement of Colquhoun and the influence of his utilitarian philosophy as well as that of Jeremy Bentham

(1748–1832), his close friend and associate, on Joshua van Oven, a surgeon and leading figure in the Anglo-Jewish Enlightenment, as well as a communal worker and representative of the élite in social and educational matters.

This chapter shows that the failure of this scheme was related to resistance encountered by other attempts of Bentham and Colquhoun to implement similar ideas on the British scene, stemming from the opposition and suspicion of the wealthy British class to centralized governmental interventions and the delegation of corporative power during this period.

The educational arrangements for the poor are covered in chapter 3. At the very beginning of the nineteenth century those arrangements hardly affected the children of poor immigrants and the least Anglicized poor, who were in the most acute need of education. Later, during the nineteenth century, the establishment of the Jews' Free School (1817) represented the most concentrated effort of the Jewish élite to help the younger generations of the poor to escape poverty. The rapid increase in the rate of enrollment proves the extent of the previously unsatisfied needs in this area.

This chapter discusses the patterns of poor relief provided by the synagogues, the severe defects in its distribution, its inadequacy, and the neglect of the poor by a Jewish élite very much preoccupied with its struggle for political emancipation. It also deals with the characteristics of the newly formed Jewish philanthropic institutions, not necessarily connected with the synagogues and somewhat secularized. The initiatives of the poor in response to their unmet needs, as reflected by the inadequacy of the relief provided them, as well as their vital need for institutional care are also covered. It was Roth's opinion that 'to some extent the poor Jewish immigrant of the East End suffered and paid the price for the prominence enjoyed by his plutocratic co-religionists' (Roth 1961: 291).

Chapter 3 also describes and analyzes the extensive, however abortive, scheme of Henry Faudel. The class basis of his planning and the doctrines that influenced his frame of reference are examined. The preferences of the élite during the 1840s, as discussed in this chapter, can explain the postponement of the implementation of some elements of Faudel's scheme until the establishment of the Jewish Board of Guardians in 1859.

Chapter 4 explains the causes that influenced the establishment of the Jewish Board of Guardians, its organizational structure and centralized bureaucratic system. The Board did not strike out in a novel direction, but rather followed secularized ideas consolidated in the theory and practice of the voluntary and mandatory arrangements in Great Britain during the first half of the nineteenth century. As shown in the chapter, the Board regarded itself as rooted in the bedrock of Judaism; however, it did not develop a synthesis between the obvious influences of contemporary trends and the traditional ways of Jewish charity. The individualistic and other contemporary doctrines and models that were adopted by the Board through temporization are discussed. The tactics that both served and perpetuated the implementation of its ideological perspective are explored. The Board had been the symbol of the élite's beneficent patronage, its efficient mechanism of control and supreme domination over the poor. Backed by the continuous economic success of its oligarchic leaders in the host society, its self-righteousness and excessive pride in its accomplishments, the Board was characterized by a strong confidence in its intentions, policies and methods of implementation.

It also focuses on the significant issue of immigration which continuously faced the Jewish élite to different degrees. The Board considered any immigrant who would burden its financial resources as undesirable, but it could not legally prohibit immigration. The severe socioeconomic problems of the immigrants were perceived by the élite as dangerous to its reputation and to the conditions under which it could continue untrammeled economic and social activities. When such danger was felt, the élite was more motivated to active intervention, sometimes of a deterring and punitive character.

This chapter covers the struggle of the élite to make use of the unions' workhouses, to institute labour tests for the able-bodied Jewish poor, and to receive subventions from parochial authorities for outdoor relief. The intensive efforts in this area had preoccupied the élite and the Board for more than twenty years and to a large extent overshadowed all other philanthropic activities. The Jewish poor were reluctant to enter the workhouses. Members of the Jewish middle class bitterly resented such placements for the poor. This subsequently led them to establish an independent Jewish workhouse. Special attention is given to the contradictions in the statements of Board leaders in dealing with various aspects of the use of the unions' workhouses.

Chapter 5 considers the strategies and tactics of the élite to avoid, inasmuch as possible, the overburdening of its charitable funds. One strategy was to reduce allocations during increased waves of immigration. This continuous policy of the Board merged harmoniously with the contemporary doctrines of aggressive individualism and the legitimacy given to attempts to diminish social expenditure, which was regarded as getting out of control.

Chapter 5 also examines the provisions made by the Board for loans and work. The Board's policy as reflected in these two areas of allocation, demonstrated a preference for 'the better class of the poor'. The consequences of this policy are analyzed. After its establishment, the Board was motivated to institute medical services of its own and take over the medical relief which continued to be administered by the three City Synagogues that founded the Board. However, in view of the cost involved in such expansions, the leader of the Board shifted the burden back onto the tax supported parochial infirmaries and other voluntary medical institutions. With regard to the extremely severe housing conditions which affected the poor, the Board limited its responsibilities to sanitation. The chapter provides evidence that the élite was not ready to become involved in non-profit housing projects and did not respond to this collective need of the poor and of immigrants until the very end of the century, when it was more willing to moderate the discontent of the poor.

This chapter focuses on the efforts of the élite around the turn of the century to use the elementary school system, clubs and youth brigade to discipline the Jewish poor, condition them to be docile, punctual, and a clean and grateful workforce; and to accept their subordination to the communal leadership of the élite. The chapter makes reference to the Jewish press which, by and large, supported the élite's policies in their entirety, especially with regard to acculturation to the host environment.

This chapter also considers the arrangements and organizations initiated by the poor themselves or sometimes in cooperation with members of the middle class. The latter were characterized by more reciprocal notions of paternalism, traditional and personal ties. The chapter discusses the extensive attempts of the Board to control and coordinate the activities of the different Jewish philanthropic institutions according to its overall policies. Jewish immigrants were undergoing complex processes of proletarization and urbanization. By the end of the century they were divided into rival classes (including some pauper against pauper antagonisms). The mass immigration added a radical new dimension to the political structure. However, even earlier, from the 1870s onward, socialist leaders sought and found the support of Jewish workers.

It also discusses the persistence of the élite in maintaining the exclusiveness of its institutions, dominated for more than half a century by the same wealthy families. Such tenacity had created inequalities and mutual distrust for more than half a century. In spite of the remarkable increase of the working and poor Jewish classes and their relative independence, the élite continued to perceive them as dependants or retainers, and excluded them from the decision-making processes relevant to their lives. In this context the assistance offered by the Board continued to emphasize subordination to the wealthy class. In spite of the social changes in Great Britain which were an expression of more collectivist, egalitarian and democratic ideas, the Board remained authoritarian and estranged from the poor, perpetuating its power through paternalistic philanthropy. This chapter shows the ways in which the working class and the poor succeeded in exercising influence by creating their own alternative institutions, and how developments and events significant to those classes emerged. This process forced the élite to renounce some of its exclusive prerogatives. The compromises of the élite were made through an intermediary arriviste group of the élite, accompanied by some internal frictions. However, those tensions did not prevent the cohesive pursuit of the élite's primordial interests.

The book concludes with a chapter which synthesizes the strands of the arguments.

SOURCES

Some of the primary sources are the main schemes advanced for reforming the philanthropies of the Jewish élite at the very beginning of the nineteenth century as well as the reactions to them from different quarters. These have been preserved in pamphlet form. The works of Bentham and Colquhoun, containing their influential philosophies, have been in publication in various forms since the last quarter of the eighteenth century. The laws and regulations of the main Jewish charities have been obtained from the Mocatta Library, University College, London and the British Library. They give account of their policies and organization, including the voting system upon which many of them were founded. Nineteenth-century material dealing with Jewish as well as non-Jewish London charities in terms of their origin, philosophical bases and functions are reviewed in such contemporary periodicals as the *Monthly Magazine*, the *Quarterly Review* and the *Philanthropist*. Other relevant contemporary sources are the extensive reports on Jewish poverty by Henry Mayhew (1851–1862), J. H. Stallard (1867), whose superlative description of the Jewish Board of Guardians should be approached carefully, Beatrice Webb, née Potter (1858–1943) and Charles Booth (1891–1903). Further evidence has been gathered from the publications of the London missionary societies.

The proposal of Ephraim Alex (1800–1882) in a pamphlet entitled *A Scheme for a Board of Guardians to be formed for the relief of the necessitous foreign poor* (1859), has been preserved, as well as the Board's *Laws and Regulations – Orchim* (Heb. guests – a term that indicated 'foreign' poor); also in their revised and enacted form of AM 5627–1867. The Board published *Half Yearly Reports* from the time of its establishment in 1859 and successive *Annual Reports* from 1860 onward. The complete set of these reports are held in the archives of the London Jewish Welfare Board. They are a significant source of material for this book and were used as basic points of reference, especially with regard to the under-researched first twelve years of the Board's activities. Each one of these reports commences with a survey of the year's occurrences and developments, then explains and interprets them. In addition, each *Annual Report* contains detailed special reports of the Board's various departments. The minutes of the Executive Committee however, do not detail policy discussions. For that reason, they are less valuable than the reports written by the reporters of the *Jewish Chronicle* who gave many detailed descriptions, often almost verbatim, of the Board's official meetings. Old issues of the *Jewish Chronicle* are at the Collindale branch of the British Library and are important in the context of this study in spite of limitations in coverage (see Chapters 5 and 6). Board Minute Books, Minutes of the Sanitary Committee and Letter Boxes, as well as other material can be found in the Jewish Welfare Board's archives. Further evidence has been extracted from the memoirs of some 'self-made' middle-class immigrants who arrived penniless in London, and other biographies of members of the élite. Secondary works that reveal responses to the causes of poverty as perceived by members of the élite, of the Jewish middle classes and other social observers throughout the nineteenth century have been consulted and are used to illustrate and analyze the decision-making processes of the élite.

Obviously, the historical sources on which this book is based lack the voices of the poor, which were rarely recorded, as no case records or papers relating to the period researched appear to have survived. The 'begging letters', a method strongly opposed by the Board, have not been preserved in the archives. They disappeared almost without trace and were not quoted. Nor were any verbatim accounts reflecting the grievances and other expressions of the poor recorded in the detailed, ample Annual Reports and other commemorative publications. The absence of more direct expressions of the poor such as, their choices and opinions in the archival material can also be explained by their severe culture shock, often lack of the English language and adequate access to the Jewish press. Additional reasons were most probably related to their fear to complain and the overhelming impact of poverty, their preoccupation in obtaining the barest essentials required for their daily needs, long working hours in sweatshops, or their continuous search for work.

1

Jewish Philanthropy: Power and Interests

HISTORICAL PERSPECTIVES

In Judaism, as in many other denominational conceptualizations, there is no monolithic approach to dependence and poverty. The development of the Anglo-Jewish philanthropy in the nineteenth century and its corresponding ideologies and justifications can best be understood in the context of class tensions and conflicts. According to Mahler (1950), one hundred years after the democratic achievements of the French Revolution, most of the Jewish communities all over the world were still dominated by hierarchies of powerful wealthy men, a far cry from the political regime that was the vision of the Prophets. Mahler asked 'what is the advantage of boasting that we are the people of the Prophets and the inheritors of their ideas about social justice? All those explanations of the particular content and entity of our culture were advanced only to conceal the sad realities of the upper-class regime' (Mahler 1950: 253).

Mahler suggested that the Conservative movement disguises reactionary concepts opposed to the ideas of equity and social justice by presenting them as progressive, national or religious (p. 255). He regarded the protests of the Prophets and their uncompromising struggle against the oppression of the poor classes as an important Jewish national heritage of the biblical period that strongly influenced the Christian popular sects and religious social movements. Mahler criticized the automatic, superficial use of the prophetic ideals and the rationalistic movement, which assumed a superiority of the wealthy and educated classes over the poor, and lacked the ideas of democratic equality and social justice. His critique also concentrated on the Jewish Enlightenment that until the first half of the nineteenth century followed the enlightened absolutism of the eighteenth century, according to which 'everything should be done for the people, nothing by the people' (Mahler 1950: 264).

During the nineteenth century and in the early twentieth century, the poor Jewish class in London was composed of significant groups of immigrants who were at the bottom of the socioeconomic ladder. Their ethnic and cultural background and circumstances of work and life were sharply differentiated from those of the native Jewish wealthy class. As such, they constituted a particular ethnic group. Ethnic groups can be delineated in accordance with Schermerhorn's definition (1970) as a 'collectivity within a large society, having real or putative ancestry, memories of a shared historical past and a cultural focus on one or more symbolic elements' (Schermerhorn quoted in Entzinger 1987: 5).

The overlapping of poverty, immigration, ethnic and cultural backgrounds and the relationship of these different aspects to each other and to the domineering Anglo-Jewish élite were blurred by the perspective of national solidarity, based on an axiomatic hypothesis according to which a singular Jewish interest dominates all intra-communal Jewish questions, as well as the relationship between Jews and Gentiles. According to this view the monolithic interests led to a unified policy aimed to promote them. N. Kokosalakis (1982) writes:

> regarding the solidarity amongst Jews the world over... which sometimes has been advocated... by many Jews... in its more popular form 'Jews always stick together', that they help each other financially... that there are scarcely any poor Jews, that there are no class or status divisions worth talking about in Jewish communities. (p. 81)

Such an ahistorical perspective was derived partly from an incomplete analysis of Jewish life in the pre-emancipation era and the assumption that because all Jewish classes were subject to legal discrimination, identical interests might have developed. Elements of Jewish solidarity did not diminish the practical importance of class interests and this solidarity is not in contradiction with class conflict amongst the Jewish social classes. Jewish solidarity is seen in this book as a function of rival socioeconomic and other interests and their impact as reflected in the organization of philanthropic institutions. Those interests created corresponding conflicting concepts and ideologies with regard to the definition of national solidarity and the limit of its comprehensiveness.

Since most of the Jewish immigrants to England were almost destitute when they entered Britain, they required assistance for a considerable period afterwards, and their ethnicity was effectively a class attribute. The immigration from eastern Europe is regarded as an effort made by a whole class which had preserved their national identity in the struggle for existence.

Social history has provided a reappraisal of the way the immigrants were looked upon (Zunz 1985: 62–3). Rather than seeing them as uprooted and passive individuals, social historians regard them as clever, motivated and, by and large, more active when compared with those who did not have the energy to leave their depressed native environment. It is possible that the way in which immigrants have previously been regarded by historians was partly influenced by the lack of confidence of the élite in the power of the poor immigrants to overcome their predicaments. Jewish immigration to England was a collective, not only an individual, enterprise and, as such, included chain migration with a strong element of reciprocal help.

The immigrant poor were able to think about their collective interests *vis-à-vis* the élite and to furnish some of the resources needed to protect them. Structural factors became enmeshed with the immigrants' cultural backgrounds to produce the élite's ideology of a differentiated superior class. The élite placed much of the blame on the deficiencies and differences attributed to the poor immigrants as a group. Such a perception was embodied in the repressive policy of the Board of Guardians as the main institution of the élite intended to deal with immigration. The policies of the Board were presented by the élite in positive terms and legitimized as being in the interests of the potential immigrants, those already living in Britain and all the strata within the Anglo-Jewish community.

Ethnicity is viewed by Katz (1985) as a temporary element (albeit with long-range traces), and as such, a secondary one, and so a less valid analytical category (quoted by Zunz 1985: 89). Katz was, however, criticized by Zunz for treating ethnicity 'as a simple, uniform reflection of nationality and religion, not as a complex attribute worthy of careful definition' (Zunz 1985: 90). Karl Marx (1818–1883) advanced the hypothesis that 'the Jew' was a socioeconomic category and, at the same time, a religious entity. What Marx implied in his 'On the Jewish Question' was that Jewish culture and solidarity were all epiphenomena of widespread socioeconomic conditions and conflicts.

According to the analysis made by Irwin Kohn, writing in the early 1920s, Marx knew nothing about Judaism, especially of the Jewish masses, but only of a few wealthy Jews in Western Europe. In Kohn's opinion, Marx's essay reflects a *salto mortale*, a break with his Judaic ancestry. Marx regarded 'Jewish economics' as fiendish (Kohn quoted in Carlebach, 1978: 282). His view is partly derived from his unreal conception of Jews as forming a unitary category of economic action in a larger stagnant and uniform economic context. In fact, Marx was indifferent to Judaism but was aggravated by the abilities of some Jews to adjust comfortably to the grande bourgeoisie. Isaiah Berlin summarizes Marx's essay and its anti-Semitic tone as a shallow and dull composition aimed 'to kill the Jewish problem once and for all' (Lesser quoted in Carlebach 1978: 282–3).

Since the 1970s a few historical studies have been published on the period of mass immigration, which emphasizes instances of a 'bitter class struggle transcending any concept of national unity' (Newman 1985: 133–5). William Fishman, in his book *Jewish Radicals* (1975), rejects the notions according to which aspirations and lack of class consciousness characterized most of the immigrants. Joseph Buckman, in *The Jewish Immigrant in Leeds* (1983), relates the integration of the Jewish immigrants in Leeds during the last quarter of the nineteenth century to their working-class status and self-perception. He claims that the Jewish upper class acted out of 'short-term class interests' with regard to the poor immigrants. Buckman criticizes both Lipman's *Social History of the Jews in England* (1954), and Gartner's *The Jewish Immigrant in England* (1960, rev. 1973), for their conclusions as to the predilection of the Jewish poor for the bourgeoisie and the blurring of the identity of the Jewish working class:

> The conclusion that the economic struggle had utterly overridden ethnic and religious bonds, and that it presented the key to the very articulation of the various parts of the community, became inescapable. Against this, a strange quietus inhabited the literature of the subject. Cemented into eclectic postures and disabled by an institution-centred and establishment-oriented methodology, it seemed unable to conceive of a Jewish proletariat having an existence as a separate and distinct historical class. Hence a class conflict model finds no place in the standard accounts of Jewish communal life, in which the Jewish bourgeoisie, occupying the entire foreground, exists in an anti-dialectal void with no sociohistoric counterpart in the shape of an immigrant proletariat. Bourgeois communal institutions, especially those concerned with 'philanthropy', are never considered from the standpoint of their function as agencies of social control but are, instead, promulgated as the bases of spurious claims to pre-eminence as 'protectors' of the aliens against the hostility of British society'. (Buckman 1983: viii–ix)

While Buckman himself concentrates on the conflict between the

Jewish workers and their Jewish employers following the classic Marxist model, he does not see the philanthropy of the élite as an epiphenomenon in the development of socialism but as an important mechanism deliberately used to control the Jewish working class and poor, long neglected as a subject for the scrutiny of historical research.

Buckman further writes that 'Professor L. P. Gartner, at once the leading exponent and victim of this static method, considers that the alien worker "did not regard himself as one endowed with a fixed station in life", and thus accepted long hours and irregular seasons' (Buckman 1983: 6). He refers to the profits made by the Jewish élite, arranging loans to the Tsarist regime under which the Jewish population faced cruel discrimination and officially sanctioned massacres. Negating the notion of mutuality, Buckman concludes that the absorption process involved strong conflicts between the interests of the working class, their employers and the élite.

Another historian in this group, J. White, author of *Rothschild's Buildings* (1981), argues that the Jewish élite adopted the conception of the host middle classes, according to which the poor were to be disciplined into an obedient working class who could be exploited as a measure to prevent complete disorder in society. In the framework of such discipline, attempts were made to condition the poor ideologically, as evidenced by the conditions of eligibility for philanthropic services. The writings of Buckman and White expose the community's social dynamics and relate them to a political rationale that had contradicted the assumption of class cooperation.

Other historians reject the interpretation of narrow class interests motivating power that is suggested by Buckman and White, claiming it is 'rooted in their ideological prejudices and derived from their own stand in the political debate over current immigrant policy in Britain' (Gutwein 1992: 19). Newman accepts the known facts about the errors made in the absorption of the immigrants and the 'cold' approach towards them (Gutwein 1992: 19–20). Endelman regards Buckman's interpretations as a 'Marxist presupposition', but concedes, with White, that the élite attempted to inculcate the immigrants with middle-class values (Gutwein 1992: 20). Still other historians detect class motives in the philanthropic activities of the élite as well as class tensions, but underestimate their total impact. They note the efforts of the élite to find a *modus operandi* to support the process of absorption without resorting generally to the Poor Law and, in this way, preventing further class antagonism.

Although it can be argued that some embourgeoisement had infiltrated into the Jewish poor class, and second and third generations of immigrants were able at a later period to abandon manual labour as a result of economic opportunities and social mobility, this does not mean that during the nineteenth century large numbers of immigrants did not harbour a deep resentment towards the philanthropic institutions established by the élite, or that class tensions did not exist.

The nineteenth century is characterized by hectic changes of economic and social circumstances that forced the immigrants to leave their familiar environment for other countries, with all the subsequent upheaval involved, in employment, social status and lifestyle. This upheaval was accompanied by internal struggle within Jewish society. The changes had various effects on the Jewish social structure. The Jewish upper and middle classes were generally able to make a comfortable adjustment to the capitalist régime while the Jewish proletariat lived on low-paid, intermittent work. These class discrepancies between the assimilated Jewish bourgeoisie and the Jewish masses further weakened feelings of Jewish solidarity.

Ideological expositions and practical decisions taken by individuals or groups with regard to philanthropic actions are often representations of different, divergent or conflicting views of 'doing good'. Active or latent conflicting interests in philanthropic actions may be reflected in the negation of values and competition over resources. In theory and practice, the exclusion or resolution of such conflicts is hampered by the difficulty of establishing hierarchies of values and ordering priorities. In spite of such pluralism, which has affected philanthropy (especially in modern times), philanthropy was generally based on some unifying assumption emphasizing religious and/or public, secular philosophy and aspirations for 'doing private or common good'.

As generally represented, the theory and practice of Jewish philanthropy assumes cohesiveness, convergence and coherence between the diverse moral aims and virtues that it attempts to accomplish. The underlying socioeconomic factors related to *tzedakah* (defined both as social justice and charity), were especially obscured by the issue of Jewish ethnicity, obligatory and voluntary religious commandments and national solidarity. Many studies on Jewish philanthropy have concentrated on influential wealthy donors and important events, sometimes of a celebratory nature, when portraying the élite and the institutions through which it functioned. Scant attention has been paid to the mistakes made by the élite with regard to the poor, effectively marginalizing the concerns of the poor in historical accounts. Such narratives have overt and covert conservative implications; for instance, that the needs of the poor were simply not as important as those of the wealthy middle class. Ample description is rendered of the support extended to the Jewish poor in the field of income maintenance and education, thus minimizing class antagonisms and confrontations. Jewish philanthropy was often explained in traditional terms as an imminent phenomenon rather than in the context of the exogenous influences it experienced. Many narratives and studies of Jewish philanthropy have omitted dissonant facets of Jewish belief, to avoid controversy likely to undermine the representation of a unified Jewish community. Most of those sources relate to generalities and lend themselves to sweeping sentimental statements.

Idealizations, sometimes of a legendary and nostalgic nature, permit misleading interpretations, which conceal the contradictions between the philanthropists and those that most needed their services. Also, Jewish inequality has been presented as an impermanent phenomenon by historians who base their explanations on a middle-class orientation of the Jewish poor, emphasizing their later upward mobility. Modern Jewish philanthropy, as differentiated from mere charity, is presented in such narratives as rational, enlightened, and *ipso facto* as useful and progressive. Elusive, liberal and individualistic assumptions, combined with conservative views, create the impression that what was good for the bourgeoisie was good for the proletariat and the poor.

The philanthropic arrangements have often been presented in an affirmative manner, whatever they were, emphasizing the generosity of the rich rather than the needs of the poor, thus not relating to the extent to which generosity could be extended further to meet more adequately the needs of the poor. For example, Jewish charitable relief given to immigrants is described by Gartner as 'extensive and generous' (Gartner 1973: 162–5).

It is not only Jews who have held to this idealized cliché of Jewish solidarity among the Jewish social strata, oversimplifying this image to the point of untruth. Rather than a 'pessimistic' interpretation which might stress the economic and social hardship of the poor, the impression is given that this was readily believed by the Jewish philanthropies.

The positive impressions of non-Jewish observers are often mentioned emphasizing the superiority of Jewish charity. For instance, no beggars nor Jews requiring relief were found according to the Aristedes (530?–468? BC), Tacitus, (55?–118? AD) and the Roman Emperor Julian (331–63 AD) as quoted in Epistle XXX: 49. Similar accolades for Jewish charitable institutions were expressed by Lancelot Eddison in *The Present State of the Jews of Barbary* (1675); Jake Surim, the

Protestant leader, and others who, in spite of being sometimes highly critical of Jews in other respects, admired their charities (quoted in Bergman 1942: 147). Amalgamations and centralization of Jewish philanthropic institutions were regarded as a subject around which cohesion were forged, that is, as a unique catalyst, building bridges between Jewish communities formerly characterized by divisive rivalries between different élite groups and associations, who generally tended to remain aloof from one another.

In view of the distinct importance that Judaism always attaches to charitable concepts and activities, and the high esteem with which they are regarded, it seems important to review the critical discussions and research of Jewish charity with particular reference to its redistributive aspects. In his study, *Social Work and Jewish Values: Basic Areas of Consonance and Conflict* (1959), Alfred Kutzik, a social worker in the Jewish communal service in the United States and lecturer at the University of Connecticut School of Social Work, adapts the critique of Thorstein Veblen with regard to the worth of the social worker or philanthropist and the devaluation or negation of the work of the beneficiary. His approach derives from the upper-class character of social work agencies and the lower-class nature of their clientele. Kutzik contends that anti-democratic values of the nineteenth-century charity movement, such as the Charity Organization Society, had been transcended by the contemporary social work practice. He concludes that both Jewish and social work values consist of sets of democratic values coexisting with opposing anti-democratic ones. Moreover, the democratic values are not monolithic, containing differing degrees of democratic values. The democratic Jewish values are reflected, among others, in the philosophy of Hillel (*c.*110 BCE – *c.*10 CE) with regard to the equality of individuals and its corollaries, the love of one's fellow men and the pursuit of peace. While in Judaism the individual is identified with the Jewish community, in theory and in practice, the superiority of the communal rights is an integral part of Jewish communalism reflected throughout Jewish history, for instance, in the primitive communism of the ancient Jewish tribes.

However, any value system or law cannot presuppose universal compliance to its terms, necessarily containing antagonistic anti-democratic values; that is, any set of values is not exclusively virtuous, implying the rejection or devaluation of other systems. For example, in the approach of the Prophets to the crucial principle of equality, there are marked differences between the egalitarianism of the sheep-farmer Amos, and the liberalism of the aristocratic Isaiah; between the chauvinism and fanaticism of Ezekiel and the cosmopolitanism of Jonah. The resistance to their prophecies indicates the persistence of the severe exploitation of the poor, the social corruption and perversion of justice. Other Scriptures reveal, amongst a preponderance of democratic and humanistic values, prejudices against the poor, disguised as criticism of their ignorance (Kutzik 1959: 31).

Kutzik was influenced by the critique of the predominance of wealth over learning in the value hierarchy of the *shtetl*. I. L. Peretz (1947), stressed the detrimental effects of affluence on the Jewish upper-class ('the bigger the businessman, the smaller the Jew'). Kutzik also came under the influence of the anthropological study of Zborowsky and Hertzog on the eastern European *shtetl*, primarily before World War I, and the general concept of American political democracy directed towards the enhancement of human life.

Kutzik emphasizes the religious benefits and status earned by individual donors of personal charity – as opposed to communal public charity – in the form of *mitzvot* and *yikhus*, as well as the loss of status of recipients of material help. However, Kutzik omits the detrimental redistributive aspect of personal charity (1959: 44). He does not define democracy; while the term is meant to have a favourable connotation (for instance, people deciding the way they are governed), it has been used very freely, even by opposing social and political persuasions.

George and Wilding (1976) point out that the socialist emphasis on democracy is a consequence of the belief in equality, and its essence is the enlargement of democratic principles to include previously neglected vital aspects of socioeconomic life (George and Wilding 1976: 67). In a later study they write 'there are understandable differences of opinion as to what constitutes acceptable or unacceptable inequality. Taking wealth and income as examples there is no agreement on the dividing line between the acceptable and unacceptable face of inequality. Those are matters to be decided not *a priori* but in the democratic process of policy' (George and Wilding 1994: 97). Kutzik writes correctly that, 'since the entire ideological superstructure is ultimately based on the socioeconomic practices of the groups of people who develop values . . . practice rather than ideology will be looked to for the ultimate validation of our thesis' (Kutzik 1959: 8). However, the authentic evidence that he cites to differentiate the anti-democratic Jewish values from the history of American Jewish charities and their actual practice are few. Their importance is exemplified by the following secondary source quotation, revealing a primary concern for the worth of the donors. A poorhouse was argued for, in part, on the grounds:

that many of our charitable females . . . would have opportunities of visiting and ministering to their [the poor's] health and wants. At present they are restrained from visiting the poor by the objectionable locations of their dwelling. (Schappes quoted in Kutzik 1959: 47, 92)

Although Kutzik recognizes the class origin of some conflicting Jewish values with regard to poverty, he lacks however, a historically consistent frame of reference. He writes that 'the general upward movement socioeconomically and the increasing rigidity of the social class structure of the American Jewish community has begun to make itself felt', disregarding previous significant class conflicts and tensions which could be discerned in consequence (Kutzik 1959: 35). Using the rather elusive concepts of democratic and anti-democratic as well as communal values, Kutzik reaches the unsubstantiated conclusion that 'tzedakah, charity and social justice rendered as assistance (as a right and social equality) appear to have been preserved or re-created by American Jews . . . there is no objective evidence that American Jews characteristically have acted on the basis of communal rather than personal or class concerns in the field of social welfare and politics' (Kutzik 1959: 34–5).

According to Kutzik, Jewish charity directed by the value and work of the community fulfilled the major role in maintaining the Jewish communities during many centuries of severe persecution and socioeconomic hardship in the Diaspora, supporting the national rather than the class structure and character (Kutzik 1959: 47). Again, Kutzik does not substantiate this dichotomy; that is, he omits the role of tzedakah in supporting existing stagnant social structures within Jewish communities, emphasizing its function in strengthening national solidarity instead.

Despite the apologetic remnants and internal contradictions of his study, Kutzik's work was, and has remained, an important turning point in the research of the traditional and current theory and praxis of Jewish charity and social work. The major groundbreaking elements of Kutzik's study are his coverage of several previously neglected issues:

- Exhortation and codes of charity are no proof of beneficiary-centred practice of charity among the Jews, neither are commands and code of ethics. Rather they may be interpreted as evidence of implicit criticism directed towards those that could and needed to contribute more funds for charitable purposes (p. 34).
- Anti-democratic values generated by Jewish society throughout its

history are only partly due, or are at least not necessarily due, to outside corrosive influences (p. 35).

- Democratic as well as anti-democratic values are equally traditional.
- Anti-democratic values as a rule are adopted, if not generated, by groups of higher socioeconomic status in Jewish society.
- The individual freedom of which Jews 'became so enamoured' contributed to a loss of the sense of collective responsibility.
- Individualism is essentially an upper-class value orientation generated by the need to justify and advertise socioeconomic superiority (pp. 39–40).
- Participation in the movements and organizations of the lower classes can provide a basis for fostering democratic communal values 'to which individualism in all its guises and disguises is opposed' (p. 40).
- The meaning of the word *tzedakah*, charity and social justice or righteousness, is rather a semantic argument and does not imply that Jewish charity is superior to non-Jewish charity. Such superiority is not proved by the emphasis of the *Talmud* on the right of the individual, the corollary obligation of the community to assist him, universal eligibility, adequacy of assistance and confidentiality (p. 42).
- Reactions to the malpractice of charity are an integral part of the Jewish folklore, literature and hagiography (p. 42).

Advancing these ideas, Kutzik (1959) challenged significant deep-seated beliefs with respect to Jewish charity. Regarded as important but provocative at the time of its publication, Kutzik's work is not widely quoted. Many writers on the subject generally prefer earlier non-critical compilations on the characteristics of Jewish charity such as Frish (1914), and Bergman (1942).

Defining Tzedakah

A turning point in the modern research of Jewish charity is the well-documented study of Daniel Nusbaum, *Social Justice and Social Policy in the Jewish Tradition: The Satisfaction of Basic Human Needs in Poznan in the Seventeenth and Eighteenth Centuries* (1978). Nusbaum uses the instrumental definition of *tzedakah* – social justice as distributive equality – and asks 'is social justice a Jewish value?' in order to analyze the extent to which social justice was operative in the social policies of Poznan (west central Poland) as a representative community of the late medieval period, the last period of time in which Jewish communities in Europe remained committed to their *hallachically* generated traditions.

Defining *tzedakah*, social justice, as distributive equality, Nusbaum (1978) concentrates primarily on the dispensation of life-sustaining resources for fulfilling elementary human needs. In consequence, such resources were to be supplied to the entire community before less essential, life-enhancing, resources were provided to any member. The nine basic human needs the satisfaction of which Nusbaum examines in the statutes of the Poznan Jewish community were: (1) food; (2) shelter; (3) clothing; (4) needs of the traveler; (5) health care; (6) dowry for a bride; (7) ransom from captivity; (8) support for old age; and (9) burial (p. 258). Nusbaum attempts to verify whether the implementation of *tzedakah* in Poznan translated all the above mentioned basic life-sustaining human needs into human rights.

Nusbaum's conclusion is that the communal authorities in Poznan achieved this. As evidence he considers the community's refusal to subject the satisfaction of life-sustaining resources to the arbitrary discretion of voluntary contributions and the militancy of the poor when demanding greater provisions for their food allowance and their claim to receive it at the proper time. However, Nusbaum mentions that the *gabbaim* of *tzedakah* who were members of the community council themselves, regarded the provisions as insufficient, reflecting a more generous attitude towards the poor (Nusbaum 1978: 265). Sometimes the Jewish authorities attributed such insufficiencies to the exploitation by the host community and the collective debts to the latter.

The data examined by Nusbaum reveal periods during which there were difficulties in supplying the intended provisions to the poor, but that even so:

> the communal officials sanctioned accumulation of life-enhancing resources even when encountering difficulties in supplying food, clothing and shelter, and not only when supplying those needs embraced by *tzedakah* which might be considered life-enhancing. (Nusbaum 1978: 266)

The data reveal unequal distribution of wealth and its accumulation in significant amounts by members of the Poznan community even when difficulties were encountered in providing basic provisions to the poor. While the overall system by which the community generated its revenue was progressive, its official statutes sanctioned the privileges of the wealthy and preserved class distinctions as illustrated by the differential sumptuary regulations. The general conclusion of Nusbaum's study is, that except for ransom from captivity and provision of medical care which were basically egalitarian, the provisions to the poor never provided them with more than a subsistence level of existence.

Neither is there, according to Nusbaum, evidence of conscious attempts to achieve distributive equality (Nusbaum 1978: 254). The traditional trend of providing life-sustaining resources according to social status – *lefi kvodo*, that is, provision in accordance with what the recipient was accustomed to before becoming poor – also increased the differential availability of life-sustaining provisions.

Nusbaum's (1978) conclusions are refuted by Jerome Widroff in his study, *Medieval Jewish Social Welfare Institutions* (1987). In an attempt to demonstrate that Nusbaum's definition of *tzedakah*, distributive equality, was flawed, Widroff proposes a rather conservative alternative definition of *tzedakah* as social justice. To do so he examines the context in which the term *tzedakah* was used by Jewish writers representing different aspects of Jewish life cited by Nusbaum. Widroff contends that the writers and authors quoted by Nusbaum with regard to *tzedakah* as a Jewish value of special significance, focuses their attention on one or more of the terms: civil liberty and civil rights, pro-union or working men, in favour of the welfare state etc., but not distributive equality.

According to Widroff's definition, social justice can be adequately termed a Jewish value 'if it is central to Jewish self-definition and if Jewish institutions have been organized and structured to encourage altruism, generosity towards strangers and between social groups' (Widroff 1987: 156).

Some of his criteria for testing the operational application of the value of *tzedakah* are judgements and characterizations about Jewish persons in terms of their dedication to charitable purposes. On the basis of his definition, Widroff finds that the medieval Jewish communities provided *tzedakah* in a way that was compatible with the 'institutional' rather than with the 'residual' conceptions of social welfare as formulated by Wilensky and Lebeaux (1958). Widroff writes:

> Jewish survival is one of the great wonders of history. How did this weak, small nation, deprived by its homeland manage to survive and maintain its identity, while so many greater, more numerous and more powerful nations have disappeared? (Widroff 1978: 158)

Widroff attributes the resistance to all forces that acted towards the dissolution of the Jewish people to *tzedakah* and *gemilut chassadim* (personal acts of loving kindness), together considered as one of the three pillars of Judaism together with Torah and worship. Yet Widroff recognizes that traditional Jewish society lacked social justice 'if we accept Nusbaum's operational definition of social justice – that it is equivalent to distributive equality' (Widroff 1978: 4).

Defining *tzedakah* by the exclusive meaning of distributive equality is a radical goal even for advanced socialist régimes of contemporary societies. What is evident in the effort of Widroff to refute Nusbaum's frame of reference, is that the very definition of *tzedakah* as operative redistributive equality is perceived as a threat to one of the most important Jewish values. Instead, vague and more compromising interpretations are preferred; these ethical distinctions are, however, rather difficult to apply to the everyday practice of *tzedakah*.

Widroff claims that *tzedakah*, social justice, can be adequately termed a Jewish value if Jewish institutions dispensing it 'have been organized and structured to encourage altruism, generosity towards strangers and between social groups' (1987: 156). Widroff bases his claims on Titmus's assertion that 'the ways in which society organizes and structures its social institutions, and particularly its health and welfare systems, can encourage or discourage the altruism in man; such systems can foster integration or alienation' (Titmus quoted in Widroff 1987: 10). Believing that people 'were neither altruistic nor egoistic by nature', he attributes to the ideological and ethical basis of social welfare arrangements (such as the National Health Service in Britain) the potential 'to provide institutional opportunities for citizens to show their altruistic support for one another' (George and Wilding 1994: 82). For instance, Titmus claims that the commercialization of blood-giving and receiving 'represses the expression of altruism . . . and leads to all sorts of undesirable consequences in both health care and society in general' (Titmus 1970: 277). Consequently, George and Wilding (1994) enumerate the ways in which altruism is encouraged in society as one of the important justifications of social service provision; relating to recent social welfare problems in Britain, however, they point out that 'several Democratic Socialists have come to accept that social services do not always act as agents of socialist change but as a means of social control, particularly when they are provided under strict eligibility rules' (George and Wilding 1994: 82).

George and Wilding (1994) contend that altruism and self-interest are integral parts of fellowship, which implies love for one's neighbour; but they recognize that in spite of its vital role for the communitarian appeal of socialism – as differentiated from capitalism – altruism 'is a very demanding, and some might say impossible, value in its policy implications' (George and Wilding 1994: 99). They emphasize the importance of values for directing practice, regarding them as 'broad, vague and flexible concepts which can be interpreted differently at the margins . . . ' (George and Wilding 1994: 99).

The encouragement of altruism can contribute to social cohesiveness and is an important element in the universal approach to social welfare (Crossland 1963 and Marshall 1965). However, due to its vague – not to say elusive – definition, altruism may involve no more than a limited commitment to distributive equality, and as such can be related ideologically to rather conservative movements. Karl Popper, in *The Open Society*, differentiates between altruism and egoism (Popper 1957: 99). The distinctions between these two categories may, however, be easily oversimplified and fail to consider the ambiguous nature of perceived interests – enlightened though they may be – such as class obligations (Pinker 1979: 233). According to Pinker, confrontations between adherents of egoism and altruism in their uncompromising forms are generally connected with academic and political debates. These forms are extreme; he suggests that 'it is possible to discover more by looking at the various forms of qualified egoism and altruism in the context of daily welfare practices' (Pinker 1979: 7). Pinker's suggestion is, in fact, very close to what Nusbaum attempts to do by examining the satisfaction of basic human needs in the late medieval Poznan Jewish community by defining *tzedakah* as distributive social justice (Nusbaum: 1978).

Whether or not Nusbaum properly examines the value of *tzedakah* (given Widroff's critique), he does attempt to develop an explanatory concept in evaluating redistribution in the dispensation of *tzedakah*, relating to it in terms of service organization and not only as a cherished value. Challenging Herbert Spencer's view, Durkheim in *The Division in Society* (1964), affirms the existence of altruism in every society where there is solidarity. However, as Pinker points out, neither Durkheim nor Kropotkin support collectivist intervention by the state as a basis of social policy. Rather, both Durkheim and Kropotkin rely on the spontaneous expression of human inclination for altruism (Pinker 1979: 9). Pinker concludes that the term altruism, used in an unqualified way, is largely irrelevant to social welfare because of its inapplicability to forms of social behaviour. The conditional social welfare model of altruism that Pinker advances lies beyond present purposes (Pinker 1979: 10, 47–8, 69).

Altruism in the context of European poverty and in historical perspective is discussed by de Swaan (1988). He regards altruistic motivation for charity as an 'object of collective action' rather than 'as an affair between . . . the charitable and the beneficiary' as it is customarily described (de Swaan 1988: 21). De Swaan contends that charity must also be understood in the context of collective interests, such as the maintenance of a labour reserve (de Swaan 1988: 23). This contention arises from his explanation of poverty:

> The problem of the poor is to stay alive; the problem for the rich is of distributing part of the surplus without altering the rules of accumulation and conservation . . . to pacify and terrify those who might attempt to change the rule of accumulation, and to prevent the ills of poverty – whether through crowding, contagion or discontent – from affecting the ranks of the well-to-do . . . the problem of poverty exists as distributing a minimal amount of social surplus without altering the patterns of dependency and exclusion which define the rich on the one hand, and the poor and all the others between. (de Swaan 1988: 14–15)

The collective actions of the rich were motivated, in de Swaan's explanation, by their need for conformity of action among peers and 'some rules to abide by', which were sometimes difficult to achieve; in general, however,

> when confronted with a sufficient number of visibly suffering poor or with threatening bands of the indigent, the established classes did realize that a coordinated effort was required. They found it much harder to persuade everyone in their ranks to participate in it and agree upon a distribution of burdens. (de Swaan 1988: 15)

De Swaan defines 'social consciousness' as a cognitive awareness of the interdependence between the poor and the rich, together with a readiness and responsibility of the rich to ameliorate the situation of the poor (de Swaan 1988: 253).

The frame of reference suggested by de Swaan, emphasizing worldly consideration of class interests and collective actions of socioeconomic control, can explain the morality, feelings of superiority and ideological justifications of the nineteenth-century ascending Anglo-Jewish élite's philanthropy, as it emanated from its own class interests.

In this book, the following questions related to altruistic motivations, will be asked: Were not the patrons of Jewish philanthropies motivated to help the poor by their short and long-term interests? Were not the forms of some income redistribution in the interests of the élite? These questions do not negate the existence of uncommon altruism represented by completely anonymous contributions made by members of the wealthy classes to known or unknown objects of charity. Such giving, free of *quid pro quo*, was considered by Maimonides as the highest degree of charity. Marx claimed that social consciousness can never be realized under capitalism and that the market mechanism prevents more cordial relationships between people. However, the distinction between egotism and altruism does not appear in Marx's analysis (Collard 1978: 59, 149).*

Philanthropy is closely related to altruism, generosity, charity and love. The Greek term *philanthropia* refers to a generalized attitude of kindness and consideration for a human being, and it can be displayed without the transfer of material resources. However, later, Greek *philanthropia* and its cognates tend to suggest a specific favour done by a superior for an inferior. According to Webster's definition, the English term 'philanthropy' seems to have been a conscious borrowing from the Greek in the general sense of love to humankind, practical benevolence towards people, the disposition or active effort to promote the happiness and well-being of one's fellows.

This was also the Victorian pre-Welfare State conception of the general scope of philanthropy. Philanthropy, as somewhat differentiated from the term 'charity', was characterized by more institutionalized and generalized voluntary activities, sometimes including preventive actions. Philanthropy was accompanied by paternalism and social control, to the extent that it is difficult to separate them. Although sometimes paternalism was exercised through some kind of established relationship, this is not a precondition for philanthropic paternalism.

Philanthropy is considered a moral excellence and a virtue, fostering conformity to the requirements of morality. While some virtues are very important in moral life, others are negligible. The differentiation between significant and insignificant values cannot be sharply delineated. The tendency of Christians and Jews, amongst others, is to regard philanthropy as one of the most important virtues. Jewish people pride themselves on their descent from Abraham, characterized by his care

---

*Psychological theories that attempt to interpret philanthropic motivation as mechanisms used to placate personal or collective guilt-feelings, superego demands, as well as metaphysical and religious concern with the salvation of the benefactor's soul, either during his or her life or posthumously, are not discussed in this book; however, it is not my intention to negate their importance and influence.

for the weak, helpless and unfortunate. Maimonides, relying on Rabbi Assi (*Baba Batra* 6a) wrote that 'we are duty bound to observe the *mitzvah* of *tzedakah* [the religious obligation of charity], more than all other positive commandments'.

Generally, philanthropy is considered an uncontroversial, desirable attitude; it is used to show the generous face of the 'haves' towards the 'have-nots'. As such, philanthropy can be exercised only by giving insufficient consideration to the claim of justice; this is because philanthropy presupposes a better-off benefactor enjoying a surplus beyond his or her needs, and an impoverished beneficiary. The basic question remains as to whether the inequality between a philanthropic person and the beneficiary might not be eliminated by some alternative means, and whether such alternatives could better serve the interests of the beneficiaries, by excluding their dependence on the charitable impulses of the philanthropic person. The importance of this question is also emphasized by the prevailing hypothesis of psychological studies: that philanthropy is based primarily on an emotive element – cognitive motivations being secondary. In *The Doctrine of Virtues*, Immanuel Kant critically poses the following question:

> The ability to practice beneficence, which depends on property, follows largely from the injustice of the government, which favours certain men and so introduces an inequality of wealth that makes others need help. This being the case, does the rich man's help to the needy, on which he so readily prides himself as something meritorious, really deserve to be called beneficence at all? (Kant 1964 edn: 122)

While pointing out that only inequality makes room for philanthropy, Kant regards philanthropy as preferable to no philanthropy if the conditions that made it necessary can not be removed altogether. This pragmatic approach is accepted in this study particularly as the period discussed here is pre-Welfare State.

Marx claimed that the language of moral rights is senseless and that it is a disguise of vested interests and creates confusion. Whether in the first place the philanthropists had a right to the wealth they distributed for charitable purposes or not, the following question is asked: Did the philanthropists have a right to use their wealth at their discretion, without taking into consideration the rights of the beneficiaries? That is to say, does the value of altruism based on property and wealth override other social values that may be related to the problems created by the very accumulation of the philanthropists' wealth? Historically, significant philanthropy of wealthy élites was based on conditions of great inequality of wealth, where accumulation of private property permitted or encouraged pauperism, poverty, and dependence, allowing the lower classes to remain impoverished and dependent over considerable periods of time. Characteristically, philanthropic activities were optional rather than mandatory in content and frequency. As such, in spite of continuous acts of rescue and assistance, especially following catastrophes or other severe circumstances – philanthropy was generally far from being, even in part, supererogatory, considering the large numbers of people afflicted by poverty, homelessness, disease, and the like.

Sharp divisions between a wealthy élite, including philanthropists, and the poor suffering extreme anguish, generally have underlying economic, sociopolitical and institutional causes that have to be attacked and dealt with by drastic, systematic and extensive political measures. These means require that provision for the poor should be based on mandatory welfare arrangements. Ruling wealthy élites, even when philanthropic in character, are generally hostile to the basic needs of the poor classes and underestimate the political obstacles in the way of necessary change.

This discussion demonstrates the contradictions between the ideals of philanthropy, conducive to a more egalitarian society, and the realities of inequality. Myths of philanthropy have deep historical and cultural roots in nations and religions, and they continue to be artificially created. Such myths, I shall argue, are especially detrimental, even dangerous, to the poor when they direct social policies. Moreover, when such policies are deliberate manipulations intended to impose the myths of philanthropy on large social groups, the poor may find it difficult to protect themselves against them.

This discussion will, in the next chapter, be placed in the context of the historical development of Anglo-Jewish philanthropy.

THE JEWISH ELITE AND THE JEWISH POOR

This section examines the lack of community organization addressing the problems of the poor, especially the immigrants earning their livelihood as street and countryside hawkers. This was partly due to the gradual collapse of personal charity and elements of synagogual assistance to the poor, and the general apathy regarding the problem of poverty. Significant Jewish poverty, vagrancy and delinquency were not dealt with by the increasingly wealthy, small Ashkenazic oligarchy out of the fear of attracting ever more immigrants. Instead some futile repressive measures were sporadically undertaken.

In 1656, Jewish Sephardic (Spanish and Portuguese) merchants from Amsterdam were granted legal rights to resettle in England. This step was taken by Cromwell in order to broaden overseas trade and to facilitate competition with Holland. A corollary of this policy was a liberal individualistic approach expressed in continuous toleration of Jews in England, a toleration that continued throughout the period discussed in this book. The Sephardic community had developed a more comprehensive system of relief and mechanisms for maintaining class control, which were economically and socially motivated. As early as 1663 the Sephardic élite adopted a severe ordinance prohibiting the communal board from liberating delinquents; 'They shall consent that he be punished by the law according to his crimes as an example to others, and that thereby the stumbling block in our midst be removed and God's people be free' (*El Libro de los Acuerdos* 1931: 12, Article 3). The regulations also prevented the giving of *tzedakah* to poor Ashkenazic immigrants, called *Tudescos* (Germans) and *Polaccos* (Poles), but allowed its use for permitting them to leave England (1931: 28). However, the Ashkenazim increased considerably and by 1760 there were about eight thousand. The Sephardim numbered only two thousand, but still they were the most influential. Most of the Jews were concentrated in London. The Ashkenazic community did not develop a system of relief able to cater to the large number of poor, a situation that continued well after the Ashkenazic élite gained ascendancy in economic resources and political influence.

From 1675 onward, Jewish Sephardic magnates began to buy country houses (Brown 1984: 20). Two of the most conspicuous financiers were Sir Solomon de Medina and Samson Gideon (1699–1762). Gideon was a loan contractor, stockbroker and financial adviser to the Pelham administration. He assisted the government in fighting the French fleet and also with the invasion of the Young Pretender. Gideon and others invested enormous amounts of money in great houses, works of art, racehorses and so on, following and reaching out to the landed aristocracy. Such expenditures and the magnates' physical separation from the concentration of the Jewish poor population affected their sense of responsibility towards the poor. Some of the members of the Sephardic élite did not find sufficient scope for their political and social aspirations within the community and disengaged themselves entirely by converting. This adversely affected the resources available for the

Jewish poor. The Seniors, Ricardos and D'Israelis are the best-known examples. Samson Gideon reared his children in the Christian faith but continued to pay anonymously for his seat in the synagogue (*Jewish Encyclopaedia* 1935, vol. 5: 66). In 1740, he provided an annuity for Captain Thomas Coram, founder of the Foundling Hospital. Gideon himself was worth £350,000, 'more than the whole land of Canaan' as Horace Walpole wrote when informed that the bulk of his estates, including the Belvedere in Kent, was left to the Duke of Devonshire (Aris 1970: 48). Gideon bequeathed £2,000 to the Sons of the Clergy, £1,000 to the London Hospital and £1,000 to the Sephardic congregation.

In 1753, Henry Pelham agreed to the petitions of Jewish merchants and manufacturers to advance the Jews' Naturalisation Bill, intended mainly to permit wealthy Jews born outside the country the rights of buying land (an entitlement which was legally uncertain). The bill passed into law in 1753, but in 1754 it was repealed following petitions from all the cities of Great Britain, raising considerable public excitement prior to the general election. The agitation increased popular hostility and temporarily endangered the lives of itinerant Jewish pedlars, especially 'old clothes' men, no matter how long they had been known as harmless on their beat. The adversaries of the bill claimed:

> such a naturalization would deluge the Kingdom with brokers, usurers and beggars that the rich Jews, would purchase lands and even advowsons, would interfere with the industrious natives, and by dint of the most parsimonious frugality, to which the English are strangers, work at an underprice, so as not only to share, but even in a manner to exclude them from all employment. (Smollett n.d., II: 336–7)

This quotation reflects the restrictionist economic views which emphasized the obligation of the state in protecting the English working class by limiting foreign manpower competition. It also expresses the expectations of English merchants that the state would protect their privileges and monopolies. As pointed out, the bill was not intended to promote general naturalization or to encourage Jewish immigration to England, but was initiated by a group of Sephardic magnates headed by Joseph Salvador (1716–1886) as a limited concession to which they felt entitled as compensation for the services rendered to Pelham's administration. The resentment aroused by the bill reflects that, in English eyes, during this period the distinction the Jewish élite sought to make between itself and lower-class Jews was not entirely accepted. To be blunt, the images of the upper-class Shylock and the lower-class Shylock were similarly perceived. To counteract this dual image the Jewish wealthy class did not intend to alter their pursuit of economic enterprise (including large scale speculations), but rather to seek to control the poor. During the outburst of anti-Jewish feeling related to the Naturalization Bill, the Great Synagogue (established in 1722), the main communal centre of the Ashkenazic community, attempted to placate the resistance directed towards all Jewish classes by excluding from relief immigrants that, according to the synagogues' consideration, were not compelled to leave their native countries. Such measures proved, however, generally ineffective (Hyamson 1908: 236).

In 1771, a robbery and murder was committed in Chelsea by a gang of eight vagrant Jews (*Gentlemen's Magazine* 41, 1771: 521). The wide publicity given to the crime, the reward offered for information and innovative methods of detection used for the first time (by Sir John Fielding, magistrate of the Public Office on Bow Street), aroused strong feelings against the Jews. The damage was caused in the first stages of the investigation when every Jew was implicated in public opinion and, probably more than at any time before, Jewish immigration appeared as a serious social problem. According to Francis Place 'the derision "go to Chelsea" was a common exclamation when a Jew was seen in the streets and was often a signal of assault. I have seen many Jews hooted, hunted, kicked, pulled by the beard . . . without any protection from the passersby or the police' (Add. MSS. 27827, fol. 146). The cooperation of the 'principal Jews' and their 'laudable conduct' during the prosecution was complimented and the hope was expressed that the whole nation would not be thusly stigmatized. Such situations gave the Jewish élite a strong justification for social control.

Five years previously (1766) during a crime wave in London, the Ashkenazic leaders offered their help to eradicate Jewish receivers of stolen goods and other malefactors; the wardens of the Synagogue expected 'to receive the applause of every Jew who is not totally ignorant of . . . his own religion to the true regard for public justice, and the obedience due to the laws of the Kingdom' (quoted by Roth 1938: 155–7). The meaning of the moral support and identification requested by the Jewish élite from the Jewish public can be better understood in the article by J. R. Marcus, 'Shed a Tear for a Transport' (1974), based on a Yiddish letter sent from London to a relative in the British American province of Pennsylvania. According to this letter a fifteen-year-old Jew, Feibel Fibeman, had been sentenced to seven years service (equal to exile and slavery) as a 'transport' in British North America for pickpocketing a handkerchief worth ten pennies in December 1771. Marcus concludes that 'although no previous crimes were committed by the teenage lad the Ashkenazic leaders refused to interfere on his behalf and added in their refusal to evince any sympathy for apprehended evil doers, the London Ashkenazim . . . were only following in the footsteps of the socially dominant Sephardim' (Marcus 1974: 56).

Following the Chelsea murder, the Home Office protested to the Great Synagogue with regard to the large number of shiftless poor. In response, the Ashkenazic leaders blamed the English government for the lavish distribution of free passages to England in Royal Packet Boats to impoverished Jews abroad. Moreover, the Great Synagogue petitioned the Home Office to stop completely the immigration of Jewish poor. The restrictions suggested by the wardens were that no Jews should thenceforth come to England unless they paid their full passage and were furnished with passports by the British ministers abroad (Wolf 1934: 194). As a result of this presentation the Post Master General was instructed accordingly (Roth 1949: 334). At the same time the Lord Mayor of London offered free passage to Jews accepting repatriation. However, probably only the war with revolutionary France induced the more effective Alien Bill of 1792, which temporarily stopped Jewish immigration. In correspondence with Sir John Fielding and the Earl of Suffolk, Secretary of State, the Elders of the Great Synagogue expressed their views that Jewish immigration was pulled by the assistance offered to immigrants in England as much as it was pushed by the disquiet in Poland following the War of 1768. It was the Elders' opinion that the users of free passage were vagabonds unable to earn a living (Letter of Sir J. Fielding to the Earl of Suffolk, S.P., Dom. Geo. III, Parcel 8).

The Elders also claimed that their relief funds were on the verge of bankruptcy and suggested that immigrants should provide evidence to the Home Office as to the business that necessitated their presence in England or alternatively, evidence as to their ability to find employment prior to their embarkation. According to Wolf (1934: 194) raids were actually made on Jewish pedlars all over the country. While some difficulties in Poland were recognized, the immigrants as a whole were represented to the English authorities as a group of people who came to obtain their subsistence through begging. The economic causes of vagrancy were not recognized.

The constant fear that England would become an 'El Dorado', attracting continual influxes of oppressed poor Jews was aggravated by the anti-Jewish feelings following the brutal Chelsea murder and the increasing concern of the élite over the rising rate of criminal acts committed by Jews. But according to Wolf, the restrictions introduced by the Ashkenazic authorities in the distribution of relief, or the total refusal of relief ostensibly to deter potential immigrants, 'made matters worse. The destitute strangers, knowing no trades, and possessing no friends, either peddled on the highways or drifted into crime' (Wolf 1934: 193). Wolf severely criticizes the Ashkenazic establishment for prolonged apathy, refuting the claim that funds were exhausted:

> The problem of the poor, which had been growing daily more serious for eighty years does not seem to have excited the slightest intelligent interest among the leading Ashkenazim, while the Sephardim had equipped themselves with a number of fairly well managed schools and other charitable institutions including an orphan school, a hospital and an institution for lending money to respectable poor and for apprenticing poor children, the German Synagogues although numbering a much larger congregation, had done scarcely anything to prevent their poorer members from becoming paupers or to save the children of the poor from growing ignorant and shiftless. They could not plead the excuse of poverty, for although the majority of their members were the reverse of affluent, the well-to-do and even wealthy families were certainly not few. (Wolf 1934: 194)

It seems that the Ashkenazic élite tended to enforce 'police actions' using the central and municipal authorities. In *Desultory Reflections on the Police* (1785), Sir W. Blizard mentions a plan designed by the Earl of Suffolk for the regulation of the lower orders of Jewry. His friend, a 'worthy respectable Jewish gentleman', assured him 'that the respectable part of the body would do all in their power and be happy to advance such a good design, but that the undertaking would be far more arduous' because of the extent of the Jewish involvement in crime (Blizard quoted in Rumney 1933). The order of the Secretary of State, the Earl of Suffolk, to the Post Master General of December 1771 to charge the Jewish poor with full passage (at the request of the Jewish élite) was carefully formulated so as not to imply any change in England's liberal policy on immigration – 'the industrial poor of all other nations could be transported to England gratis' (Roth 1949: 334). At this point it is interesting to bring in the interpretation of Josiah Tucker, published in his pamphlet, *A Letter to a Friend concerning Naturalisation* (1753), which related to the problem of the repatriation of poor Jews. His support of an open economy, so crucial to the Jewish élite, included a free immigration policy:

Perhaps you may imagine, that the law empowers proper Officers to send such indigent foreigners to their native countries . . . But there neither is, nor ever was, such legal power subsisting by virtue either of the statute, or Commander of the Realm. (Tucker 1753)

This liberal policy continued after the Napoleonic Wars until the late nineteenth century, emanating from the belief in the beneficial contribution of immigrants to the economic progress of England. This view persisted even through the period of fear prompted by Malthus' theories of over-population (Trevelyan 2nd edn, 1946: 474).

This parallels the recognition of free migration as a legitimate right which was the corollary of the perception of the worth of untrammelled trade. Although Adam Smith did not discuss the subject, a positive view of human mobility was implicit in his writings and strengthened by the American Declaration of Independence. As pedlars, Jewish immigrants expanded the markets of newly developed consumer goods and recycled used goods and materials. But towards the end of the eighteenth century, and at the beginning of the nineteenth century, there was a feeling that the Jewish poor could not be absorbed by the economic growth, especially when, due to lack of sufficient support, they presented social problems. In spite of the fact that during this period many of the Ashkenazic leaders were themselves immigrants or first-generation natives, they adopted this pessimistic view that, among other reasons, influenced the inadequacy of the system of relief. Taking into consideration the élite's background, one assumes that it was aware of the ways in which the immigrants, as European city-dwellers, were affected by the changes brought about by the Industrial Revolution. But, like their contemporaries, non-Jewish middle-class capitalists, the élite was to a considerable extent preoccupied with hectic economic enterprises. Provisions for the poor, as an integral part of synagogual funds, were as nowadays, 'sustained exclusively by men engaged in this acquisitive process . . . among the more favoured members of society, economic interests have eclipsed all others' (Rabbi Mordecai Kaplan 1972: 30).

In terms of relief, the crisis of 1771 did not impel immediate action by the communal leaders. Eight years elapsed until, under circumstances of severe distress, the first significant Ashkenazic charity, the Meshibat Naphesh or Bread, Meat and Coal charity was established. One of the founders and the first president was Levi Barnet Cohen, born in Amsterdam in 1740, son of a wealthy trader. He arrived in England in 1778 and during the late 1790s was considered one of London's leading merchants. Levi was the father-in-law of both Nathan Mayer Rothschild and Sir Moses Montefiore. In 1859, his grandson Lionel Louis Cohen, later the Conservative MP for North Paddington, was one of the founders of the London Jewish Board of Guardians and its vice-president. (Since 1869 and until the 1940s all the presidents of the Board were the descendants of Levi Barnet Cohen.) This institution was not, however, designed for, or capable of, dealing with the distress of the poor in any important way.*

The incessant influx of homeless immigrants and the fear of attracting even more, scarcely provided an incentive for adequate charitable provision. Other factors that influenced the Jewish élite during the Napoleonic Wars in curtailing assistance beyond the bare necessities, included the resentment about the large expenditure on poor relief, agricultural depression and social unrest.

At the beginning of the nineteenth century Colquhoun (1796) estimated that there were between twelve and fifteen thousand Ashkenazim in London. The large number of poor among them encountered serious difficulties in providing their children with secular and religious education. Such educational facilities were created too late and were too small. They met the needs of only a fraction of the Jewish population. The majority of the poor children were employed in street trades to supplement the meagre incomes of their large families. Many of those children were no longer influenced by the traditional restraints of their parents and religious institutions. It was only natural that they moved into street callings, which enabled them to establish some independence with a small amount of capital.

The situation was complicated by the fact that the efforts some Jews were making to make a bare living raised some public discontent. Some of the immigrants belonged to a category denoted as *Betteljuden*. *Betteljuden* were small groups of Jews who moved continuously from Jewish community to Jewish community seeking charity after being uprooted from Poland and other countries by persecution and economic competition. They lived for long periods as transients in Germany and underwent a process of disorganization prior to their immigration to England. Some of the *Betteljuden* were rejected by their original communities because of various transgressions (Moses Avigdor Shulvass 1971: 85–101). Members of the Jewish upper-class showed a persistent

---

*For some other Ashkenazic charities see S. Stein (1964), 'Some Ashkenazic Charities in London at the End of the Eighteenth Century and the Beginning of the Nineteenth Century', *Transactions of the Jewish Historical Society of England*, 20: 63–81.

tendency to regard the majority of immigrants as belonging to the *Betteljuden*. In fact, most of the immigrants were impoverished Jews who believed that England would offer better economic opportunities than Germany and Holland, or who could not obtain settlement in Germany. Still others planned to transmigrate further to America. Their outlandish look – long Polish-style gabardine, beards and sidelocks (at a time when faces were generally clean shaven) made them more visible than the Irish immigrants, who also followed street vocations.

The lack of openings in industrial and mechanical occupations forced the Jewish poor into street-selling. In addition to old clothes, oranges and lemons, the Jewish pedlars sold buttons, sealing wax, pencils, spectacles, cheap jewelry and pictures, etc. Other Jews were employed in pencil-making, embroidery, glass-engraving, diamond-cutting, watch-making and repairing; the total number of Jewish artisans, however, was small. Street trades involved some *deformationes professionelles*. Many Jewish crimes were typical of the English urban poor and mainly committed as a direct consequence of hunger and the inability to provide the most elementary necessities in a socially acceptable manner. The legitimate returns in peddling and street-trading in second-hand clothes, were small.

In terms of entertainment, by the beginning of the nineteenth century, the Jewish poor had acquired some of the values and morals prevalent in their surroundings, this is, the English class of which they increasingly became a part. The customs that the poor internalized were remarkably different from those practiced by the élite. This process was accompanied by a growing indifference of the Jewish poor toward the patronizing élite. The physical violence used in self-protection and protest on the streets became a characterisic of the Jewish poor classes, as it was of the English poor. Modes of amusement such as boxing – still very brutal and rowdy – became common amongst the Jews. Renowned Jewish prize-fighters, such as Samuel Elias (alias Dutch Sam), his son and, above all, the most outstanding and sophisticated 'scientific' pugilist of England at this time, Daniel Mendoza (1763–1836), provided the Jewish poor with ethnic pride and important models of identification. Jewish pugilists and their peers were involved in the Old Price Riots at the reconstructed Theatre Royal at Covent Garden in October 1809. To counteract public protest against a sharp increase in the price of theatre seats, Jewish pugilists and other Jews were hired by the management as 'bruisers' against the 'ringleaders' of the protest. In derision, Jews were called 'old clothes', 'bad shillings', 'oranges and lemons' and so on. The contemporary *News* reported:

the high priest of the Jewish synagogue has caused one hundred itinerant Jews to be struck off the charity list for six months for making a noise at the Covent Garden Theatre. He has also warned them of excommunication in case they should be guilty of the like again. (quoted in Roth 1950: 208, 211)

Such external developments and rigorous collective repercussions caused great concern to the élite. Most aggravating for the Jewish élite was the fact that the Englishman in the street did not distinguish between the wealthy Jews (associated with money-lending and speculative transactions) and the poor offenders, despite the advanced acculturation of the former. In a way, no matter how far they moved from their residential concentration in Whitechapel, Houndsditch, and Spitalfields, nor how isolated they became in their country estates, nor how much they internalized the stigma-free image of the English gentleman, the real image of the Jewish poor stuck to them. This image was presented to the English public in a distorted form by newspapers and periodicals in caricatures, popular songs and shows. At the beginning of the nineteenth century, the image of grasping and unrestrained Jewish economic self-interest was already stereotyped. In different tracts such as *The Commercial Habits of the Jews* (1809), written anonymously, the Jews were presented as excessive, aggressive, dehumanized capitalists who functioned under the guise of their utility to the successful state of the Empire, leaning on theories of economic liberalism.

The financial activities of the brothers Goldsmid and, later in the century, of Nathan Mayer Rothschild, became a popularly propagated theme. According to this view, Jewish money endangered the state and the Church. The apparent threat of Jewish takeover was posited, *inter alia*, by the connections of Jews in England with Jewish financiers abroad. Their presumed lack of national and social ties to England and its masses, were regarded also as evidence of this menace. These arguments were reinforced by anti-capitalist radicalism as well as by the resentment towards the Jews *per se* as expressed by William Cobbett (1835). The anti-capitalist trend of Cobbett was based on physiocratic doctrines, which were applied to the total Jewish population in England and not to Jewish financiers alone. According to this doctrine, Jews did not really contribute to the English economy but exploited it by not creating goods by work (Cobbett 1967 edn: 34–36). Such views were shared by other nostalgic radicals and exacerbated by the acquisition of some country estates by Jewish financiers, which was regarded as usurpation of the traditional paternal, rural ownership. In spite of the economic freedom and prosperity the wealthy Jewish class enjoyed in England, it was exposed to anti-Jewish sentiment that was reinforced in England at this time by the nationalist movement and the Napoleonic Wars.

However, anti-Jewish feelings in spite of their ample expression, did not lead to the same political and social limitations that prevailed in other European countries. The ideas adopted by the English aristocracy can largely be defined as non-interventionism. However, Jews were generally expected to control the situation of their poor classes so that they did not present a social problem affecting the general public. Under the impact of capitalism, the English social environment at this time provided a rationale for a liberal frame of reference, de-emphasizing religious and other differences between individuals. There was a spirit of opposition to Church and central government interference. The emphasis was rather on local government responsibility with regard to the maintenance of charities, health and educational institutions. The Church of England at this time also assumed a more worldly outlook. The stress was now more firmly on the obedience to the Civil Law, social responsibility and voluntarism.

In light of these values the Jewish élite was expected, under normal circumstances, although unofficially, to take care of their own poor. The image of avaricious Shylocks with ample international connections in novels, comic magazines, on stage, daily papers and in pseudo-scientific tracts induced some of the wealthy Jews to maintain a low profile. Many others, however, felt that this image of making money malevolently should be counteracted with an image of the wealthy Jew as a 'big giver' and scientific philanthropist. For the very wealthy, money was the *carte de visite* for entering the non-Jewish upper-class *bon ton* society, but generous philanthropy was needed as well. Moreover, as the social acceptance of Jews was always incomplete, they remained in many ways marginal.

Less wealthy Jews were accepted as governors of non-Jewish philanthropic institutions and as overseers of the poor in the parishes in which they lived. While antipathy, suspicion and hostility continued and were possibly even more traumatic for the Jewish upper class (taking into consideration their social ambitions), the Jewish élite learned to live within these predicaments. After Waterloo, the Jewish wealthy class improved its economic position and English society was even more open to accepting their members into its ranks. During this period, the Jews belonging to the upper-middle class and the middle class continued to move away from the Jewish East End. In this way they separated and estranged themselves from the Jewish poor, and from the circumstances of daily life and East End Jewish institutions, to which the poor applied for help.

During the last part of the eighteenth century the Ashkenazic synagogal charities were at a very low point in terms of resources and administration. In ways similar to the English boroughs, they were not stimulated by pressure from a central authority. A striking account of the consequences of this disorganization in terms of Jewish delinquency, want of skill and illiteracy was given by Patrick Colquhoun LLD (born in Dumbarton, Scotland in 1745) in his book, *A Treatise on the Police of the Metropolis* (1796), which attracted widespread attention through its relatively objective and comprehensive disclosures on delinquency. His detailed, methodical descriptions and remarks with regard to the different categories of offences, forced the Ashkenazic community into the light of fierce public criticism. Colquhoun's official position in the city magistracy increased the authoritativeness of his book. In the context of this alarming quantitative account, Colquhoun estimated the number of itinerant 'Jew Boys' dealing in counterfeit money, purchasing articles stolen by servants, and so on, to be two thousand (1796, 3rd edn: vii).

Colquhoun regarded the offences committed by the 'lower order of the Jews' as one of the 'chief sources of that depravity which prevails in the metropolis, and is to be considered as one great cause of the increase of petty crimes.' He attributed the delinquency of the Jewish poor to their faulty education, lack of occupational training and resources for honest employment (1796: 41), and therefore considered them redeemable. He was aware that:

> their Sabbath prevents them from placing out their children as servants, or apprentices, or binding their sons to mechanical employments, or indeed to any useful art, by which they can assist in increasing the national property – instead of which they diminish it by living upon the industry of others. (1796: 159)

Colquhoun denounced 'the system, which now prevails in the education and habits of this numerous class of people and which is directly hostile to the interests of the State and to the preservation of morals' (1796: 40). In his Treatise, Colquhoun admitted that the police system was unable to control the numerous, partly minor transgressions of the low-income urban class, including the Jewish poor.

He dealt with all groups of the population and Jews were not treated worse than other sectors. Beyond the accusations directed to specific groups, Colquhoun stigmatized the whole working class, presenting it as composed of potential criminals that need to be controlled by a regime of hard labour. However, unlike other contemporary magistrates, Colquhoun did not limit himself to police measures but suggested preventive intervention through education, savings banks, provision of employment and a uniform national poor rate. Colquhoun related to the 'lower order' as a separate entity; however, in other passages he placed the Jewish poor and the middle classes on the same continuum of immoral commercial practices:

> From the orange boy to the retailer of seals, razors, glass and other wares in the public streets, to the shopkeeper, dealer in wearing apparel or in silver and gold, the same principles of conduct too generally prevail . . . the mischiefs which must result from the increase of this depraved race, arising from the natural course of population . . . that a remedy cannot be too soon applied . . . Those belonging to the Dutch synagogue, are in a peculiar manner, rendered objects not only of commiseration but of serious attention on the part of the legislature. (Colquhoun 1796: 160)

In yet another paragraph, Colquhoun makes an analogy between Jews and gypsies. The criticism and admonition of special legislation to restrain Jews or to interfere with their internal organization was directed only to the Ashkenazim, who unlike their Sephardic co-religionists, did not establish sufficient institutions to educate and help their poor. Colquhoun's quasi-official remarks with regard to specific legislative measures were without precedent, as the autonomy of the Jewish élite vis-á-vis philanthropy and education was considered unquestionable. Neither did the English authorities interfere in Jewish internal community conflicts. As to the solutions proposed by Colquhoun, he regarded the Jewish élite as unwilling, rather than unable, to reform its poor, in this way contributing to London's crime and social insecurity. For this purpose he intended to superimpose the wealthy on the 'lower ranks'. Colquhoun believed that 'they [the wealthy Jews] cannot but view with horror and distress, the deplorable conditions and growing depravity' of the Jewish poor (Colquhoun 1796: 160). Considering his proposals to establish various institutions for the assistance of the poor, it is possible that the paragraphs relating to the situation of the Jews were aimed deliberately at creating an unprecedented embarrassment, to provoke the emotional reactions needed to force the wealthy Jews into concrete action.

What Colquhoun criticized and expected to change in the situation of the Jewish poor can be understood by looking at his general approach to popular education and employment. In his article 'Propositions for Ameliorating the Conditions of the Poor, etc.' *Quarterly Review* (December 1812), Colquhoun proposed a national education scheme in a paternalistic framework as the fundament on which a superstructure of prosperity and happiness could be erected solidly, followed by a disappearance of want 'in proportion as the lower classes are instructed in their duties' (Colquhoun 1812: 323, 354). Claiming that the improvidence and vices of the poor were a result of their utterly neglected education, Colquhoun placed, at least indirectly, the responsibility for their situation on the well-to-do who were able to support such education (1812: 319). Colquhoun was himself criticized for supporting the public education movement (the plan designed by Dr Andrew Bell). The criticism came from George Ensor in *On National Education* (1841), who believed that every man must buy instruction, as any other commodity and 'if he cannot afford it he must go without it' (reviewed in *Quarterly Review*, 1811: 431). Considering the economic causes of poverty, Colquhoun was also concerned with the fluctuations in the number of the poor in England and their uncertain sources of income. 'The true essence of government', he asserts, 'was to guide by imperceptible means, the working classes into channels calculated to enable them to render their labour productive' (1818: 22). Such ideas were compatible with those of the *haskallah* – the Jewish enlightenment movement in Europe, which propagated the aim of making the Jewish masses productive.

Colquhoun was aware that the Anglo-Jewish élite was given an almost free hand in managing matters of philanthropy. It was recognized and legitimized by the relevant English authorities. At the beginning of the century, philanthropy was tied to the synagogues and financed through membership taxes and foundations. Each synagogal congregation functioned autonomously. Through the synagogues, the oligarchic élites continued to dominate the infrastructure of the Jewish community in England.

During the first half of the nineteenth century, the great majority of the community accepted the élite submissively. The mainsprings of the power of the Jewish élite were both spiritual and civic, but the élite's rule lay in character rather than in rabbinical authority. With respect to philanthropy, most of the voluntary contributions usually centred around the synagogue, and the wardens of the synagogues were often also charity wardens. Most governments did not make provision for the specific needs of the Jewish communities who continued to cater for the poor within the framework of their remnant autonomy. For that reason, the communities were forced to fall back upon the resources of their wealthy members and to accept their authority. Such élites succeeded in maintaining a relatively firm grasp over most of the educational and socioeconomic aspects of Jewish life.

The voluntary loyalty and dependence of the members of the Jewish communities enabled the élites to exercise comprehensive powers over them. During the nineteenth century, Russia and other East European countries, from which the Jews arrived to Britain, generally remained medieval in character permitting internal self-government among the different corporate groups. More modern emancipated states did not perceive the autonomy of the Jewish community as a usurpation of their power and continued to expect, and even stipulate, that Jews would take care of their own. In such circumstances only the very courageous would occasionally dare to scold the oligarchic leaders or get involved in some aggressive protest against them.

The establishment of the Jewish Board of Guardians in 1859 reflects three parallel processes: (1) the secularization of the aid system; (2) the rationalization of its application; and (3) the emulation of the concept of an aid system and organizational structure prevalent and preferred by the host society. This was therefore a relinquishment of traditional forms of collective and individual philanthropy. However, a series of actions intended to bring about these changes was evident from the very beginning of the nineteenth century, when the doctrines of Colquhoun and Bentham were incorporated by Joshua van Oven – the representative of the London Jewish élite.

Since the late eighteenth century, there was a gradual disuse of Hebrew and Yiddish (written in Hebrew characters) in the traditional and philanthropic terminology. In lieu, English philanthropic terms were borrowed. Beyond the semantics, English contemporary concepts of philanthropy were adapted especially as they generally fitted the interests of the Jewish bourgeoisie anxious to imitate its non-Jewish counterpart.

As presented in the following discussions, because of the important role played by the rapid acculturation of the Jewish élite, concepts of philanthropy were generally constructed on the same basic considerations that prevailed in English philanthropy; they developed and functioned much in tandem. The similarities between the different aspects of English and Anglo-Jewish upper-class philanthropy are indeed striking. Both were largely unanimous in their characterization of the 'lower social orders' and in aiming to replace the values of those strata with English bourgeois values, rather than with a specifically Jewish system of traditional values. Moreover, there were almost no organizational forms of uniquely Jewish characteristics established by the Anglo-Jewish élite during the second half of the nineteenth century. This is demonstrated, for example, by the separatist Orthodox community that developed in the East End, namely *Machzikei Hadath* (Heb. Upholders of the Religion), in the last quarter of the nineteenth century, which fiercely condemned the Anglicized form of Judaism promoted by the élite, including its philanthropic aspect. The preservation of some specific Jewish aspects of Jewish philanthropy was rather related to the observances of strict religious commandments such as the *Shabbat*, Jewish festivals and dietary laws.

Throughout the nineteenth century, some of the members of the élite felt that by manifesting their willingness to resemble their British counterparts and culture as much as possible, they were fulfilling the expectations of the host society. Others felt that by doing so they were actually implementing Jewish traditional values, that after undergoing a metamorphosis they became an integral part of the modern bourgeois thinking. Beyond this there were sporadic attempts to connect directly Anglo-Jewish modern philanthropy with traditional Jewish values based on the universal and humanistic common denominators of general philanthropic notions. Thus, for instance, rabbis quoted biblical verses and *hallachic* texts relating to *tzedakah*. However, in instances of conflict between the concept of Jewish and non-Jewish philanthropy, the Jewish élite followed the English precedents to which they were keenly alert. The involvement of Jews in non-Jewish philanthropies continuously reinforced this trend.

In this book it is claimed that while the Jewish élite identified itself with the general principles of English philanthropy, the selection of these principles for actual implementation was based on class interests as they appeared to the élite in the historical circumstances that prevailed.

This chapter has shown the constant fear of the Jewish wealthy class that public opinion might identify the 'enlightened' and assimilated Jewish bourgeoisie with the 'undesirable' hawkers and itinerant mendicants. However, additional pressures from the host society were required in order to motivate the Jewish élite to undertake the planning of financial and social responsibility for the poor, as reflected by the Colquhoun–van Oven scheme to which we now turn our attention.

2

The Colquhoun–van Oven Scheme

This chapter focuses on the readiness of the Jewish élite to adapt an innovative and comprehensive English organizational model designed by Patrick Colquhoun. The scheme was intended to empower the Jewish élite to support, educate and combat vagrancy and mendacity by using quasi-police measures. It also included the establishment of an exclusive indoor institution for the Jews. The scheme was to be legalized by Parliament. The basis of opposition to the scheme and the reasons for its failure will be explored in the following discussion.

BACKGROUND TO THE SCHEME

The campaign to obtain the funds requested for a large plan to reform the Jewish poor was started in 1795 when the brothers Benjamin (1755–1808) and Abraham (1756–1810) Goldsmid, who by this time were involved in large transactions in government loans, were able during two consecutive years to collect the amount of twenty thousand pounds sterling that was invested in Imperial 3 per cent. More than half of this money was raised within an amazingly short period of time from Jews and non-Jewish philanthropists, their banking friends. Unfortunately the outlines of this plan are unknown and so is the dispute that induced the brothers to postpone the use of the capital and the accumulated interest until 1807 when it was ultimately used for the erection of the Jews' Hospital. According to Alderman (1983: 9) the scheme failed because it was considered to attract large numbers of Jewish poor from abroad.

The brothers Goldsmid were born in Holland. Their father, Aaron, settled in London around 1763, starting in *c.*1777 as a somewhat unknown bill broker in a modest office in Leman Street, close to the East End where he lived in Goodmans Field. Abraham and Benjamin extended the business their father established. During the Napoleonic Wars they overpowered the domineering Stock Exchange banking clique, and in association with a non-Jewish firm, were successful bidders for huge national loans. Both brothers were determined to win a place in non-Jewish aristocratic society. In 1792, Benjamin bought and remodelled an extravagant thirty-bedroom mansion at Roehampton, decorated with famous works of art, which Thackeray dubbed a banking colony (Arkin 1975: 160). Abraham acquired a country house at Morden in 1805 and later Merton Place, the country house of Nelson's mistress, Lady Hamilton (Brown 1984: 33–4). The Goldsmids entertained lavishly, giving splendid fêtes. Among their guests were the Prince of Wales, George III and Queen Charlotte, and Nelson.

Philanthropy to non-Jewish causes was a way of counteracting the image of the Jews as merciless usurers and the feelings of non-Jews that the Jewish wealthy class reserved its generosity for their own philanthropies. During the 1790s, the brothers Goldsmid and some of their Jewish partners became governors of the Foundling Hospital. When the Naval Asylum was established in 1798, Benjamin contributed £2,000 and was instrumental in raising an additional £2,600 from other Jewish financiers in 1806. According to his biographer in 'Memoir of the Late Abraham Goldsmid' (*Gentleman's Magazine*, 1810, LXXX, 2nd part: 382–5) and the *Dictionary of National Biography*, (VIII: 81), Benjamin was the real founder of the Naval Asylum. Abraham gave £700 to the Society for the Deaf and Dumb, and to many other charities. The participation in non-Jewish philanthropy received commendations in the general newspapers and, to some extent, created and maintained good relations between the Jewish and the general communities as well as on a more interpersonal level.

However, meteoric success, the amassing of huge capital and the ostentatious way in which donations were made, raised suspicion from some non-Jewish quarters. An anonymous publication, *The Commercial Habits of the Jews*, commented:

> One of these gentlemen [A. Goldsmid] (who it must be confessed, if we remove out of the consideration the rapidity and manner in which his immense property has been acquired has been liberal in his charitable donations) has been exhibited in the windows of the print-shops with scrolls of paper dangling out of his pockets ... The indelicacy of this exhibition is sufficiently obvious, but our contempt and disgust are excited when we learn that it was not the result of gratuitous adulation, but a wretched design and plot upon the admiration of the publick. (1809)

William Cobbett expressed his deep contempt for Abraham Goldsmid even more bluntly, by emphasizing the exploitation involved, in and disguised by, his charity: 'a man acquiring such immense wealth must see that something was necessary to keep the public from grudging . . . [Goldsmid] merely tossed back to the miserable part of us in the shape of alms, the fraction of pence upon the immense sums of money that he got by his traffic in loans and bills and funds' (quoted in Emden 1943: 93). Such accusations could not be easily dismissed. Beyond the deep dislike Cobbett felt for Jews in general and his description of them in derogatory and misleading terms, his campaign was an integral part of an attempt made by the radical opposition to stop the system that Pitt initiated for financing the war, by which the wealthy capitalists exploited the state. (Cole 1938: 118–19). Yet, large-scale philanthropic donations impressed the contemporary social mind as an effort to correct and ameliorate social conditions out of a sense of *noblesse oblige* and many newspapers considered Abraham's benevolence genial and respectable. Such laudatory articles motivated Cobbett to devote an issue of his weekly *Political Register* to combat Goldsmid's popularity as a philanthropist.

A contemporary Jewish critique was expressed by the London Jewish printer, Levi Alexander, 'As for their charity . . . they like the pomp and stance of a printed subscription, where their names blazoned in the front of a newspaper tells the world so much good has been done' (Alexander 1802: 22). As a traditionalist, Alexander's strictures were based on the *hallachic* principle of giving without making one's identity known. Lucien Wolf, writing in 1934, considers the donations to non-Jewish charitable causes during that period as jeopardizing the needs of the Jewish poor: 'Those, however, who know from the pages of Patrick Colquhoun . . . how terrible was the condition of the German Jewish poor of London at this period, can only marvel at Benjamin Goldsmid's misdirected altruism' (Wolf 1934: 196). Wolf differentiates between the approach of the brothers, regarding Abraham as 'delighted in succouring the needy' and 'truly attached to his community'. According to Emden, the tendency of Benjamin to combine charity with his own personal advancement was severely criticized in Jewish circles (Emden 1943: 90). Both brothers committed suicide; Benjamin in 1808, presumably due to gout and melancholia, and Abraham in 1810, subsequent to an alleged conspiracy of other speculators and stock collapse.

Situated at the higher level of the power structure, the Goldsmids were consulted with respect to the situation of the Jewish poor, but out of an unwillingness to face excessive attention and possibly due to lack of time and expertise they frequently acted through Dr Joshua van Oven (1766–1836), surgeon and Honorary Medical Officer to the Poor at the Great Synagogue. Joshua van Oven was not a member of the higher economic circles but had a more direct knowledge of the situation of the poor, acquired through his contacts with them as a surgeon. He was not a deep thinker but possessed the knowledge of modern philanthropic doctrine and social thought necessary for helping the élite choose between alternative modes of action.

His job security, however, depended upon the leaders of the Ashkenazic community who ultimately took responsibility for the implementation of any project. Joshua van Oven was the second president of the Bread, Meat and Coal Charity (Wolf 1934: 187). At the beginning of the nineteenth century he was a leading figure in philanthropic and educational reforms. His father, Abraham, graduated at Leiden and was appointed physician of the Great Synagogue in 1767. He translated into Hebrew the *Oeconomy of Human Life* written by the moralist, Robert Dodsley, among other works. Joshua's son, Bernard, followed the same professional and communal career, and was active in the élite's struggle for political emancipation.

In 1815, van Oven translated from Hebrew into English, the *Shoreshei Emuna, Elements of Faith* by the 'enlightener' (*maskil, aufklärer*), Shalom Cohen. (Contact between van Oven and Cohen was established in 1813 when the latter attempted to found a Hebrew school in London, prior to his return to the Continent). The *Elements of Faith* is a moderate orthodox Jewish catechism, parallel to those used during this period in Christian Charity Schools. Despite being based mainly on the Bible, it received the approbation of the Chief Rabbi, Solomon Hirschell, subsequent to the pressure raised by influential financiers (Roth 1950: 68). Twenty years later, van Oven published the *Manual of Judaism* as well as other Hebrew writings that he translated into English. Joshua van Oven attempted to modernize Judaism in England sharing the tendencies of the *haskalah*, the Jewish enlightenment movement in Germany (Roth 1967: 345–76). Although the *haskalah* emerged as an integral part of the general enlightenment movement of eighteenth-century Europe, it was characterized by the special circumstances of the Jewish people. As an adherent of this movement van Oven was concerned with assimilation with respect to language, manners and the productivization of the Jewish poor (by introducing changes in their occupational structure and promoting mechanical crafts and agriculture).

Such a change was deemed by some circles, Jewish as well as non-Jewish, as a precondition for bettering their character and situation.

Generally, the *maskilim* accepted this implied critique and propagated this view in their social and economic doctrines, sometimes overlooking the real conditions of the low-income Jewish class and their inability to obtain employment of any sort, even when fairly skilled. At the beginning of the nineteenth century this doctrine was implemented in Western Europe by societies for apprenticing and promoting industry amongst the Jews, especially in manual work. In the eastern and other parts of Europe the *maskilim* were often supported and maintained by wealthy Jewish merchants; consequently, in their writings they reflected the ideals of the rising Jewish middle classes, presenting them as a model to be imitated by the poor. In their view the Jewish masses were ignorant and arrogant.

R. Mahler writes about their approach to the poor: 'Enrichissez vous! the motto of the rising capitalism was also the motto of the *maskilim* . . . wealth is a natural reward for economic initiative . . . poverty is the result of indolence, inertia and illiteracy' (Mahler 1972: 80–1). According to Mahler, 'the productivization of the masses was also directly in the interests of the rising Jewish capitalist class, for the impoverished non-productive elements constituted a handicap to the expansion of the internal market' (Mahler 1972: 82, 84–5). As a consequence of their approach to the poor, some *maskilim* regarded Jewish philanthropy as an incentive to idleness. Even when the approach of the *maskilim* to the Jewish wealthy class was more ambivalent or critical, it still reflected the hope that their resources could be used for improving the situation of the Jewish masses. The indifference of the host régimes towards the vast poverty of the Jews and the long-standing tradition of 'Jews take care of their own', only increased the dependence of the *maskilim* on the wealthy Jewish class.

The influence of this movement on van Oven facilitated the incorporation of contemporary ideas on education for the poor and relief of poverty. However, there is also evidence of internal struggle which sometimes underlined the writings of European *maskilim*: some of them identified with the poor class and criticized the wealthy Jewish domineering class in Eastern Europe. In 1780, during a visit to different European countries, Benjamin Goldsmid established contact with prominent *maskilim* with a view to use their methods in England. In *Memoirs of the Life and Commercial Connections of Benjamin Goldsmid of Roehampton* (1808), Alexander comments:

His views [Benjamin Goldsmid's] were directed to the remotest points of moral perspective as the greatest means of reducing the whole to a uniform practice of beneficial improvement. The principal object of Mr. Goldsmid's inquiry was the situation of the individuals in foreign countries. He felt for their state at home as well as lamented their abject depression abroad, but above all things he wished to observe was their mode of educating children … in order, if possible, to alleviate their condition at home on his return. Thus he invited philanthropy and philosophy for application to the best of purposes. (1808: 24, 25, 27)

The emphasis of his inquiry abroad was on the education of children, reflecting a more sceptical view of education of the adult poor. In 1788, the two brothers Goldsmid, their two brothers-in-law and other financiers, reorganized the small Ashkenazic Talmud Torah School (established in 1732, as a traditional Jewish religious school for poor boys), by adding and emphasizing practical subjects, but this institution accepted a very limited number of boys whose parents could not pay for private tutoring. The school accepted only children of 'respectable families', rejecting homeless and destitute children. Illegitimate children were to be *a priori* excluded from the screening process, as were children whose parents were not legally married, all in accordance with the prevailing social philosophy of nineteenth-century philanthropy.

By 1801, in spite of the severe situation of the Jewish poor and the high rate of offences committed by Jews, no agreement was reached between the Jewish financiers as to the proper use of the £20,000 which remained in abeyance since its collection in 1797. Additional editions of Colquhoun's book continued to present Jews of all classes and Jewish philanthropy in derogatory terms. The leaders of the two Ashkenazic synagogues, in Fenchurch Street (Hambro Synagogue) and Leadenhall Street (New Synagogue), refused to share the expenses incurred by the Great Synagogue in maintaining the 'strange poor' who swarmed the streets, peddling and begging. Under these pressures, van Oven met Colquhoun (who presided as a police magistrate at Queen's Square, Westminster) in March 1801, and in collaboration with him designed a comprehensive scheme that (as described later) was based on the ideas of Colquhoun and Bentham and supported by Abraham Goldsmid and the Ashkenazic élite.

The correspondence between van Oven and Colquhoun was summarized in the publication: *Letters on the Present State of the Jewish Poor in the Metropolis with Proposition for Ameliorating their Conditions by Improving the Morals of the Youth of Both Sexes and by Rendering their Labour Useful and Productive in a Greater Degree to Themselves and to the Nation* (London, 1802), by Joshua van Oven. The publication of the letters to Colquhoun aimed at generating, without delay, a more favourable opinion towards the whole English Jewry. They included such argumentative apologies as the causes of Jewish poverty and delinquency, the care that Jews generally take of their own poor, the potential of the Jewish poor to extend their occupational field and the ability of the Jewish wealthy class to control the poor and help them in discriminative ways, embodied in a practical scheme. At the same time Colquhoun was instrumental in rendering the scheme as a bill for presentation before Parliament (Picciotto 1875: 260).

Colquhoun's involvement in the scheme can be better understood in light of the repeated failure to implement his and Bentham's plan during the same period, the general unwillingness of the government to reform the Poor Law and the reluctance of the destitute poor to enter the workhouses. Colquhoun, possibly with the consent of Bentham himself, regarded the whole situation as an exceptional opportunity to realize some of his ideas using the material resources of the Jewish magnates and their non-Jewish partners to reform the Jewish poor. In fact, in 1778, Bentham suggested erecting a labour house for Jews to be supported by the Jewish community. This was proposed to solve the problems connected with dietary and other Jewish religious obser-vances that prevented the Jewish poor from entering workhouses. In *An Extract of a Pamphlet intituled, 'Draught of a Bill, To Punish by Imprisonment and Hard Labour, Certain Offenders: and to Establish proper Places for their Reception'* (1778), republished as *A View of The Hard-Labour Bill*, Jeremy Bentham wrote:

> As to Jews, I must confess, I can see no feasible way of making, in each Labour house, the provisions requisite for satisfying all their various scruples. As it happens there seems reason (I do not know whether to say to hope, but at any rate) to believe that of such of them as are likely to become inhabitants of these houses, there are not many on whom these scruples would set heavy. The only expedient I can think of for the indul-gence of those people, is to have one Labour house for all the convicts of this persuasion throughout the kingdom. In such case, it would be but reasonable that the whole community of Jews should be at the expense of this establishment, including the charges of conveyance. They might then have their own rabbis and their own cooks and butcher. (Bentham 1778)

In this pamphlet Bentham suggested *inter alia* to provide a new estab-lishment of Labour houses all over England. In March 1792 Bentham proposed that the government should undertake the charge of a thou-sand convicts under a new system, denoted the Panopticon. The plan of the model prison (a 'pauper' branch was planned later on) was adopted in 1794 by an act of Parliament. In 1795, Bentham prepared the adaptation of the Panopticon prison's plan to workhouses. His plan was extended gradually to comprise two hundred and fifty houses of industry to be established throughout England. Bentham was assisted with his plan by Colquhoun who collected information and agreed to sponsor the Panopticon Plan. According to Poynter (1969: 200), when Jeremy Bentham had enlisted Colquhoun's aid in 1796, 'it was not as a mere assistant but almost as a patron, for Colquhoun was already much more widely known as an authority on such subjects than was Bentham himself'. However, Bentham and Colquhoun were to be disillusioned because they could not recruit new supporters amongst the philanthropists and few parishes cooperated in providing information (Poynter 1969: 141, based on Bentham Papers, CLI: 102–5). Under the circumstances described, and in view of the optimistic financial prospective of the brothers Goldsmid during this time, the Jewish Askenazic élite was willing to adopt Colquhoun's ideas.

Principal Proposals of the Scheme

The scheme proposed to establish a corporative body, authorized by Parliament, and empowered with a quasi-governmental prerogative for the supervision of all matters relating to the Jewish poor in London, regulating their economy, promoting industry and productive labour among them. The board was to be entitled to purchase lands, not exceeding one hundred acres in extent, upon which buildings would be erected from time to time as to be found necessary. In the first phase, four buildings were to be erected (*Substances* 1802: 1, 2):

> an asylum for the aged and the infirm persons; a hospital for the sick, maimed and diseased; a school for the education of children and for the instruction of the mechanical and other useful arts; an institution of industry for vagrant poor and such as are able but not willing to work for their living.

In addition, a burial ground was to be purchased or rented for burying those who may die in any of the places belonging to the establishment, unless removed by their relatives to be buried elsewhere at the family's expense.

Colquhoun and van Oven's scheme was inspired by the arrangements for the poor at Shrewsbury. According to the parochial survey of Sir Frederick Morton Eden (1928), at the end of the eighteenth century, the six parishes of Shrewsbury had been united by an act of Parliament, and among other arrangements a joint house of industry was built (1797, abridged edn 1928: xxxv), 'designed on sound lines and under . . . able management . . . this Poor House became almost a municipal work-shop'. Due to the earnings from the sale of manufactured merchandise the yearly poor rate was reduced (a fact, however, considered by Eden to be unrelated to the value of work done by the inmates). In compar-ison with other workhouses, those of Shrewsbury provided a relatively high standard of accommodation, and reflected the rise of public conscience regarding conditions under which the poor were main-tained. Eden, however, concluded somewhat sceptically, that 'a kind of glare, which obscures the truth, has been thrown upon workhouses . . . the advantages are only negative. This is the merit of the much taunted workhouse of Shrewsbury' (1928 edn: 127).

Colquhoun had no good opinion of the contemporary workhouses and, no doubt, wanted to create something quite different. It was true that beyond its intrinsic defects, whether a workhouse reformed by educating and providing work for the able-bodied, punished, deterred or solely maintained the poor more comfortably than elsewhere, depended less on statutory provisions and regulations than on indi-vidual management and parish leadership. Colquhoun hoped to achieve more ambitious aims by establishing a system of securing effi-cient, properly motivated and resourceful governors. However, he did not consider other aspects of the contemporary practices such as the demoralizing cruelties and tyrannies of the contractors to whom the poor were to be 'farmed'. As envisaged by Bentham and Colquhoun, workhouses were to become institutions that the nation could be proud of. They were to combine productivity and usefulness, rehabilitate the able-bodied poor and provide separate accommodation for the impov-erished but previously independent labourer, using a differentiation based on moral traits. The separation of the honest victims of difficult times from those who lived depraved lives, was regarded by Colquhoun as one of the main advantages of his proposal. The houses of industry were to improve the conditions of life of all inmates; for instance, by reducing working hours, providing healthy food and so on.

The operation of the whole scheme was to be carried into effect without interfering with 'the general system of Jewish oeconomy' (*Letters* 1802: 2) and without obstructing the Jewish religious practices (*Letters* 1802: 17). The aim of the scheme was to operate powerfully 'not only promoting the cause of humanity but also in rearing up the infant poor in habits of useful industry and in restraining the adults from acts of nature, criminal and nauseous to the society' (2: I). In cases of illegitimacy the directors were to be entitled to act for children in the same way as church wardens and overseers (6: XVI).

The directors were to be empowered (6–7, XVII) 'to appoint officers, who are to have the authority for apprehending persons of the Jewish persuasion committing acts of vagrancy and carry them before the magistrate to be dealt with as the law directs'. Determined to combat Jewish vagrancy in the densely populated metropolis, van Oven regarded the substitution of the functions discharged inefficiently by the police as rather promising. Moreover, putting into practice some of the theories that Colquhoun had advanced, even on a limited scale, could raise Abraham Goldsmid and himself in public esteem as outstanding philanthropists and reformers, far beyond the sphere of the Jewish community:

> I am persuaded, that if the scheme was fairly laid down, and its consequences fully made out, it would be embraced with avidity by the best informed and most important part of the nation . . . A system like this . . . would be an exemplary proof of justices of the plan for consolidating the metropolitan parishes into one Board for the affairs of the poor as proposed in your excellent work of the Police. (Letters: 21)

It is worth noting that in the wider general context of poverty, the plan of the Panopticon included measures for apprehending beggars and vagrants. In addition to its power to incarcerate the dependent and punish the criminal, the Board was also to be invested with power 'to inquire into the circumstances of the poor', to differentiate between the 'idle and disorderly persons' and 'the deserving poor'. The latter were to be helped by occasional relief (*Substances*: 4, VIII; *Letters*: 19, 28). The model for this provision was also borrowed from contemporary innovative practice (*Letters*: 18): 'a method of assisting the out-door poor with occasional relief, somewhat familiar to that adopted at Shrewsbury'. However, out-door relief was considered rather secondary. Bentham contended that a system of out-door relief (which he designated as 'Home provision') could not be universal, as the so-called impotent and homeless needed institutional care anyhow. He also thought it could not employ paupers efficiently and it could not be combined with education. In *Pauper System Compared*, Bentham expressed his opinion that out-door relief could 'do tolerably well for the strictly virtuous', but a

system based on institutional care and publicly run in large establishments was controllable and perfectible. (CLIIb: Bentham Papers: 454–9,
509–15; also quoted by Poynter 1969: 123).

Activities of the Calquhoun–van Oven scheme were to be conducted
by a Board of Presidents of the four main synagogues, twelve
Ashkenazic and four Sephardic representatives, two aldermen of the
City, two magistrates for Middlesex, Kent, Essex and Surrey, and the
four presidents of the City synagogues. The executive body was to be
constituted of eight directors (two elected representatives of each
respective congregation). All members of the synagogues who paid an
annual fee of three guineas were eligible for election.

To support this scheme Jews of the metropolis were to become a separate fiscal unit. The activities of the centrally-led institutions were to be
provided from a Jewish Poor Fund established by an act of Parliament.
The following sources of income were proposed:

1   Compulsory, synagogal levies and, if they were insufficient, an
     individual tax on the incomes of all Jewish householders in London
     assessed by three committees to be balloted for from the Board of
     Directors.
2   An appropriation of one half of the poor rates paid by Jews to their
     parishes of residence which were, with very few exceptions,
     without recourse to their poor co-religionists, due to the long tradi-
     tion of 'Jews taking care of their own.'
3   An option to borrow up to £10,000 for the purpose of purchasing
     land and erecting buildings.
4   An appropriation of the funds used by the synagogue to assist their
     attached poor.
5   Donations, bequests, legacies and any other voluntary contribu-
     tions were to be accepted.

The proposal to replace voluntary contributions for the maintenance
of the poor by compulsory levies to provide adequate relief on a steady
operational basis stemmed from deep dissatisfaction with the exclusive
reliance on contributions that were insufficient and fluctuated
according to the decisions of the donors.

Voluntary contributions, especially at the 'top level', were, to a large
extent, based on personal discretion, clique and business relations, and
rivalries over hierarchic positions and honours in philanthropic institutions. The contributions were further hampered by the atrophy of
charitable instincts and unwillingness to devote surplus resources to the

needy. In contrast, the members of the Sephardic congregation were paying a progressive income tax, *'imposta'*, based on financial transactions and an additional fixed tax, *'finta'* (Ascamot, [Heb. Agreements] revised edn 1906: 1–6). This social arrangement of the Sephardim was a continuation of the traditional Jewish *tzedakah*.

Voluntary financing of the poor was fraught with the dissatisfaction of the wealthy with the gratifications the community could offer. In this regard van Oven wrote to Colquhoun:

> I do not think that the support of an institution of such consequence *can or ought to rest on such* an uncertain footing *as occasional elemosynary subscriptions.* The plan is for the effectual relief and maintenance of poor which is an absolute duty not an act of generosity and liberality . . . experience has too fatally evinced how unstable a basis elemosynary contributions proves, being too much subject to the changes of caprice, and too liable to have its resources withheld from opposition, whom avarice and sometimes interest. (Letters, 24 March 1801: 18, 31–2: emphasis in original)

This bitter critique of the prosperous Jewish élite is evident throughout his letters. On the other hand, van Oven's letters to Colquhoun anticipate the reluctance of parishes to lose a part of the poor rates paid by the Jews, of which they benefited in their entirety, especially 'wherein the majority of the Jews reside, which may oblige us to wait the period when the reform you suggest shall take place and open a door for the admission of such a claim' (Letter of 27 March 1801, *Letters* 1802: 21). Joshua van Oven also feared that such parishes would have to reassess all their inhabitants, non-Jewish included, in order to make up for their income, 'a measure, in the present high state of the rates, extremely unpopular, if not oppressive, besides its producing a revival of prejudices and hatred against the Jew, which is now happily fast diminishing' (Letter of 21 December 1801, *Letters* 1802: 31). Consequently, that proviso was altogether omitted from additional formulations of the bill.

OPPOSITION TO THE SCHEME

Fully supported by Abraham Goldsmid, the scheme was endorsed by the three main Ashkenazic synagogues and presented to the Chancellor of the Exchequer, Henry Addington, for approbation by Parliament. It was, however, strongly opposed by the Sephardim, who petitioned

Parliament. They regarded themselves as both more Anglicized and more organized than the Ashkenazim, and resented being identified with the limitations of the Ashkenazim in terms of philanthropic organization and being forced to contribute disproportionately to the scheme. The charitable efforts of the Sephardic community were recognized by the pamphleteer, Levi Alexander (1802: 30), yet this community also faced a severe problem of poverty.

Rumney (1933: 90) estimates the number of Sephardic poor at 1,100. According to Roth (1964: 239), during the last quarter of the eighteenth century, many wealthy Sephardim lost as much as 90 per cent of their capital as a result of the crisis in the state of affairs of the Dutch East India Company, leaving the finances of the Sephardic community in disarray. The immigrants were mainly Ashkenazim, and due to a lack of solidarity between the two élites, the Sephardic élite was determined to preserve financial independence and to remain a separate 'political body'. To justify this trend, differences in religious rituals were overemphasized. The Sephardim blamed the Ashkenazim for the unfavourable change in English public opinion towards Anglo Jewry, and indicated their wish to avoid the imposition of public policy. They regarded the plan as an intention to use their funds for encouraging Ashkenazic immigration from Europe. Mr. Pierce, a solicitor, was instructed by the Sephardic élite, led by Isaac Aguilar, to prepare a clause requesting the exclusion of the Sephardim from the bill and to forward it to Mr Hobhouse, the MP in charge of the bill in the House of Commons.

Still another conflicting pressure with which van Oven was faced came from the wealthy Jewish group itself, concerned about the authority given to the Board to assess and tax them. This is reflected in the second letter of van Oven to Colquhoun:

> how trifling and nugatory does a burthen of a moderate taxation appear as an objection. I say a moderate tax for it cannot, and must not, be a heavy one, no tax for charitable purposes ought to be so large as to excite sentiments militating against these benign ideas of charity . . . (Letter of 21 December 1801, *Letters* 1802: 34–5)

Although the financing of the plan was to be based on more progressive and obligatory taxes, the inherent unwillingness to burden the wealthy Jewish class and to protect its interest is reflected throughout the approach of van Oven and this was probably the main obstacle to the implementation of the scheme.

Following the opposition of the Sephardim, and in spite of intra-élite controversies, a plan was prepared by Colquhoun and van Oven for the 'general oeconomy' of the Ashkenazic poor only. It was entitled *Substances for Clauses to Frame a Bill to be brought into Parliament for the Better Providing for the Poor of the German Jews in the Metropolis and the Bills of Mortality, including St. Pancras and Marylebone.* This category of the poor included those British-born and foreigners. But opposition from other quarters further reduced the momentum of the scheme. Finally, only a brief petition of the German Jews, resident in London, was presented to the House of Commons on the 25 February 1802, in which was stated:

> although the Jewish Poor have an equal right with other members of the community to Parochial Relief when in Distress, yet the peculiar Circumstances of their religious Rites and Diet completely shut them out of all Places established for the Relief of the Poor, and the same Cause deprives them (when afflicted with Sickness, or maimed by any Accident) of the Benefit to be derived from medical Aid administered in the different Hospitals in this Metropolis, and prevents the Children of Jews from being bound to mechanical and many other Employments, by which they might be enabled to become useful Members of Society; and that, in the present State of the Class of the Jewish nation, of whom the Petitioners form a Part, there is no Asylum to which the aged and infirm can resort for Succour and Protection when Disability assail them, nor any place for the Education and Maintenance of the Infant Poor; and that the Relief afforded by the Synagogue is, under the present Circumstances, very inadequate and for Want of proper Regulations, is inefficiently applied; and that the Petitioners conceive it will be highly advantageous to the Persons denominated German Jews, residing in the City of London . . . if Power was given to regulate and maintain their poor, and to promote Industry and the knowledge of useful and productive labour among them and thereby render them more useful members of Society than they are, or can be, under the present peculiar circumstances and therefore Praying, That Leave may be given to bring in a Bill for the purposes aforesaid . . . Ordered, That the said Petition to lie upon the Table. (*Commons Journal* 1802: 172)

George Tierney did not act to bring in a bill that would incorporate the scheme's proposals. By moving to lay the petition on the table, he indicated that at some future date he intended to refer it to a committee prior to its presentation for parliamentary approval in the form of a bill based on the Colquhoun–van Oven scheme. However, no further proceedings took place on the petition and no letter was required for its withdrawal. There are no verbatim accounts of debates in this period, and the standard edition of Parliamentary debates (*Parliamentary History*) has nothing noted for 25 February 1802 when the petition was presented. On 22 April 1802, at the Coachmakers' Hall, the scheme was totally abandoned following a decision taken by the Ashkenazic leaders who had supported it (Board of Deputies of the British Jews, Minute Book 1, 1760–1828, *The Parliamentary Register* 1802: 63–4).

One of the main factors accounting for the failure of the scheme was the reluctance of the Ashkenazic élite to authorize the Ashkenazic establishment as a distinct fiscal body, subject to the interference of the state. The élite suspected that an obligatory levy, although proposed as moderate, would not be limited to the relief of the poor, but would eventually be extended to encompass other fields of communal activity, such as education. This aspect of the scheme was regarded by the Ashkenazic élite as unfeasible and even dangerous to its vital interests (Letter of 21 December 1801, van Oven *Letters* 1802: 34–5).

The obstacles encountered by Colquhoun and the Ashkenazic establishment, which was represented by van Oven, in implementing the scheme, even in a limited form, exposed the conflicting interests and ideologies within the structure of Anglo-Jewry as well as the positions of Jews of different social strata *vis-à-vis* the host environment. These reactions were published as pamphlets. The opposition of Levi Alexander to the scheme reflects the traditionalist approach combined with a sympathy for the poor, and a rejection of the scheme's repressive measures, designed to control the poor, and a sarcastic critique of the wealthy class struggling to legalize its power over the poor.

Levi Alexander was a printer, and bitter pamphleteer, of Whitechapel. His father, the English-born Alexander Alexander, was the first Jewish typographer in England. In 1770, Alexander Alexander translated the Ashkenazic liturgy into English. Levi prepared and printed a revised edition. In 1808, Levi Alexander published a pamphlet critical of Solomon Hirschell, the chief rabbi of the Great Synagogue, which referred to his want of charity in a particular case (1808b: 16). In his pamphlet, *Answer to Mr Joshua van Oven's Letters on the Present State of the Jewish Poor in London . . . with a Word to P. Colquhoun* (1802), Alexander vehemently criticized the elements of coercion and punishment included in the scheme:

> the rich impose too often the iron hand of power on the weakness of the poor . . . but oppressing the poor without legal power and causing for legal assistance to do it to a greater extent, is worse than amassing fortunes by indirect means . . . The men, or bodies, who grow rich every day . . . deceive

themselves when they think because it is so, that they are better than their less fortunate neighbours. (Alexander 1802: 41–2)

Alexander described the tyranny already exercised by the synagogal authorities to obtain considerable burial taxes from the lower middle class families of deceased persons; beyond this, his fears of authoritarian policies can be understood in the context of the historical experience of the Jewish people. As a representative of the lower middle class, and taking into consideration the structure of the Jewish community at this time, which consisted of a small upper and middle class versus a large number of poor, Alexander was alarmed by the burden of the prospective compulsory taxation (Alexander 1802).

At the same time Alexander suspected that 'If . . . an asylum . . . could be accomplished, the influx of foreigners from all parts would be drawn to this centre and it would require above a *treasury loan* to supply all their wants. Yet I must confess these exotics are better learned than our own natives' (1802: 22).

Like the wealthy class, Alexander regarded the financial burden imposed by immigration as insupportable but as a traditionalist, and in contrast to the Jewish élite, he viewed the integration of the immigrant poor as a two-way process necessitating a thorough understanding and appreciation of their Jewish education. In contrast, the Jewish élite demanded the overall 'regeneration' of the immigrant poor without specifying what mores were to be the target of change. In an open letter to Colquhoun, Alexander accepted his conclusions with regard to the educational deficiencies of the poor in modern and secular terms, but rejected the stigmatization of the poor and contested the practicability of the proposals included in the scheme: 'why brand and maculate a proportion of the human species . . . with an indelible mark of approbrium, for what is not to be alleged against individuals as a fault, but only to their mode of education, the prejudices of which if they are so lawful, are too formidable for any Police bench to reform' (Alexander 1802: 34–44).

Alexander stated bluntly that the Jewish poor did not derive any advantage in terms of employment from their geographical proximity to rich neighbours, thence he concluded that the proposed vocational training was futile. The viewpoints expressed by Alexander reflect the insularity of the Jewish élite from social realities and the extent to which democratic and traditional practices such as providing employment to the poor were lacking in the Jewish community. Alexander regarded the poor with compassion and even saw himself as a representative and instructor of the poor in avoiding oppression:

> In this place I think myself intitled, as well as called upon by strong conviction of duty, to admonish, and as far as I can, instruct my poorer brethren upon the nature of the mischievous measure that is about to be circled about them; for should the Synagogue obtain the wished-for power, what will be the consequence only time can shew. (Alexander 1802: 42)

Both van Oven and Alexander were among those who at this period in England were knowledgeable of the Jewish scriptural assertions on poverty and the practical ways the *hallachah* suggests in dealing with the poor. But van Oven's position as an employee of the Great Synagogue and his functions as representative of the Ashkenazic establishment account for the differences in their approach. Alexander related the reaction of the poor to their situation in another pamphlet 'Though the mob are blind enough, yet their optic are not so thick . . . ' (1808b: 16). The deprecation of the masses was characteristic of some of the early nineteenth-century Jewish intellectuals and was adopted by the *haskalah* (Enlightenment) movement. The direct opinions of the poor about the scheme are not known as they did not possess the means of the wealthy to immortalize themselves. The social structure as a whole discouraged the poor's expression in the contemporary media.

An additional reaction to the scheme of van Oven and Colquhoun came from Philo Judaeis, an anonymous non-Jew in his pamphlet, *A Letter to Abraham Goldsmid, Esq. containing Strictures on Mr Joshua van Oven's Letters Pointing Out the Impractibility of Ameliorating their Condition through the medium of Taxation and Coercion, etc.,* London 1802. The basic premise of the writer is that the Jewish poor were already provided for quite adequately and consequently there was no need to impose an additional burden on what he considered 'the frugal and the industrious part of the community, who already groan under the pressure of Parliamentary and Parochial Taxes' (V). The writer suggests the establishment of a seminar for the education of the new generation to be financed by voluntary donations. Philo Judaeis did not object to the repressive feature of the scheme, rather his skepticism was based on the inefficiency of the legal confinement of mendicants:

> If British jurisprudence, with all its advantages has hitherto been found inadequate, to coerce them [mendicants] into habits of industry. How can it be expected, that your proposed Directory with limited powers will be able, especially after they are reinforced by fresh importation of alien

Jewish vagabonds, Surely Mr van Oven will not, assert that the young and profligate Jews will tamely submit to such an incarceration. If Mr Wood [the Director of the Shrewsbury House of Industry] is drawn so pathetically to complain of the insuperable difficulties in establishing proper discipline. (Philo Judaeis 1802: 11–12)

On the basis of his knowledge regarding the feelings of the English poor towards the workhouse, Philo Judaeis asked 'is it your intention to require Parliament to arm you with the invidious power of compelling adult Jews to become inhabitants of what, I am convinced, they will in spite of your benevolent intentions, view as a prison?' (p. 18). Regarding unemployment amongst the able-bodied poor as irreversible, he did not see any strength in van Oven's proposals for outdoor relief:

If you cannot comprehend all your Poor, in your proposed operations, where is the utility of restoring to partial remedies? and shutting up one part in the House of Industry, while you leave the remainder to their former habits of vagrancy? Such a step will at once defeat your main object – which is to regulate the oeconomy of the Jewish Poor. (p. 22)

Philo Judaeis regarded such power as was requested by the Ashkenazic establishment in the scheme to be in direct contradiction to the spirit of the English law. He doubted whether 'without trenching on existent laws, which ought neither to be modified nor repealed, merely to enable your nation to impose a tax on yourselves' (p. 26), and also whether the 'legislature . . . will delegate an authority to the opulent Jews, to assume an unconstitutional controul over their poorer brethren' (p. 18). Finally, Philo Judaeis suggested giving up the proposal in order to avoid the dangers inherent in opening 'a new channel of Fiscal resource' (1802: 24). The ideas included in the pamphlet reflect the reluctance of the English middle classes to allocate power to the centralized authorities.

While some interest aroused by the *maskilim* in the reform of the spiritual and material life of the Jewish people was still current, the attention of van Oven, as the delegate of the Ashkenazic élite in charitable affairs was attracted to the philosophy of Colquhoun, himself inspired by Bentham. As van Oven and the Ashkenazic élite accepted his ideas and were ready to implement the scheme on their basis, the social ideology of Colquhoun will be considered in some detail. Colquhoun can be considered an incipiently moderate collectivist; his confidence in economic individualism was tempered by the recognition of the utter exploitation of the working classes, especially children, and his sense of justice. Yet beyond their moderate collectivism, and rejection of the more cruel exploitation, Bentham and Colquhoun shared the common doctrine of the nineteenth century, that the paupers should never be relieved of their poverty above the level of scanty means of supporting life. Bentham also asserted that, at no time should a person be granted from public funds relief to an extent that rendered him in general more eligible upon the whole, than that of persons maintaining themselves by their own labour (Bowring 1833–1846, I: 32). Colquhoun attempted to differentiate between 'indigence' – a state wherein a person is unable to maintain himself by his labour – and 'poverty' as the state where a man's manual labour support him, but no more; 'the other when there is a surplus from his labour' (*Quarterly Review* 4, 1818: 103). Bentham considered poverty as the main incentive to work. Colquhoun in his *Treatise on Indigence* (1806), writes:

> Without a large proportion of poverty there could be no riches, since riches are the offspring of labour, while labour can result only from poverty, poverty therefore is a most necessary and indispensable ingredient in Society without which nations and communities could not exist in a state of civilization. (Colquhoun 1806: 7)

After four decades these definitions were adopted by the Royal Commissioners of 1832–4. The existence of poverty and inequality as a basic premise of social existence was manifestly acknowledged by the Jewish élite. It was considered to be conducive to an harmonious society, supposed to prevent indigence and help the already indigent to become self-sufficient, but no more. Poverty was seen as an insoluble chronic problem, but indigence and crime were acute states that required greater bureaucratic control to substitute the personal and more informal pattern of relationships between social classes in the Jewish community. Van Oven and the Jewish élite accepted, apparently without second thought, Colquhoun's inclination to deal with the relief of indigence and the problems of delinquency in the same frame of reference. The differences were obscured by the overemphasis of control elements in the relief of the poor. To the extent that control was not to serve the interests of the dominant class *per se*, it was deliberately minimized. The models chosen for the reformed house of industry, and other main instruments for moralization and subordination reflect the tendency to maintain the poor by their own work and in this way reduce the poor rate and synagogal fees.

These models also expressed a growing awareness of urban disorganization (the Jewish London poor included) and recognition of the insufficiencies of the old Poor Law arrangements. As Colquhoun did not explain how the passage from poverty to indigence had occurred or how to prevent it, this theoretical lacuna was reflected in the contradiction of van Oven's explanations. On one hand, the negative characteristics attributed to the Jewish poor were described as caused by the unfavorable circumstances of their lives in the Diaspora, and by the adverse influences to which they were subject in an oppressing society (that amongst other prohibitions did not permit Jews to work in agriculture). Van Oven wrote to Colquhoun: 'The inability to work for a livelihood is not occasioned by a want of industry in the poor, it is a combined effect of some transient local and some permanent religious causes' (Letter, 25 March 1801; *Letters* 1802: 10). But on the other hand, van Oven was disposed to assert the necessity of improving 'the habits of the lower classes . . . to support those measures which shall convert idleness into industry' (pp. 3, 4). Behind this contradiction was a confluence between van Oven's *haskalah* (which basically defended the principles of Judaism but overemphasized the need for productivization of the Jewish poor and generally regarded the lower classes as inferior groups), and the individualistic doctrine according to which poverty implied some falling short in moral conduct or judgement, or some social defect in terms of willingness to work.

EFFECTS OF THE FAILED SCHEME

The 1802 Colquhoun–van Oven plan to authorize social control of the Ashkenazic élite over its poor failed. However, many of the elements of social control reflected in van Oven and Colquhoun's scheme were incorporated in subsequent plans dealing with the situation of the Jewish poor. It is worth noting that fifty-seven years later, the newly established London Board of Guardians for the Relief of the Jewish Poor in its *First Half-Yearly Report* regarded its emergence as a direct realization of the comprehensive proposition made by van Oven to establish 'a Poor Board for the entire management of the poor' (1860: 8).

Some of the powers requested by the plan were invested in the European *kehillot* (Jewish communities) that obtained autonomy in pre-national decentralized and privilege-granting states. As a *maskil*, van Oven based his thoughts on the social philosophy of Bentham, and was interested in modernizing Jewish life. Joshua van Oven was not interested in a revival of the *kehillah* but in adopting an ultra-modern philosophy of welfare that assumed maximum control over the Jewish poor. However, the obligations of the middle and upper Jewish classes were also to be increased by some compulsory financial measures.

The plan of van Oven and Colquhoun had a clear tendency towards secularization of poor relief and its gradual separation from the synagogues. This was in line with the general atmosphere in philanthropic endeavour. While in Catholic countries the Church, in the main, continued its educational and charitable functions with minimal control, in England, private charitable donations were expected to provide important social and economic needs under public rather than religious supervision. As a general result of Protestantism, the secularization of social welfare, including philanthropy, attained a high degree of congruity in England, and the disunity of English religious organizations made the secularization of philanthropies even more necessary. The scheme reflects an open criticism of the particularistic trend of the different Anglo-Jewish sub-groups, and the negative impact of this on the relief of poverty:

> These synagogues are, generally speaking, independent of each other, and of course involve distinct interests. All their reliefs to the poor are dispensed in money, at the discretion of the overseers . . . This relief is far short of being even temporarily effectual, both from its inadequateness to the extent required and from the vague manner of its dispensation. (*Letters* 1802: 9–10)

Van Oven hoped to obtain a consolidation of all the funds of the synagogues, comparable to those of all parishes suggested by Colquhoun in his tract, *The State of Indigence and the Situation of the Casual Poor* (1799: 29).

The failure of the Colquhoun–van Oven Scheme discussed in this chapter, reveals the different interests of the Jewish strata and groups. In the final analysis, the Jewish élite regarded the obligatory additional tax to be imposed by the scheme as contradictory to its basic class interests. Rather, the élite preferred a continuation of the voluntary arrangements, permitting maximum leeway in terms of its obligations. The consequences of the scheme's failure are discussed in the next chapter. The fear that excessive power of the Jewish élite would lead inevitably to the abuse of the poor, expressed by some opponents to the scheme was justified by subsequent developments as we shall see in the following chapters.

3

Wealth and Poverty: A Widening Gap

EDUCATING THE POOR

The aim of this chapter is to examine the efforts made by the élite in educating the poor, which also included philanthropic provision such as apprenticeships, clothing, meals, and so on. The elementary education specifically designed for the poor was considered by the élite to be the greatest Anglicizer for the children of the immigrants and the native poor. The poor were acculturated to the values chosen by the élite as necessary for the 'humbler classes'.

A small-scale implementation of the van Oven and Colquhoun plan was the Ashkenazic Jews' Hospital at Mile End, established in 1801. The number of 'inmates' was limited to ten elderly persons, ten boys and eight girls. The intention of the founders to create a model institution is also evidenced by its administrative structure and personnel, as shown in *The Rules for the Management of the Jews' Hospital in Mile End, London Called Neveh Zedeq 'Abode of Righteousness'* (1808). Many of the hospital's arrangements were comparable to those of the charity schools and, indeed, the motto of the institution was: '*Homsum, humani nihil a me alienum puto*' (I am a human being and consider nothing human alien to me).

The impetus to establish this institution was partly due to the Christian conversionist activities amongst the Jews. The £20,000 plus interest collected by the brothers Goldsmid from Jews and their non-Jewish business associates in the late 1790s, were finally used by Asher Goldsmid, the third brother, and his three brothers-in-law with the help of Joshua van Oven and others, to establish this institution. Admission to the Jews' hospital required that candidates be of good character or from parents 'belonging to one of the three established synagogues in

London and born in or have been ten years resident in London' (Rules 3, 5). Rule 6 added 'those are to be preferred who shall prove to have been reduced in life, from a respectable situation, denominated *evionim* (a term used by the élite for the 'stipendiary' poor). Other prerequisites included the ability to read Hebrew prayers and English (Rule 73). Admittance was further limited by the voting system (Rule 6), as we shall be discussing. Homeless and destitute children were excluded, as well as those considered to have a limited potential for industrial training. No preference was given to orphans. The curriculum included a limited general education (arithmetic, English language and a religious education, mainly prayers) and elementary training in a few trades such as furniture-making. By the age of twelve to thirteen, the boys were apprenticed to artisans, while the girls, aged thirteen to fourteen, were placed in Jewish homes as servants.

A manual prepared for the girls by 'A Daughter of Israel' entitled *The Jewish Preceptress: Elementary Sessions Written Chiefly for the Youth of the Female Children Educated at the Jews' Hospital* (London 1818), published by an anonymous wealthy Jewish woman, presents the set of values and attitudes that servant girls were to acquire in the institution. These included, besides the moral implications of Jewish religion, a strong emphasis on thrift, gratitude, subservience and industry, which were considered 'as an efficient remedy for abating laziness, immorality, poverty and criminality and restoring prestige of the London Jewish community' ('A Daughter of Israel' 1818: 52). Also writing about industry, she comments that it 'is admirable to observe the gradations of industry by which ... the labour of the mechanic ... are rewarded by the purchase of their industry by the affluent. The affluent ... are occupied by the peculiar duties of their station' ('A Daughter of Israel' 1818: 52–9).

The general purpose of the institution was to keep Jewish children off the London streets and at the same time 'to improve the morals and social habits of the children' in such a way as to maintain the social structure and the subordination of the poor to the wealthy class. To ensure the admittance of their children, parents were requested to renounce their rights over their children. Children were referred to as 'inmates' and were confined to the premises of the institution.

According to the prevailing middle-class standards of the period, the Jews' Hospital was highly regarded by non-Jewish philanthropists, as shown in the book of A. Highmore, *Pietas Londinensis* (1810, vol. 1). Among the instrumental supporters of the institution was Augustus Frederick, the Duke of Sussex (1773–1843), the sixth son of George III and uncle of Queen Victoria, who supported the cancellation of civil disabilities of Catholics, Jews and Dissenters and the abolition of the slave trade. He was also a reputable Hebraist and active in Jewish philanthropic schemes.

A more flexible approach to the occupational mobility of the female inmates was made evident when Henry Faudel was nominated by the House Committee presided over by Baron Anthony de Rothschild to investigate the system of this institution. In 1844, Faudel anonymously published his *Brief Investigation into the System of the Jews' Hospital with a Proposition for Improving the Management and Extending its Benefits, by one of the members*. He suggested that only some of the girls should be fitted for servants, while others 'could be apprenticed to respectable trades . . . would after a few years produce a number of superior nurses and other governesses and teachers, now very much wanted by the Jewish community and they would find really good and well–paid situations' (Faudel 1844).

Faudel deplored the insufficient contribution of the vocational programme of the Jews' Hospital to the occupational structure of the community: 'the Jews would at the present moment hold a different place in the Kingdom, if at this time five hundred mechanics existed among them, drawn from the poorer classes, who must otherwise casually obtain their living . . . ' (Faudel 1844: 21). With regard to the policies of the Jews' Hospital, middle–range donors were excluded *a priori* from the process of decision making. To insure this, Rule 6 in respect of Governors stated: 'Subscriptions of Half a Guinea per annum will be received; but such persons cannot have any vote in the concerns of this Charity, nor be elected to any honorary office' (Rules 1808). The rules do not present any pretence of democracy, rather, inequalities in wealth and their implications in terms of power were regarded as natural and ordained by God. Two hundred and twenty three children completed their studies and were apprenticed from the time of its opening in 1807 until 1844. Obviously this institution did not meet the needs of the large number of neglected Jewish children. The fear that assistance to newly arrived immigrants might encourage others to come to England acted against such preventive interventions on poverty.

Even with regard to the children of the so-called 'respectable poor', the tendency was to separate them from their parents and their environment. The limitation of the main educational efforts to the children of the 'respectable poor' reveals the conceptual frame of reference of the Jewish élite. The contradictory set of distinctions with regard to the poor, reveals an approach that viewed poverty as the direct effect of vice, however, that the industrious poor could be rendered functional by fulfilling the specific tasks assigned to them in a rather stagnant society. By inference, a distinction was introduced between the 'respectable', 'honest' or 'worthy' poor and the 'unworthy' poor. Only the respectable possessed the social characteristics that entitled them to the sympathy of the élite, but they too were not to be trusted. The distinction between the 'respectable' and 'unrespectable' was not the same as the distinction between the rich and the poor, therefore this interpretation of poverty connected the two categories 'respectable' and 'poor', that is, the poor could not be genuinely 'respectable'. In this evaluation the most evident contradiction was idleness. Respectability meant respect for work, independence and concealing as much as possible the external evidence of poverty. According to this 'double bind' interpretation the scope of the educational and philanthropic institutions was to enforce the work ethic amongst the poor, not to enable them to escape poverty but to perpetuate their situation, albeit as 'respectable poor'.

During the first quarter of the nineteenth century, English charity schools provided simple education – the inculcation of religious and moral values, and fulfilled an important task in preparing the children of the poor for earning their livelihood. Boys were apprenticed. Charity schools were under the wing of the Church of England; Catholics, Non-Conformists and Jews had to provide their own services. The expansion of Jewish popular education followed closely the overall English trend. In 1812, Joshua van Oven initiated the establishment of a school for the Jewish poor based on the Lancasterian model. The Jews' Free School (a name taken from the British educational system), was opened in 1817. After a few years it moved to a more spacious building in Spitalfields. Conversionist institutions founded somewhat earlier were considered an important contributory factor. The Jews' Free School fed the pupils, and Baroness de Rothschild provided them with clothing, so in this sense it too can be regarded as a charity institution. As such it was to a considerable extent used as an instrument of social control. It is worth noting that Francis Place and others who feared that the Lancasterian schools could hurt the feelings of the poor, deliberately avoided the use of the words 'poor' and 'labouring poor' in the by-laws of the Royal Lancasterian Society (Letter of E. Wakefield to F. Place quoted in Graham Wallas, 4th edn 1925: 95).

The adoption of the Lancasterian system by the Jewish élite is not surprising. In the first quarter of the nineteenth century this movement was supported by wealthy dissenters such as the Quaker, William

Allen, the editor of *The Philanthropist* and one of the first subscribers to The Jews' Hospital (Rules, 1808, XI). The Jewish élite also cooperated in other areas with non-conformists who stood outside the Established Church. The Lancasterian movement was supported also by the Whigs, who believed that through popular education the working classes could be brought to be an integral part of the social order, but the Whigs were at the same time interested in preserving the supremacy of the landed aristocracy.

The curriculum of the Jews' Free School included a strong component of Anglicization and embourgeoisement, persistently impressing respect for middle-class values. In fact, as late as the 1850s the Jewish wealthy class which patronized Jewish charity schools (and, on a small scale, some non-Jewish schools around their country homes), was frightened by the possible results of popular education as exemplified in the *Memoirs of Annie and Constance, daughters of Sir Anthony de Rothschild* [Mrs Eliot Yorke and Lady Battersea]. Both daughters had been greatly interested in the education of the poor, having started a village school at their mother's house at Worth before they married. This suspicion is reflected in the following remark:

> Richter disapproves of education for the poorer classes. I think he is quite right in saying that reading and writing may be dangerous acquisitions to them . . . They are either too much, or not half enough. If you teach the poor to read, you must give them . . . sufficient moral and religious instruction to make good books welcome to them. (Lucy Cohen, *Lady de Rothschild and Her Daughters* 1935: 69)

After Annie's death Constance resolved to devote 'more time and thought to her children and the poor at Aston Clinton and Halton must now claim my care and our own poor Jewish brethren . . . ' (Cohen, 1935: 69.

Such a manifest statement would generally not have been made by Jews permeated with the often repeated *hallachic* injunctions with regard to the education of the poor as reflected in the long accepted tradition of Hillel. Like its non-Jewish counterpart, the Jewish élite was swept up by the social philosophy of the period and its ambivalence towards the education of the poor as illustrated by the request of some unions to omit writing from the instruction programme in order not to offer the indoor children greater advantages than to other poor children. This was a matter of principle and unrelated to budgetary considerations.

Henry Mayhew in his *London Labour and London Poor* (1851), regarded the Jews' Free School, around the middle of the nineteenth century, as the largest Jewish educational institution. It was designed to educate up to 1,200 boys and girls but had an average attendance of about 900. Mayhew noted that the children of the Jewish poor often left school in order to help their parents. He writes of the indifference of the Jewish wealthy class: 'Even if they subscribed to a school, they never cared whether or not it was attended' (Mayhew 1968 edn: 128). Taking into consideration the estimates of the Jewish poor population in London, their geographical concentration and their inability to pay for private education, it is evident that only a small percentage of the children of the poor were able to attend schools. The basic elementary education and skills provided by this school contributed to some change in the occupational structure of the Jewish poor. The establishment of the Jews' Free School and then the Jews' Infant School can be regarded as more useful, although limited, attempts of the Jewish élite to subsidize the education of poor Jewish children. Yet by the end of the second quarter of the nineteenth century, the majority of the poor children remained untouched by the programmes that van Oven had designed on behalf of the élite.

In 1841, the Jews' Infant School was established as one of the earliest schools of its kind. The attention to the need for infant schools was drawn by Robert Owen's New Lanark experiment. One of the school's founders was Francis Henry Goldsmid who, together with his father, Sir Isaac Lyon Goldsmid and his sister, Anna Maria, were interested in educational questions and were close associates and friends of Owen (Emden 1943: 111–12).

Francis Henry Goldsmid (1808–1878), afterwards Barronet, MP, was born in Spital Square, Spitalfields. Later on, the family resided in St John's Lodge, Regent's Park. His father also possessed the Wick at Brighton and Somerhill near Tonbridge (Emden 1943: 112). Francis received 'a very careful private education'. He was the first Jewish barrister (1833) and Queen's Counsel (1858). In 1860, he began his parliamentary career as a moderate liberal. Francis pursued his father's deep interest in the University College and its hospital as treasurer and chairman (in 1870); a ward was named after him in recognition of his services. As a minority group struggling for the right to parliamentary careers, the Jewish élite was predisposed to embrace Owen's humanist philosophy (borrowed from Joseph Priestley and others), based on rational education and attempting to uproot superstition and preconceived ideas. On the other hand, characteristically in contradiction with this declared humanism, in 1858, Francis Henry stressed in his reply to Ephraim Alex, the founder of the London Jewish Board of Guardians, the importance of checking foreign immigrants by refusing them all relief until they had been in England for three or five years (Lipman 1959: 25–60).

The Goldsmids were exposed to the ideas of David Ricardo (1772–1823), with whom Isaac Lyon Goldsmid corresponded intensively. Ricardo was of Jewish birth, and remained Jewish until 1793. He opposed religious oppression in Parliament (Heerjte 1970–3: 73). Ricardo adopted Malthus's theory of population:

> If it is part of the plan . . . to feed . . . and educate the children of three years age and upwards belonging to the poor, I see the most serious objections to the plan and I should be exceedingly inconsistent if I gave my countenance to it. I have invariably objected to the poor laws and to every system which should give encouragement to an access of population. (Sraffa, edn *The Works of David Ricardo*, VII: 359–60)

Malthus himself favoured the establishment of a system of parish schools believing that in such schools the children of the poor could acquire the virtues of sexual restraint (*Malthus*, 1878 edn: 436–41). The correspondence between Isaac Lyon Goldsmid and Ricardo is not extant but there is no evidence that such views were refuted by the Jewish élite as contradictory to the *hallachah*, rather, this élite was the main supporter of bourgeois assimilation (the process by which one transfers one's identity from one ethnic community to another).

In 1844, Isaac Lyon Goldsmid opposed the establishment of an institution designed to provide lecturers for the adult Jewish poor. He expressed the fears of the wealthy class that such an institution might promote separation between the Jewish and non-Jewish poor and unduly encourage their exclusiveness. Goldsmid's proposal to remove the word 'Jews' from the name of the Literary and Scientific Institution was opposed by a certain John Michael who stated that he represented the Jewish working class and 'that the rich were ashamed of the name of Jew' but he claimed 'the rest of the community was not' (*Voice of Jacob*, 15 March 1844). This is evidence of the fear of the Jewish élite, that the establishment and support of Jewish services might be interpreted as an unpatriotic act. Sharp differences in terms of feeling toward Jewish ethnicity were an integral part of general class tensions and made application to and the use of the services provided by the Jewish élite uncomfortable and repulsive. The deplorable lack of *Yiddishkeit*, and the constant preaching about the duties and values of the middle-class further estranged the different social groupings.

A severe critique appeared in a spirited article entitled the 'Baron Rothschild and the Phanthom' by Hertz Ben Pinhas published by the *Jewish Chronicle* early in 1850. It illuminates the ways in which the poor were accused by the élite and deserves an extended reproduction:

Panthom: True thou art charitable, pious and liberal . . . because you art an honest, upright and honourable Jew, the first among thy race, they have chosen thee . . . Look at yonder pale face wretch as he descends the 'vale of years' as regular as the fingers on thy gold repeater . . . on his beaten tract, neither rain nor snow can stop . . . And for what? To obtain that miserable pittance which every fellow obtains in the dungeons . . . And what has he done to deserve such a fate? Had fate but made him thy father's son and taught him the value of shares, and the rules of compound interest, and the use of vulgar fraction, he too might have been a 'gentleman' . . . Take the restless tiger from his wide forest, place him in van Hamburgh's cage and bid him rest, such is the Sabbath to the itinerant Jew! . . . there actually is such a place as a synagogue . . . then he looks at his clothes, they are so 'shabby' how can he be seen among so many 'gentlemen'. He reflects, too, that he is a 'sinner' and . . . there is no synagogue for 'sinners', the house of God belong to 'saints', sinners must not show their faces therein . . . Why do they seek the gambler's den and the drunkard's grave . . . Is it because these poor wretches have no souls for intellectual bliss? O no . . .

Baron Rothschild: [Roused with indignation . . . replies] And what would'st thou have me do with the scum of my race? Where I to divide my gold among them, and waste the fruits of a life's labour upon these vagrants . . . ? Is not my purse ever open to every charitable cause? . . . Is not my name inscribed in letters of gold upon the tablets of charity? . . .

Phanthom: Hear me. Thy ire I neither fear nor invoke, thy hand cannot reach me, neither in bounty nor in wrath . . . Listen, to feed the hungry is not to find food for the body alone . . . When a few moments ago thou didst dilate with honest pride upon thy manifold bounty thou didst utterly forget to relate thy liberality expended on food for the hungry mind. I heard . . . nothing of what is termed Jewish Press . . . Baron it looked not well for a Jew to have to go to the Gentile press to read thy electioneering speeches. (Quoted in M. Margoliouth, *History of the Jews in Great Britain* 1851, II, 177–83)

To the extent that some effort was made by the élite to relate to the 'hungry mind' of the poor, it involved an inculcation of respect for property and its preferential status.

The educational arrangements for Jewish upper and middle classes reflect the rigid stratification of the London Jewry. The wealthy who supported and patronized the charities and the Jews' Free School in the East End provided a liberal education for their own children, a privilege they could afford by paying for private tuition and schools selected for their standards and reputation. To accommodate such pupils, a Jewish school named Academy was established by Hyman Hurwitz, a Polish-born *maskil*. Apparently, some middle-class parents at that time were sending their children to non-Jewish schools including those belonging to the National School Society – a branch of the Church of England.

In 1845, the West Metropolitan Jewish School was established under the patronage of the West London Synagogue of British Jews, led by Francis Henry Goldsmid. This school later became the West Metropolitan Jewish school for Middle Class Pupils, and in 1878, The Jewish Middle-class School. Most of the parents supported the school as subscribers. The Chairman 'disliked the system of ragged schools in which education is cast to the poor as we cast alms to the beggar' (*Jewish Chronicle*, V, 39: 311). In the same period two other Jewish schools at Borough and Stepney were designated for the working class. The contributions to the Jewish Middle-class School burdened the parents and brought some grudging contemplations at the exemptions accorded to the poor:

> This class deserves more sympathy than it receives. With the poor, who cannot or will not pay for the education of their children, there is almost unlimited sympathy. To such an extent is it carried that from pure benevolence large classes of the poor have been pauperized (for there is a distinction between poverty and pauperisation) and indeed almost demoralized, for they have been led to imagine that no portion whatever of the duty or cost of educating their children falls on them . . . Heaven forbid that we should write a word or think a thought unkind to the poor, but still we cannot help feeling that it is a duty on the part of the so-called better classes to endeavour to educate the parents as well as the children of the poorer classes to foster amongst Jewish Englishmen that spirit of independence and self reliance which is one of the noblest characteristics of our Anglo-Saxon brethren . . . (*Jewish Chronicle*, 270: 138)

This furnishes additional evidence of middle-class moralism and friction between the middle class and the poor (which shall be discussed later in greater detail).

A serious disability that concerned the Jewish élite was the policy of Oxford and Cambridge to reject Jewish candidates as well as Dissenters and Catholics on religious grounds. This continued until the University Test Acts of 1871. However, the University of Edinburgh had graduated Jewish physicians (Henriques 1974: 208–10). Isaac Lyon Goldsmid took an important part in the foundation of the University College, London (1825), then called the University of London, giving the necessary impetus to the acquisition of the site on Gower Street (University College Report for 1859). Goldsmid enlisted the support of Aaron Goldsmid, George Magmus, Nathan Mayer Rothschild and the Sephardic financiers, Abraham Lindo and Moses Mocatta, as well as non-Jewish bankers.

Isaac Lyon Goldsmid da Palmeira (later Sir J. L. Goldsmid, Bart. (1778–1859) was the nephew of Benjamin and Abraham. As a partner of Mocatta and Goldsmid, bullion brokers to the Bank of England and the East India Company, as well as through his investments in London docks and railway construction, Isaac Lyon amassed a large capital. He conducted many of his other financial activities in Spanish and Portuguese countries and South America together with his son, Francis, and Bernard van Oven (the son of Joshua). Isaac Lyon invested a great deal of energy in introducing the Jewish Disabilities Bill (1830, 1833) and induced various politicians to take an interest in this question that concerned the Jewish élite. He was made baronet in 1841, the first professing Jew to receive an hereditary title in England. In his London and country houses, Isaac Lyon entertained politicians, musicians, artists and educationalists; Louis Napoleon, Metternich and Queen Victoria (in 1853) were amongst his guests. Isaac Lyon represented a degree of theoretical sophistication that the Cousinhood attained during the first half of the nineteenth century. The concepts of contemporary philanthropy were an integral part of this trend:

> On the political sciences . . . Isaac Goldsmid bestowed particular attention. Political economy was only one of these that he had deeply studied . . . his association with Ricardo made him familiarly practised in the theory and discussion of the leading questions of political science. (Clarke 1859: 377)

In 1834, Isaac Lyon supported the establishment of the University College Hospital and served as Treasurer (1839–57). The foundation of University College represented a new system of education fitted to meet the needs of the affluent and ambitious members of the upper middle and wealthy classes. In this framework Benthamite concepts were widely applied. Among the supporting members of the original Council, were leading philosophic radicals and also dissenters, Catholics and Jews. The First Statement of the Aims of the Council of London University (1827) assured that no religious tests and teaching were to be imposed on the students. Isaac Lyon and his friend, the poet Thomas Campbell who was one of the founder, agreed to this (Emden 1943: 115).

Isaac Lyon rose to considerable eminence as a philanthropist. He supported Owen's experiments by acting as one of his treasurers. In 1839, he leased one of his properties in Hampshire to establish a community and housing project after the model of New Lanark (Emden 1943: 112; Life of Robert Owen, I 1857: 150). However, a more proper perspective of his social thinking is revealed in his position towards the proposals for national prosperity of Napoleon III while the latter requested the financier to assist him in his scheme:

> Perhaps what affected Goldsmid more than anything was the sham philanthropy of the prince, his socialist professions, and his plans for the benefit of the working classes. It might have been thought a capitalist was the last man to whom communistic invitations could be addressed, but Goldsmid really and legitimately wished that each man should attain property . . . So far from thinking that the possession of wealth gave him the right to domineer, he rather felt more humble in the fear he might be deemed purseproud or neglectful of his duties. (Clarke 1859: 451)

Isaac Lyon also supported and was active in the campaigns of the leading Quakers such as the manumission of the Negroes, and in the reform of the penal code and improvements in prison conditions, in collaboration with Peter Bedford and Elizabeth Fry. We read about his ambiguous personal involvement: 'nothing was more repulsive to him than the associations of a prison, but he spent many an hour not only in the jail of Newgate but even in the cells of the condemned. Here he obtained practical evidence which made him more constant in the movement for the restriction of capital punishment, which Mr Secretary Peel influenced' (Clarke 1859: 449). But philanthropic connections were beneficial to business interests: 'the Frys had introduced Mr Goldsmid to Sir William Congreve, and among other undertaking supported by that great projector and his connection was the Imperial Continental Gas Society . . . Mr Goldsmid joined in the direction' (Clarke 1859: 450).

Characteristic to the approach of the Jewish élite, Isaac Lyon Goldsmid's motivation to help children was dominated by a scepticism and contempt towards the adult poor: 'he felt strongly that the mass of ignorance and vice was rather to be overcome by the careful training of children than by combating with the fixed habits of the adults' (Clarke April 1860: 382). His attitude towards the poor was described as 'very thoughtful, ready to reprove in providence, warm in assisting the claims of the poor aged, the widow and the orphan but still more happy if he succeeded in obtaining permanent and effective relief. As a proprietor of a manorial property he increased the salary of the incumbent and in another town estate dedicated a large site for a church' (Clarke April 1860: 222–3). The geographical distance from the East End and consequently the lack of an undivided contact with the Jewish poor increased the social differentiation.

With regard to his contribution to Jewish charities, Clarke, the writer of the memoir, did not have too much to say, except for some support for the Jews' Infant School and the Jews' Hospital established by his uncles. Clarke himself concludes, that as far as Jewish charities were concerned (Clarke 1859: 221), 'he rather held back from the main body of public charities, any new design for improving the condition of the poor or alleviating distress was sure to receive a warm and early welcome'; but it was exactly those Jewish public charities which needed the support of the wealthy as their exclusive source for maintaining the poor. Notwithstanding the fact that he was acquainted with philanthropic schemes, he neither came forward with such a scheme nor supported the ones that were advanced during long periods of time despite his tremendous wealth.

This discussion shows that in spite of the patronizing character of the educational programmes designed for the poor, a variety of useful services were provided, however the facilities could accommodate only a very limited number of the poor.

THE RICH IN SEARCH OF POWER

The following discussion attempts to demonstrate that having acquired considerable financial power, the Jewish élite embarked on prolonged efforts to obtain the political power so far denied to it. Concentrating on its political aspirations, the Jewish élite largely neglected the social problems of the community. There was a lack of sufficient resources for existing philanthropic schemes, and the poor themselves took some initiative in establishing necessary services.

The oligarchic and plutocratic ruling of Jewish communities in the Diaspora was a long- established pattern. The rigidity of the social stratification of the Jewish community in London and its predisposition to adopt, en masse, laissez-faire theories and their actual implementation, was dictated by the major changes in the economic activities of the Jewish élite. In pre-capitalistic Jewish communities the wealthy merchant bankers purchased goods and services (for their own use), extended credit and invested capital by employing merchants and pedlars as purchasing agents, retailers and in many other ways. In doing so they supported the less prosperous and the poor themselves. The Jewish community was, socioeconomically, an interdependent unit, living and fulfilling economic functions in the host community. In nineteenth-century England, the Jewish merchant bankers moved increasingly into modern large-scale financing, including government and ministerial loan-contracting, investment in insurance, gas, railways, docks and in foreign countries. This process led to the breaking of old economic ties within the Jewish community; an effect aggravated by the dispersal of the well-to-do. In an attempt to refute the accusations of van Oven and Colquhoun, Levy Alexander mentioned Jewish artisans and servants whose services were not used by their rich co-religionists and therefore could not make a decent living:

> a long list might be made out of the unfortunate Jews who have attempted in vain to live by professional exertion. I must ask you here what is to become of the female sex when thought to execute women's arts, they must still remain unemployed, and our nation you know prefer English servants in every capacity but that of cooks. (Alexander 1802: 25–7)

Mayhew, fifty years later, thought that 'if they [the wealthy] cared more about employing their own people their liberality would be far more fully felt' (1850: 123b). However, the middle-class did employ Jewish workers, to some extent, increasing direct intra-group exploitation. London economic life permitted a gradual enlargement and prosperity of the Jewish middle-class: contractors, import and export merchants, shippers, wholesalers and warehousemen, ready-made clothing and cigar manufacturers, etc. Two large factories owned by Jews, Moses and Company and Benjamin Hyam, employed thousands of people. The number of Jewish artisans, shopkeepers, grocers, stall-holders and the like, with a more stable income, also increased. At the same time, the poor Jews were much less occupied in street trades (where they were replaced by the Irish) and other *lumpen* proletariat occupations. The 1840s witnessed a rapid process of manual labourization of the Jewish poor, which resulted in the emergence of a Jewish working class, increasingly employed by other Jews in cigar and hat making, clothing, boot and shoe sweatshops, also as carpenters, upholsterers, carvers and so on.

Influenced by the moralism of the Victorian upper-classes, many of the contemporary observers regarded the Jewish poor as provident, sober, self-disciplined and highly motivated to escape poverty. As such they were generally contrasted with the Irish. By implication Jewish workers were regarded as individualistic and latent bourgeois. In an attempt to explain the subsequent disintegration of the Jewish working class, the Smilesian characteristics* were repeated by historians using a more modern terminology overstressing ethnicity but omitting common denominators of social structure. In more recent studies, Gerry White, Bill Williams and Joseph Buckman challenge these views. It seems that the relatively small capital needed, rather than the Smilesian virtues, enabled some numbers of Jewish workers and ambulatory traders to become 'bedroom masters' and stallkeepers.

This process coincided with the introduction of the sewing machine and the band knife cutting machine (*Jewish Chronicle*: 27 January 1856). On the other hand, the mechanization of the boot and shoes trade in which the Jews were an important factor caused an abrupt rise in start-up capital required. The consequence of this was some decline of Jewish workers in this sector. In the clothing trade most of the work was done at home, and the small masters remained dependent on the highly competitive wholesale clothiers, who were under constant pressure to cut labour costs, and to work their employees ever harder. In this field there was almost no direct competition with non-Jewish tailors. The significant cheapening of mass production through the subdivision of labour was achieved at a high price of exploitation of semi-skilled Jewish males, females and children working as tailors, machinists, pressers and messengers. After a twelve hour day of work many of them continued to work at home until midnight in order to support themselves. In his famous pamphlet, 'Cheap Clothes and Nasty', Charles Kingsley describes the terrible conditions of the London sweaters-tailors: 'What is flogging or hanging to the slavery, starvation, waste of life, which goes on among thousands of free English clothesmen' (reprinted in Alton Locke 1877: LXVIII). Induced to bring relatives over from the old country, to pay excessive rents and to save themselves or their children from wretched conditions, the

*Samuel Smiles (1812–1904), British journalist and administrator, best known for ideas propagated in his book *Self Help* (1859), p. 70.

Jewish workers accepted exploitation. In 1858, one of the first known disputes between Jewish cigar-makers and their employers took place. According to a letter addressed to the editor of the *Jewish Chronicle* of 8 January 1858, a cigar-maker complained about his master's practice of travelling to Holland and other European countries in order to bring cigar-makers to London, promising them advantageous conditions, but after their arrival paying them lower wages than English workers were ready to accept. The editorial comment supported the masters, accepting their arguments as to the fluctuations in the trade and its semi-skilled nature. The Jewish poor were exploited as pedlars outside the sweatshops. Evidence presented by Mayhew in his series of letters to the *Morning Chronicle*, disclosed that some of the Jewish middlemen supplying relatively cheap ready-made garments to West End shops, employed as many as three hundred hands -'many of those so employed setting their wives, children and others to work' (Mayhew edn 1971, Letter 11 December 1849: 227). Mayhew left his readers to decide 'how much of the pauperism arises from deficient wages and how much from those habits of improvidence which are the necessary consequence of uncertainty of employment.' (Mayhew edn 1971, Letter 12 December 1850: 181)

During the great cholera epidemic of 1830 a Jewish East End cucumber-seller, Abraham Green, drew Jewish public attention to the wretched condition of Jewish orphans. Honen le Yetomim (Pardon for the Orphan), the institution established in 1818 by the Great Synagogue for relieving and educating orphan children, was restricted in the numbers of orphans it could accommodate. Green's *rachmunes* (compassion) was aroused by three destitute orphans named Assenheim whose parents had died during the epidemic. Green left his stall to collect money in his cucumber basket, for the maintenance of the children, carrying two of the children and leading the third. Largely through the support of Isaac Valentine, founder of the Jewish Chronicle and Green's brother-in-law, additional funds were collected for the establishment of the Jews' Orphan Asylum in Godman's Fields, later the Norwood Jewish Orphanage (Roth 1950: 221–2). A similar earlier initiative of a certain Nathan Barnett is mentioned by Roth (1950: 222). In 1884, a Jewish baker provided new immigrants with accommodation in the East End. Although the premises were closed by the Jewish Board of Guardians as allegedly unsanitary, the attempt prompted the foundation of the Jews' Temporary Shelter. The élite was afraid that such an institution in general, and especially under its own auspices, could be a direct encouragement to Jewish immigration. Green's initiative represents many other less-known and unknown efforts of charity that remain unrecorded due to a lack of interest in the life of the masses and grass-roots movements. However, such efforts involved greater personal effort and expressed more genuine compassion than those made by committees of philanthropic businessmen. Henry Faudel, in a more critical account towards the Jewish wealthy class, describes the initiative of the poor as widespread and predominant:

> many sources of relief, it is reported, have been commenced by those who are but little elevated above poverty in the neighbourhood where the distress has been most evident, and maintained subsequently by the personal interference of individuals, and the stringent appeals of private friends, which could not have been refused if wished, which dared not be neglected. (*Suggestions to the Jews* 1844: 26)

However, such initiators of limited means were not accepted as partners into the administration of the charity they created as soon as such charities were subsidized by the élite. The original arrangements established in this way were necessarily improvisations, considering the lack of sufficient resources in terms of time and money of the poor Jewish class. During the first half of the nineteenth century and well afterwards, the élite continued to maintain exclusive control over all community issues and to demand strict institutional conformity.

Christian missionary activities amongst the Jews did not counterbalance the general non-interventionist trend of the English environment. However, these activities did enforce the philanthropic endeavours of the Jewish élite by raising communal concerns and motivation to change the social conditions that were used by the conversionists in their actions among the Jewish poor.

Towards the end of the eighteenth century, as a consequence of evangelistic development, the London Society for Promoting Christianity among the Jews was established by the London Missionary Society to work among the Jews of London. The leading missionary was Joseph Frey (born 1771), a convert from Judaism, who created a Free School for the Jewish poor children in 1807. According to Roth (1950) very few pupils were Jewish or from the 'lowest section of the population' (p. 227). Salman writes:

> As is well known, the moral Jew, however poor, is not easily bought over, recourse was had to the lowest order of society. You [Frey] converted a number of ignorant, friendless children, the paupers of vice, these poor, miserable wretches, for the most part illegitimate . . . were glad to be

received in any society that did clothe and feed them. (Quoted by Levin 1957: 17)

The Society for Promoting Christianity among the Jews, however, increased its activities, especially in the educational field, by opening two additional schools by 1812. The *Twelfth Report of the Society for Promoting Christianity among the Jews* regarded the neglect of the Jewish poor children and youngsters as a moral justification for the missionary activities:

> Instead of their youth being bound apprentices to handicraft trades, they are sent forth to gain their livelihood by the lowest description of traffic. One of the best means the Jews could employ to raise their nation from its present degraded state would be to give a moral education to their youth and afterwards bind them apprentices to trades. (Twelfth Report: 1812)

In reaction, the Great Synagogue sent a delegation to present its abhorrence before the Society for Promoting Christianity among the Jews, and Rabbi Solomon Hirschell issued a ban on the Missionary Schools in a Sabbath sermon and later in a caution printed in English and Yiddish. Hirschell scorned all who sent their children to Missionary Schools:

> As if they had themselves forsaken their religion and been baptised; and shall lose all title to the name of the Jews and forfeit all claims in the Congregation both in life and death . . . everyone . . . is reminded of his duty to warn everyone who may be ignorant . . . and acquaint him thereof, that he may escape the snare laid to entangle him. (Exhortation delivered Sat., Jan. 10, 5567 [1807])

According to the *Narrative of Joseph Frey, 1813*, 'opposition of the Jews, alas! had its desired effect, for two full years after the opening of the Free-school, notwithstanding zealous exertions, no one child was added to the original number' (pp. 65–6). Besides the 'Hebrew Schools', in 1814 the SPCJ established the Episcopal Jews' Chapel. (The first stone of this institution was laid by the Duke of Kent, father of Queen Victoria, who was also a patron, while William Wilberforce was vice president.) An Operative Jewish Converts' Institution, 'to provide a place of refuge to Jewish believers', was established in 1831. Some of the inmates were trained as printers and bookbinders. An additional institution named 'Asylum for Jewess' functioned in Palestine Place, the headquarter of the SPCJ (Ayerst 1848: 421–6).

In 1847, the budget of this society was £29,000 (Historical Notices of the London SPCJ: 2–9). John de la Roy (quoted in Levin 1957: 16) estimated the number of Jews converted by missionary activities before the end of the nineteenth century at 3,500, apparently most of them poor.

The submission of the official religious functionaries to the élite is evident from a bitter critic of the spiritual leadership by Solomon Bennett (1761–1838). According to Bennett, the Chief Ashkenazic Rabbi, Solomon Hirschell (between 1802 and 1842) lost much of his influence and moral standing as a result of his subordination to the Jewish financiers, and this subservience was not divorced from personal and pecuniary benefits (*Netzah Israel: The Constancy of Israel* 1817). Bennett accused Hirschell of condoning the magnates' serious transgressions (such as transacting business on the Sabbath). He also charged that Hirschell obtained his position as Chief Rabbi as a protégé of the Goldsmids through their connections with German Jewish merchants (*The Present Reign of the Synagogue of Duke's Place Displayed*, London 1818). The neglect of the poor was one of the features of Anglo-Jewish life that Bennett condemned. Due to the subservience of the rabbis to the wealthy class and in the absence of countervailing forces, the *hallachah* was interpreted in a way that supported and legitimized economic enterprise, accumulation of wealth and individual rather than collective responsibility. The following excerpts are from the 'Subjects For Moral and Religious Discourses' published in the *Jewish Chronicle*, on 21 January 1842:

> Query – Is a desire to be rich compatible to virtue? – answered in the affirmative, Effects of prudence, temperance, and industry contrasted with their opposites, Doctrine of chance refuted. Man's fate in most instances shown to be his own working . . . Distress to be relieved. Industry to be encouraged, and the institutions of the country supported. Riches shewn to be an aid to virtue!

This departure from some of the concepts of the *hallachah* was part of a gradual and complex process connected with the changes in the socioeconomic situation of the wealthy Anglo-Jewry. Doctrines of charity were not discussed in the context of real situations. The demands of the *hallacha* with regard to the responsibilities of wealth towards the poor were stated in broad terms, and sometimes ignored. However, resentment over Jewish disorganization persisted as a counterbalancing force. Charity was not rejected publicly. It is worth noting that some important members of the élite (such as Baron Lionel de Rothschild MP and Sir David Salomons MP and the Lord Mayor of London) were radical secularists and the obliteration of Jewishness was, in their view, the best way towards assimilation.

The London Jewish community was a conglomerate of separate semi-voluntary organizations. Membership in the synagogue was partly enforced by the situation of the Jews as a religious minority. The synagogues and their affiliated charities functioned as discrete institutions serving their own members. The synagogues did not have any legal authority to implement judicial and administrative control. Functions such as marriage, burial, and mutual aid, representing the very preservation of Jewish identity, were concentrated under the auspices of the synagogue, enabling it to maintain control over its affiliated members. The expectations of the wealthy class were strongly reflected in synagogal life and rituals. The Great Synagogue was enlarged in 1790 through a donation of £4,000; this appeared to symbolize increasing trust and confidence in the future. The wealthy group of 'free members' determined the policy of the synagogue and, to a large extent, the arrangements for all the Ashkenazic poor in London in terms of relief. From this group, the *parnasin* (wardens of the synagogue) were elected. The ratepaying seat-holders, mostly middle class, were not represented in the decision-making body. Honorific practices acknowledged the status of the wealthy members demonstrating their supposed worth and superiority and insured continuous contributions (partly made during the services before the entire congregation possessing some compulsory elements). Such donations were an important source of funds for the maintenance of the synagogue and its poor.

In the eastern part of the City there were three main Ashkenazic synagogues, the Great Synagogue (established 1690), Hambro Synagogue (1707) and the New Synagogue (1761). For the purpose of relief, the synagogues divided the poor into three categories:

1   'Stipendiary poor', receiving fixed monthly allotments, were those who by themselves or through their families belonged to the synagogue, and as members, were entitled to claim relief from donations and trusts.

2   'Casual poor', not entitled to the benefits of the first category. Such poor had claim on the congregation because they or their parents rented a seat in the synagogue for at least six months, or were married in the synagogue.

3   'Strange poor' or Orchim (guests or wayfarers), who had no claim on a particular synagogue.

The assistance to the 'stipendiary' and even the 'casual' poor included elements of mutual aid which to some extent limited their humiliation under the tutelage of the wealthy members. The stipendiary poor who resented attending synagogal prayers were forced to do so in order to complete the *minyan* (quorum needed to make public prayer possible). The forfeit for non-attendance was a deduction from their allocation or complete deprivation of assistance.

According to an arrangement between the three synagogues in the later part of the eighteenth century, the Great Synagogue contributed half of the expenses incurred in helping the 'foreign poor', while the other half was shared by the other two synagogues. Within this arrangement the poor were obliged to apply weekly to all the three synagogues in order to obtain sixpence each from the first and threepence from the second and third. An agreement of 1804 meant that the Great Synagogue assumed responsibility for assisting the 'foreign poor', the other two synagogues contributing each a quarter of the expenditure. The cost of 'paupers' burials' was to be defrayed in the same manner by turn (Roth 1950: 230–3). This centralizing process was intended to prevent indiscriminate relief but its dispensation continued in a vague and insufficient manner.

The dedicated financial resources were far from being commensurate to the needs of the poor. Disputes and bitterness between the three synagogues over the responsibilities towards the poor were a continuous feature accompanied by occasional quarrels such as, in 1790, when a coffin was left unburied. It is worth noting that such tensions were sometimes temporarily eliminated by intermarriages between the members of the families of wealthy leaders of disputing synagogues competing for pre-eminence within the community (Roth 1950: 232–3).

The determination of eligibility for synagogal assistance was comparable to the gaining of a 'parochial settlement' under the provision of the old Poor Law. It often involved fierce debate (Roth 1950: 232). The honorary officers responsible for the relief of the poor were styled 'Overseers of the Poor'. The relinquishment of traditional terminology and the adoption of a new one were not only semantic processes, rather, they facilitated and accompanied the identification with concepts alleging the pre-eminence of the wealthy over the poor.

The feelings of the poor were revealed in a letter to the editor of the *Jewish Chronicle* in which the absence of the poor from religious services is explained: 'our poverty is thrown in our face at the Synagogue, we are all heaped together in a cluster at the bottom of the Synagogue in a corner, whilst at the top the benches are empty' (*Jewish Chronicle*, 4

January 1850). Dr. Hermann Adler, Chief Rabbi, wore the attire of a bishop of the Church of England; this was probably viewed with suspicion by the poor. Generally the poor did not receive *aliyot* – honours given during the reading of the *Torah* (presenting blessings, etc.).

Within the Ashkenazic élite, the status of the Rothschilds was undisputed. Nathan Mayer Rothschild (1777–1836), later Baron, was born in the ghetto of Frankfurt. He emigrated to Manchester bringing with him £20,000, of which a fifth was his own, to establish himself as a textile merchant. He moved to London and married a daughter of Levi Barnet Cohen, of one of the most prestigious Ashkenazic families. Not unlike his poor immigrant co-religionists whose lives he was going to control, he was described as 'having a strong German-Yiddish accent' (Aris 1970: 64). Not many years later he was one of the principal members of the London Stock Exchange and an official bullion broker to the English government.

Some historians suggest that together with the Continental branches of the families, the Rothschilds were able to influence to a considerable extent the direction of European history. Nathan died in 1836 leaving a capital of between £5 and £6 million. Unlike other wealthy Anglicized Jews, the Rothschilds remained somewhat separate from the more extended Cousinhood, preferring to marry their close cousins only, possibly with the intention of creating an eternal financial empire with a family dynasty. Appeals from Jews of England and all over the world were addressed to the New Court, the headquarters of the 'House' [of Rothschild] and one of the international money centres close to the Bank of England. With respect to appeals from non-Jewish institutions, Emden writes that Nathan, not always very accessible, was interested in Robert Owen's scheme at New Lanark, and helpful to it (1943: 112). Apparently many applications for help were declined. The Jewish informants of Mayhew complained:

> apart from conventionalities, they [the rich] care nothing whatever, for so long as they are undisturbed in money-getting at home, their brethren may be persecuted all over the world. An honourable exception exists in Sir Moses Montefiore, but the great Jew capitalists, with powerful influence in many a government, do not seek to direct that influence for the bettering of the lot of their poorer brethren. In fact, the Jews have often been the props of the courts who have persecuted them; that is to say two or three Jewish firms occasionally have not hesitated to lend millions to the governments by whom they and their people have been systematically degraded and oppressed. (Mayhew 1850: 126b, 127a)

As far as philanthropic activities for the English Jews were concerned, Roth (1950) points out Nathan Rothschild's lack of enthusiasm. In 1813 he had been elected *Gabbai Tzedakah* (charity collector, distributor or administrator) of the Great Synagogue, but he declined to serve and paid the substitute fine according to the regulations.

In 1818, while a warden of the Great Synagogue, Nathan proposed a savings bank for the Jewish Nation without practical results. A similar proposal to the committee of the Great Synagogue was renewed in 1822 by Samuel Samuel on Nathan's behalf. Prior to the description of the proposal itself, The *Hebrew Intelligencer* of 1 January 1823 praised Nathan's benevolence in most generous and courteous terms. According to the proposal, sums of money were to be advanced to 'the industrious poor of our nation, to furnish them with the means of maintaining their families by their own to be repaid by them in small easy instalments'. For this purpose he offered to subscribe £500. The name that Nathan proposed for the fund was *Davar Tov* (meaning 'A Good Thing'). The details of the proposal were prepared by Benjamin Gompertz, the first actuary of the Alliance Assurance Company, a relative of Nathan. However, as for implementation of the proposal, it was reported that:

> it presents some obstacles and difficulties, which we are not at present prepared to enumerate or combat with. We are aware a society of this kind exists in Hamburgh; and surely, our English Jews must be fully impressed with the utility and even necessity, of a similar one, in a country like this, where our poorer brethren stand so greatly in need of the assistance, they are often compelled to resort to means, which must retard instead of assisting the ends of industry, the plan, which we understand remains in embryo but we hope in our next, to report, that some active measures have been adopted. (*Hebrew Intelligencer*, 1 January 1823)

This proposal, too, did not have any practical outcome.

The lack of genuine interest on the part of wealthy Jews to assist the poor, is somewhat embellished by Roth: 'Rothschild's term of office was not adventurous and the most important innovation with which he was associated in conjunction with his nephew, was the establishment of the services for the poor at the Jews' Free School on the solemn occasions of the Jewish year (Roth 1950: 236). The greater prestige of the Jews' Free School afforded Nathan a way to build further his status. The information received by the *Hebrew Intelligencer*, and published in the same issue, provides an estimate of the comparative value of Rothschild's proposed donation to the unrealized 'Good Thing' Saving Bank:

'Edward Goldsmid, of Finsbury Square is about leaving the neighbourhood for Park Lane where he has purchased an elegant mansion which,
it is supposed, with the furniture will cost £10,000' (*Hebrew Intelligencer*,
1 January 1823). The reporter of one of the 'fashionable parties' in which
one hundred and thirty persons participated found that 'the dresses
were very elegant and a profusion of diamonds blazed in every part of
the room' (*Hebrew Intelligencer*, 22 December 1822).

The ability of the Rothschilds to respond more than others to various
appeals maintained their status as philanthropists amongst the English
Jews and elsewhere in the Jewish world where their wealth became a
legend. According to Roth, the continuous disputes amongst the three
synagogues of the Ashkenazim as to the ways in which their responsibilities towards the strange poor were to be discharged provoked
Nathan's 'fastidious sense of organization' (Roth 1950: 237). Through
his interventions, communications were re-established in 1824, 1825
and 1828 but no operational cooperation was obtained until 1830 and
this under pressures created by the disastrous impact of the cholera
epidemic and the subsequent appeal of the government. Generally,
calamities that affected a significant number of local Jews raised the
levels of responsibility for fellow Jews including the poor. After further
crises, the agreement reached in 1834 was mainly attributed to the influence of Rothschild. It was published as 'Articles of a New Treaty agreed
on by the sub-committees of the Great Hambro' and New Synagogues
AM 5594 and 5595' (1834–5) and after two modifications (1835–6), it was
maintained until 1859 when the three synagogues agreed to establish
The Board of Guardians for the Relief of the Foreign Poor. This ability
to mediate between opposed interests of the wealthy 'big-giving'
leaders of the synagogues underscored Nathan's position as the foremost leader of the London Jewish community by adding a dimension
of organizational leadership.

Nathan Rothschild's role in non-sectarian philanthropy remained
peripheral even when considerable donations were involved. The acces-
sibility of central positions of leadership in Jewish philanthropy
facilitated the socialization into philanthropic roles of his sons and relatives. This socialization often occurred in the ordinary process of their
business and as a family affair.

Philanthropy was an integral part of the élite's lifestyle in the formal,
as well as informal spheres, and served to promote social as well as
business connections. The leaders were chosen on the basis of visible
criteria such as wealth, reputation and decorousness. Consequently,
they tended to represent the interests of a rather narrow group. Their

commitments to give were an important factor in controlling not only the poor but the givers as well. The soliciting of gifts, apparently less conspicuous than the presentation of gifts, carried also a great deal of prestige. Persuading someone to give money meant placing oneself under the obligation of the solicited, in this way, creating a whole sequence of reciprocal claims. This sequence often reflected the hierarchy and the modes of communication used in their economic activities. The internalization of occupational qualities and roles facilitated an interpretation of such philanthropic soliciting activities in terms of selling.

The less prosperous philanthropic activists fulfilled corresponding philanthropic tasks. In this way the stratification of the London Jewish community was reflected in the philanthropic organization. The wealthier members of the élite, the 'big givers' were the trustees or officers of prestigious existing charities, which were directly or indirectly monopolized by them; the upper-middle strata were contributors to these and leaders of middle-range charities. In this framework, motives such as joining titled people in committee work and gaining public notice, were also at work. The middle-class was active in mutual aid organizations and as donors and governors of minor charities.

The ideology of the wealthy class as reflected in this framework, accepted the idea that the poor class cannot plan, think or be trusted. It was assigned a different culture for which controlling and rationalized measures were proposed by members of the élite or their professional helpers in matters of philanthropic requests.

As a result of its social structure, Anglo-Jewish philanthropy was controlled by a relatively small and stable group of affluent men. Consequently, this group had a tremendous impact on the philanthropic organization, the raising and distribution of funds, making and executing decisions, including or excluding others from important philanthropic activities. In view of the extreme centralization of the decision-making processes and the public acclaim stirred by their esteem, the leaders were tempted to believe in their own individual and institutional ethos. It seems that Jewish philanthropy enhanced its prestige by creating heroes that achieved great public aclaim and praise.

Most of the members of the Jewish élite belonged to the orthodox synagogal congregations. The most powerful sub-group, led by Louis Cohen (1799–1818) and Moses Montefiore, was orthodox. The common denominator was, however, the belief that a level of Jewish religious practice had to be protected from secular interference. The overall religious observance and knowledge of the élite itself was restricted.

Involved in a rapid process of increasing secularization, the members of the élite did not perceive conflicting elements between their orthodoxy and universalistic assimilation, nor between Jewish humanitarian concepts and the massive adoption of the laissez-faire doctrine. Unlike the contemporary German Jews, the Anglo-Jewish élite did not develop its cultural and intellectual heritage, but maintained a rather narrow Judaism based on ethnicity and religion. (German Jewry, much larger in size, developed the *Wissenschaft Haskallah*). Generally, the Anglo Jewish élite gave their Jewishness a rather materialistic and worldly meaning, which fitted their main occupations and aspirations. It was satisfied with the influence of the Mendelssohnian Enlightenment – an assimilationist Jewish European ideology that permitted Jews to change their outward appearance and lifestyle to make them acceptable to English society, and imbue the wealthy strata with a sense of social and economic success and prosperity. This was interpreted as a direct result of the strict adaptation of such values as effort, initiative and so on. The optimistic mood of the élite was generated by the appreciation of their economic endeavours, their industry and aspirations. The contemporary philanthropic thought and premises were incorporated in such an atmosphere with increasing avidity.

While the large scale philanthropic schemes designed by the Ashkenazic élite, according to prevalent English models, were abortive, there is some evidence of their limited implementation. In 1844, the Jewish Ladies' Benevolent Loan and Visiting Society was established in Whitechapel Road. The aims of the Society were to promote 'the visits of Jewish Ladies amongst their own poor, and advocating habits of prudence and economy amongst them' and to provide small loans without interest as well as a small relief fund (Low, 1850: 145–6). A small scale savings bank was attached to this association 'to enable the recipients of loans to deposit a trifle weekly from their earnings' (*Voice of Jacob*, 15 November 1844). It was an assumed truth of the savings bank movement that lack of frugality and providence amongst the Jewish poor threatened their stability. Bentham, during the early development of this movement, had a more realistic attitude towards it: 'Some are for doing everything for savings out of earnings, but this will not do very well where there can be no savings, still less where there can be no earnings' (quoted in Bowring 1962 edn 8: 367). It is possible that the savings were the price the recipients of this charity had to pay in order to benefit from the assistance offered by the society and to be able to reapply for help.

In 1855, the *Jewish Chronicle* published abstracts from the eleventh annual report of the society characterizing it as 'truly benevolent'. The concepts outlined in this report were later propagated by the Charity Organization Society. In addition to the 1844 guiding principles and the typical Victorian moralism and suspicion towards the poor, the society emphasized prevention of pauperism and immediate intervention in case of temporary distress 'by timely assistance to enable those who through sickness and other inevitable misfortunes are reduced to the verge of destitution to renew their labour' (*Jewish Chronicle*, 13 July 1855). The Society recognized the limits of rehabilitation and the consequent need for permanent relief in cases considered to belong to the 'deserving poor' and in which the principle of family responsibility could not be applied: 'there are however some cases for the relief of which absolute gifts are indispensably necessary, the cases of aged and infirm persons who being childless have none to provide for them'. According to the report, distribution of relief was 'preceded by vigilant inquiry. The committee in rotation visit the neighbourhood in which the poor are located and from personal investigation enabled judiciously to apply the finances entrusted to their care' (*Jewish Chronicle*, 13 July 1855). The Jewish Ladies' Benevolent Loan and Visiting Society was preoccupied to prevent what it regarded as the 'abuse of the bounty' of the middle-classes:

> this Society opens to them a means of dispensing their gifts, and materially enhancing the value and utility of their benevolence, the committee have much satisfaction in directing attention to the fact, as strikingly illustrative of a growing moral improvement in the principles of the poor, few bad debts have been incurred since the report published last year . . . '.
> (*Jewish Chronicle*, 13 July 1855)

The Society related to a confined number of poor persons and as such can be regarded as a small-scale extension of an operational experiment based on innovative models of English philanthropy. The principles that guided the Society were confirmed four years later by the newly established Jewish Board of Guardians which, from the beginning, attempted to implement them with regard to the 'strange' poor (having no claim of membership on the three contracting Ashkenazic synagogues). At the same time the Board made a considerable effort to persuade the leaders of those synagogues to transfer the care of their 'stipendiary' and 'casual' poor to the Board but this interference was rather 'repudiated than sought by the synagogues' (First Board of Guardians Half Yearly Report July–Dec. 1859: 17).

The incipient attempt of the Society to enlarge its control over the poor was declared as a clear and vital policy of the more ambitious Board.

> The Board seeks to draw all the poor to its own doors, it will be grateful for the information of any case of real distress to which its notice may be directed, for it wishes to establish an accurate register of all the poor, and to discourage private indiscriminate alms giving. (First *BGHYR* July–Dec. 1859: 17)

However, as far as new immigrants were concerned, the Board refused to adopt the humane principle of immediate intervention, by stipulating a six months non-interference period, that is, only after six months after immigration were the needs of any poor applicants considered by the Board (p. 19).

The increasing distance between the Jewish social classes in terms of habitation and standard of living, made the visit of wealthy women in the East End Jewish quarter quite extraordinary. The innovative practices based on harsh principles made the task even more difficult. This is evidenced by a report of the *Liverpool Mercury* about the activities of Jewish Ladies' Benevolent Institution of Liverpool (established 1849):

> the investigation of cases by untrained volunteers proved so difficult and so unsavoury, and the conflict of pity and principle involved in each decision so baffling and painful, that only the most valiant of the members continued their active service, the rest tending to absent themselves upon such reasonable excuse as their disinclination to remain in town during the insanitary summer months. The Minutes of the meetings are a tribute to those who plodded on, bravely endeavouring to reconcile themselves to the discovery that the poor were so frequently not also the deserving and to combine correct charitable practice with natural common sense. (*Liverpool Mercury*, 10 November 1858, quoted in Simey 1951: 68)

The existence of parallel situations in London is suggested by the recommendation of Faudel to use relief officers and the appointment of salaried investigation officers by the Board. Visiting the poor provided an outlet for the surplus of time and energy for the wealthy Jewish women, as well as an avenue to express their feelings of superiority, their responsibility for uplifting the poor, and getting the poor to behave and look as English as possible:

> At a time when it had not yet become fashionable to speak of personal intercourse between the rich and the needy she [Charlotte de Rothschild]

always strove to impress the great duty of cleanliness. I am *bekoved* [honoured] too, rejoined the Baroness, yet I always dust some of my things by myself. (Hermann Adler, Chief Rabbi, Central Synagogue, Sermon in Memory of the Baroness, Sabbath, 22 March in Adler 1884)

It is worth noting that the personal intercourse with the poor was presented as a precursor to a later fashion rather than as a deep- rooted Jewish tradition and its discontinuation by the wealthy class. Moses Montefiore recorded in his diary one visit to some narrow walks around Petticoat Lane in 1830:

> We there visited the rooms of about 112 persons. To 108 we gave cards to obtain relief, we witnessed many distressing scenes, parents surrounded by children frequently six or seven, seldom less than two or three with little or no fire or food and scarcely a rug to cover them, without bed or blanket, but merely a sack or two for the night, a bed being almost out of question. Few had more than one room, however large the family. (quoted in Bermant 1969: 14)

While cleanliness was no doubt vital in an era of epidemics, it seems that what was needed in order to provide the elementary wants of the Jewish poor was a continuous serious effort. Considering the tremendous wealth of some of the members of the élite, such an effort was within its possibilities.

According to different contemporary tabulations, in London there were more than twenty-five minor Jewish Ashkenazic and Sephardic charities, not including friendly societies and educational institutions. Still other charities were established and maintained by the main synagogues such as the Spanish and Portuguese Board of Guardians (established 1832). Two almshouses were founded by A. L. Moses and Joel Emanuel in 1854 (under the auspices of the Great Synagogue). Some charities included elements of insurance based on medieval corporation models according to which, needs of middle-class subscribers were considered before those of non-members (Stein 1964: 74). Beneficiaries of charity schools, for instance, were obligated to recite the mourner's prayer at the synagogal services for deceased quid pro quo, albeit posthumously. These charities provided:

1   distributions of money (pensions, loans, dowries, festival grants, etc.);
2   help in kind (food, coal, clothing, blankets, medicine, etc.);

3   utilities in kind (apprenticeship, education, medical treatment and hospitalization, nursing and lying in, etc.).

One of the early charities of the Ashkenazim, which was not strictly connected with the synagogue, was The Meshivat Nefesh (Hebrew for Restoring the Soul, taken from Psalm 19); its English name was more prosaic: the Bread, Meat and Coal Society, established in 1797. The society distributed five or six shilling tickets redeemable for the purchase of goods over twelve winter weeks. The preference of help in kind is reflected in *the Laws and Regulations of the Society called Meshivat Nefesh for the Relief of the Poor* 5540 (1780). Help in kind was considered less demoralizing than relief in cash and characteristic of the contemporary suspicion shown towards the moral values and self- discipline of the poor. The inability of the Jewish charities during the first half of the nineteenth century to apply the workhouse test often increased such suspicion. Though help in kind was accepted by the Jewish tradition along with other forms of relief, its distribution was not generally attributed to the inability of the poor to administer their life reasonably (*Laws* 1780, II).

The original regulations of the eighteenth century were patterned on the model known from the Continent. Written in Yiddish with an admixture of Hebrew, they were based on Jewish concepts of *tzedakah* and administration of Jewish institutions such as by 'seven upright men of the town'. According to the regulations in existence by the end of the eighteenth century, benefactors who had no sons were guaranteed that the poor of the synagogue would recite prayers for them regularly after their death.

The Regulations of Meshivat Nefesh and the other societies were gradually translated from Yiddish into English. This process involved, whether conscious or not, an increasing desanctification and adoption of laissez-faire concepts from the English environment, including some operational patterns of parish churches. It was the Jewish élite that took the lead in borrowing and adapting such concepts and practices to its own needs. However, the other Jewish strata too were dependent on this conditioning to various degrees. The Jewish charities were unplanned, overlapping, and responded to the diverse specific needs of a limited number of the poor. As such they did not relate to the most difficult problems of the completely and partially destitute, including those that could not become self-supporting (the very old and chronically ill). These charities were also unable to provide casual relief to the working class during sickness, unemployment and other hazards. Some of the charities, aimed at helping the 'deserving', 'respectable' and lower middle-classes, as shown by Highmore in *Pietas Londinensis* (1814), and Low in *The Charities of London* (1831). The requirement of social standing as the most important criterion for eligibility is illustrated by the regulations of the A. L. Moses Almshouses of Aldgate. Such prerequisites were mentioned by E. H. Lindo in *A Jewish Calendar . . . with a Table of Religious and Charitable Institutions of the Jews in London* (1833), for example, with regard to the Hand in Hand Asylum for the Aged and Decayed Tradesmen, established in 1840. The new immigrants were often excluded from benefits. Even when provided, the help was usually inadequate and given in a way that prevented further bona fide claims.

Notwithstanding their severe limitations, the standards of Jewish charities were highly regarded by some contemporary non-Jewish writers (such as Highmore 1814). Mayhew (1850) writes:

> The Jewish charities are highly honourable to the body, for they allow none of their people to live or die in a parish workhouse. It is true that among the Jews in London there are many individuals of immense wealth, but there are also many rich Christians who care not one jot for the need of their brethren. It must be borne in mind also that not only do the Jews voluntarily support their own poor and institutions, but they contribute – compulsorily it is true – their quota to the support of the English poor and church. This is the more honourable and the more remarkable among the Jews, when we recollect their indisputable greed of money . . . ' (Mayhew 1850: 127)

Following his survey of Jewish charities including schools, Mayhew estimated their annual cost at £14,000 (not including £2,000 representing the amount of loans lent yearly by three Jewish loan societies). At the same time Mayhew estimated that by 1849–50, there were about eighteen thousand Jews in London and concluded that the charitable donations of the Jews amounted to an approximate average of a little less than 1 pound per person and that 'the ratio of the English Christian's contributions to his needy brethren throughout the country will be very nearly the same as that of the Jews' (Mayhew 1850: 129). As far as London's Christians were concerned, Mayhew reached the conclusion 'that their munificence does not fall short of that of the metropolitan Jews' (Mayhew 1850: 129). The criticism of the Jewish wealthy class that Mayhew inserted by quoting his Jewish working class 'informants' was not reflected in his concluding remarks, wherein he rather praised the bounty of the Jewish wealthy class as well as the non-

Jewish one, implicitly accepting the sharp social differentiation involved.

As with many of their non-Jewish counterparts, Jewish charities were based on a voting charity system by which a person subscribing, for example, one guinea annually became a governor; twenty guineas usually entitled the donor to a life governorship, sometimes 'with right to name a successor in default of which his next heir according to the Jewish Law of Succession' (*Meil Tzedakah*, The Cloak of Charity, established in 1736, listed by Lindo 1838: 2). Persons donating less than half a guinea could not be elected as officers of the charity, vote, or express official opinions. The number of votes depended on the corresponding subscriptions of one guinea each, giving the donor the privilege of choosing beneficiaries. As benefits were often insufficient for all the applicants, lottery wheels especially made for drawing lots were used.

According to this system, the poor who did not have influential acquaintances to sponsor their application were discriminated against. Later, evidence of what this system implied for a Jewish widow was described by C. Rosenfeld in *Torath Ha'adam (The Law of Man) Teaching of Humanity: A Treatise Throwing some Light on Certain Movement of the Day* (1890):

> I happened to know a poor striving widow, whose child was well deserving support. Since she had no acquaintance with any member of that institution she had to advertise in the papers for votes, this entitling an expense of 16/ – After all, her endeavours proved a failure . . . but the expense . . . has devoured her only and small capital. I think in such cases it would be quite sufficient that parents should make an application in writing . . . (Rosenfeld 1890: 17)

Severe criticism of the Voting Charity System was expressed towards the end of the nineteenth century by a group of philanthropists related to the Charity Organization Society, amongst them Frederick David Mocatta (1818–1905), the most important representative of Jewish scientific philanthropy in the Cousinhood and chairman of the Charity Voting Reform Association. Mocatta considered the system irrational and immoral, permitting subscribers to select their beneficiaries, and in this way to act upon their capricious dispositions rather than on meritorious criteria. He regarded the practice of allowing any number of applicants to compete for a single vacancy as cruelty disguised as charity (Mocatta 1971: 9). The Association attempted to replace the system by introducing criteria of merit so as not to enable subscribers 'to pervert the selection process into electioneering campaign'. Mocatta did not include in his will legacies for charities based on this system. However, he emphasized criteria of merit rather than needs. The ways in which charity was distributed were embarrassing, coarse and divisive. The Voting Charity system made it even harsher. The general approach of the élite to the Jewish poor as reflected in biographies, newspapers and other extant records gives evidence of little sympathy, an unerring realism rather than idealism.

An important stage in the Jewish élite's struggle for emancipation started in 1829 under the leadership of Isaac Lyon Goldsmid. It was extended for over thirty years. In 1830 Joshua van Oven was appointed together with Goldsmid, Rothschild, Montefiore and Mocatta by the Board of Deputies to a committee that negotiated with the government the matter of Jewish emancipation which centred on the cancellation of the Christological Oath. Obviously, this was a matter of concern to the Jewish élite which aspired to political positions. (Emanuel 1920: 15). Henry Mayhew (1850) reached the conclusion that the Jewish population in the East End concerned with obtaining the basic necessities of living remained indifferent to this issue: 'I was told by a Hebrew gentleman . . . that so little did the Jews themselves care for Jewish Emancipation that he questioned if one man in ten, actuated solely by his own feelings, would trouble himself to walk the length of the street in which he lived to secure Baron [Lionel] Rothschild's admission into the House of Commons' (Mayhew 1850: 206a).

In this issue – as contrasted to the relief of the poor – there was an increasing cooperation between the various groups of the Jewish élite (Roth 1950: 238). This movement involved the establishment of administrative machinery and the commissioning of solicitors. The heavy expenses connected with the petitions to Parliament were divided between the synagogues – the Sephardim included (for instance, in 1831 in the case of Robert Grant's aborted bill). In the 1840s some letters to the editors of the Jewish press opposed the movement which regarded the solution of the problems of Jewish poverty to be much more important. The Board of Deputies that fulfilled a leading role in the movement was criticized for neglecting the widespread Jewish poverty and called to study its causes and extent, so as to draw up measures for its alleviation. Following Lionel Rothschild's election in 1847, the *Jewish Chronicle* regarded emancipation incomplete without an internal one (*Jewish Chronicle*, 18 October 1847). However, criticism that the preoccupation with emancipation consumed a vast amount of energy that could be directed towards ameliorating Jewish poverty was rejected by the Jewish élite: 'From the first, Jewish leaders strove for social improvements with no less ardour than for political enfranchisement; the chronicles who dwell, as they are apt to do, on one aspect only of their endeavours, are doing them far less than justice' (Cohen 1937: 18). Lucien Wolf (1934) regards the struggle of the Jewish élite for political emancipation as a motivating factor 'to put their house in order and so the work of internal progress was promoted side by side with the agitation for external rights' (Wolf 1934: 314).

After 1837 another domestic question that concerned the Jewish élite was the rising Reform Movement which threatened its religious unity. It is worth noting that in parliamentary debates and publications relating to Jewish political rights, the Jewish élite and its non-Jewish supporters strongly emphasized the liberality and sensitivity of the Jewish wealthy class (Faudel 1848: 7). The main opponents to emancipation were the High Church Tories who regarded the Jewish wealthy class as supporters of the liberal bourgeoisie and a threat to the Established Church. The argumentative defences used by the Jewish élite to neutralize the image of foreigners, (by which dishonesty and vulgar materialism were attached to Jews as a whole) were summarized by Bernard van Oven in a letter to the Editor of *The Times* published on 3 February 1830 (and republished as 'Emancipation of the Jews' in 1834):

> I must therefore beg of your candour to allow me . . . to rescue my brethren from the charges you have advanced against them, which include a blind and besotted pursuit of one sole and unworthy object – the accumulation of wealth. Sir, this is by no means the case. From the highest to the lowest class they may be quoted as examples to their neighbours in the important duties of husband, wife, parent and child. The annals of Newgate offer but few Jewish names courted of highway robbery, housebreaking and murder. The vice of drunkenness is so rare. His charity is universal, unbounded, the Jews contribute equally to the Church and poor's rates, without in any way benefiting from them, they maintain their own poor and all foreign poor of their religion, they have many and extensive public charities and subscribe largely to all schemes. (*The Times*, 3 February 1830)

The same counter-arguments, including exaggerations about the adequacy of Jewish relief were advanced by Francis H. Goldsmid (later baronet), in his writings in support of political rights. In this struggle the Jewish élite enjoyed the continuous support and expertise of middle-class communal workers such as the van Ovens and a more critical member of his own wealthy class, Henry Faudel (F. H. Goldsmid 1830: 12). In the struggle for political rights, Isaac Lyon Goldsmid enlisted the support of Elizabeth Fry with whom he collaborated in prison reform

(Sabbstein 1982: 67). As far as individual aspirations for political honours were concerned, philanthropy played an important part. This is illustrated by Lord Shaftesbury's recommendation to bestow the honours of the peerage to Sir Moses Montefiore (in a letter to Gladstone, 2 December 1862 quoted in Emden 1943: 164). Montefiore's generous donations were one of the main considerations. Montefiore was interested in Shaftesbury's Field Ragged Schools and supported them financially (Emden 1943: 165). Though elected several times, only in 1858 was Lionel de Rothschild fully accepted as a member of the House of Commons. Political rights were finally won by the élite. This political achievement was only partly due to the philanthropic donations through which the Jewish élite aroused a sympathetic interest in their rights. By this time the influence of the Jewish élite was increasingly felt beyond the economic sphere, as Lord Granville wrote to Queen Victoria '[Lionel Rothschild] represents a class which is great by their intelligence, their literary connections. It may be wise to attach them to the aristocracy' (quoted in *Jewish Chronicle*, 7 August 1936).

Lionel de Rothschild (1808–79), son of Nathan, was instrumental in providing the British government with the means needed to compensate slave-owners in the overseas dominions. Lionel presented this transaction in Parliament as a humanitarian and liberal act. The loan for governmental assistance during the Irish famine in 1847 was provided without commission as a philanthropic donation (Morton 1962: 141–2). The loans provided during the Crimean War and for purchasing shares in the Suez Canal were represented as a patriotic support of national endeavours and the development of the British Empire. Lionel maintained the general reputation of honest dealings. Public exposure of his huge transactions led Lionel and other members of the House to transfer their interests to mining in South Africa and Europe. Lionel was the lord of the manor of Tring, a splendid seventeenth-century mansion planned by Sir Christopher Wren as a present from Charles II to Nell Gwyn, for which he paid a quarter of million pounds. Thousands of additional pounds were paid for its subsequent remodelling (Aris 1970: 78). Lionel was considered an exemplary landlord of the estate of Gunnersbury Park which he inherited from his father and restored to sheer magnificence (Morton 1962: 143–4). The prodigious sums that other members of the Jewish élite spent on 'territorial ambitions' are illustrated by the Sassoons who bought Ashley Park in Surrey, once occupied by Cromwell, and later on, Trent Park. David Sassoon's aristocratic aspirations can be deduced from his witty saying 'There is only one race better than the Jews and that is the Derby' (Morton 1962: 143–4). The acquisition of country palaces and the extravagant way of life reflect the surplus reserves of capital available beyond investment in current business and donations to charity. They provided the Jewish élite with an even more stable and secure economic situation, less fluctuating than some of their financial enterprises, but such acquisitions were detrimental to inter-class Jewish solidarity by contributing to the increasing social distance between the rich and the poor.

The approach of Lionel Rothschild towards the Jewish poor and working class is reflected in his political campaign in which he carefully managed to disown and de-emphasize the support of the Jewish working class and even the Jewish middle class in order to avoid being identified by the English public as a leader of the Jewish electoral organized body. Consequently, during this period, the already significant Jewish constituency in the East End of London was disregarded. This attitude was reproached by the *Jewish Chronicle* (6 April 1847, 21 May 1858), which also published a reader's letter expressing scepticism with respect to Lionel's commitment to Jewish interests and his readiness to represent them in case of his admission into Parliament. However, Lionel was not deterred by the criticism of Jewish radicals nor by Jewish electoral power in the City of London, which was regarded as one of the important constituencies in England. The Jewish radicals during this period were unable to oppose this trend as represented by Lionel Rothschild. In his campaign, Lionel addressed himself to matters of general interest seen from a liberal and laissez-faire perspective, emphasizing religious freedom, property taxes and opposition to church rates. These ideas were shared by the other religious minorities and the rising middle class. Increasingly, accumulating power and security, the 'House' did not feel the need to further elevate its position by performing outstanding acts of philanthropy.

In spite of his unwillingness to strengthen ties with the poor of his own ethnic group, Lionel and other wealthy Jews nominated themselves the representatives of the Jewish poor and the community as a whole *vis-à-vis* the English authorities. The Jewish élite was ready to accept this role as a substitute or an addition to their positions in the host community. The use of the representative power enabled the Jewish élites to control the Jewish poor and prevent their immigration to England through the authority and machinery of the government. This process involved a policy of differentiation between the strata of Jewish immigrants. In 1858, this representative power was reinforced by the parliamentary positions of Lionel de Rothschild and Alderman David Salomons.

Before the struggle of the Jewish élite for election to Parliament there was a battle for the right to be elected to municipal positions. David Salomons, one of the founders of the London and Westminster Bank in 1834, became the first Jewish sheriff of London and Middlesex and in 1855 the first Jewish lord mayor. Through such involvement in the municipal higher power structure, the Jewish élite was able to under-stand better the system of money grants available, for example, for the education of the English poor. The chief powers enjoyed by municipal corporations included the superintendence of elementary education. The government of such corporations was entrusted to the mayor and a number of aldermen. In the late 1840s Benjamin S. Phillips, born in London in 1811, a partner in the financial firm Faudel, Phillips and Lows and later knighted, was instrumental in obtaining a grant of £100, for the Jews' Free School from the Common Council of the Corporation of London of which he was elected a member, in 1846, as representative of the ward of Farringdon (Mayhew 1850: 207b, 208a). This precedent illus-trates that the participation of the Jewish élite in the municipal government was accompanied by corresponding demands for munic-ipal contributions to the voluntarily supported Jewish schools. For thirty years Benjamin Phillips was an active member of the Jewish Board of Deputies which in 1849 or 1850 discussed with the Education Commissioners of her Majesty's Privy Council the possibility of obtaining a grant of money for Jewish education. According to Mayhew (1850), the grant was requested 'in the same proportion as it has been granted to other educational establishments. Nothing has as yet been given to the Jewish schools and the matter is still undetermined' (Mayhew 1850: 299b).

The increasing confidence of the Jewish élite in the English sociopo-litical environment was evident in its readiness to start a step-by-step process for acquiring equal municipal subventions for the education of children of the Jewish poor with the consequent decrease of the exclu-sive dependence of the poor upon the private resources of wealthy Jews. This confidence was largely based on the association of the Jewish élite with the important financial circles of the metropolis. The request of equal money grants reflects an additional step in the gradual departure from the practice according to which 'Jews take care of their own'. It was presented as a matter of principle. On the other hand concomitant large-scale donations to voluntary non-sectarian charitable efforts stressed that contributions of individual Jews were not confined to their sectarian charities. As an illustration, during his term as mayor, Phillips (elected 1865) personally raised £70,000 for the Cholera Fund. Phillips was succeeded in the office by his son Alderman Sir George Faudel Phillips (*Jewish Encyclopaedia* Vol. 10: 5). Both of them were presidents of the Jewish Blind Society, established in 1819 as the Institution for the Relief of the Indigent Blind of the Jewish Persuasion.

The Jewish masses were indifferent to the struggle of the élite for parliamentary and municipal positions; this constitutes additional evidence of the widening social distance that already existed in the community.

THE FAUDEL SCHEME

Now we turn our attention to a further major proposal for organizing the community to tackle the challenges as yet unmet: the Faudel scheme. This comprehensive, unimplemented plan which, as its predecessor the Colquhoun–van Oven scheme, was intended to enable the Jewish élite to reform and control the Jewish poor through registration, centralization and rationalization of services. The scheme was developed by Henry Faudel; who placed special emphasis on those children of the poor who were considered to be more educable. The detailed form of the plan enabled the identification of the Benthamite ideas and early Victorian bourgeois values that influenced the expectations of Faudel. The following discussion will show that he was also influenced by the framework of services provided by the Society of Friends.

In 1841, extracts from a large scheme of charity and education were published by Henry Faudel in the *Voice of Jacob*. The series of several articles was entitled *Suggestions to the Jews for Improvement in Reference to their Charities, Education and Government, by a Jew* [Henry Faudel]. In 1844 the articles were republished anonymously in booklet form.

Henry Faudel was from a wealthy family. In 1833, he entered into partnership with his brother-in-law, Benjamin Phillips, founding the firm Faudel, Phillips and Sons. He was considered by the Jewish élite as initiated in philanthropy and education for the poor and, as such, he investigated the conditions at the Jew's Hospital. He was active in the struggle for emancipation and published a booklet addressed to Sir R. H. Inglis, MP (1848) in which he emphasized the humane and charitable qualities of the Jewish law and people. The scheme illustrates the attempt of Faudel and the *Voice of Jacob* to bring about concerted action between the different Ashkenazic synagogues and charities, which during the first part of the nineteenth century proliferated in a chaotic fashion.

Faudel meant to create a superstructure encompassing and assimilating all Anglo-Jewish arrangements in the realm of charity and education in the metropolis and the provinces. The model for this ambitious scheme was provided by the Society of Friends:

> for they are spread over as large a surface as the Jews – consist, like them of merchants and traders – similar in numbers superior in education (although not in mental capacity) with a well-ordered and responsible government we consequently hear of no distress or disorganization among them. Yet it is not to be doubted that as many causes for interference occur in that body as in our own, but education, discipline and a well regulated system for their poor enable them to grapple with every question of good or evil. (Faudel 1844: 19)

Like his predecessors, in attempting to reform the Jewish poor and to stop deleterious competition amongst the different Jewish wealthy subgroups, Faudel was strongly influenced by Benthamite ideas. He regarded the object of government as 'the production of the greatest possible amount of human happiness. I am not far wrong in stating that the only exception in Great Britain of an extensive religious community being without a government is to be found amongst the Jews . . . the want was never so much felt as at the present moment' (Faudel 1844: 4). Faudel was not a philosopher and most probably did not read the works of Bentham deeply. Rather, he quoted passages which were regarded by the Jewish élite as justifying accumulation of wealth and middle-class prosperity. Within the framework of Bentham's utility principle the identity between self and common interests fitted the new capitalist class.

According to Bentham and his followers, the greatest happiness of England was based on the expansion of the competitive enterprise and denial of aristocratic privileges, and indeed, the representative of the capitalist interest in the Parliament used the utilitarian terminology. As was made amply evident in his booklet, what Faudel meant in his social scheme was not the socialists' interpretation of the greatest happiness of the community (such as Robert Owen's). Whittaker (1960) points out that:

> the utility derived from an addition to wealth was less for those with high incomes than for persons with low incomes, a transfer of funds from the wealthy to the poor would raise the aggregate utility of society. But Bentham backed away from accepting the equalization of income as essential to governmental reform. Such a course he said would conflict

with the principle of property if property were equally divided 'everything would be speedily destroyed . . . '. (Whittaker 1960: 131)

The idea of selective and limited interference was accepted by
Bentham's followers, for instance, Chadwick believed that in some situations only the intervention of the state can ensure the greatest
happiness of the greatest numbers (Young and Ashton 1956: p. 21).
Preoccupied with the good reputation of the Jewish élite, regarded as a
prerequisite for obtaining its political emancipation, Faudel linked the
provision to the poor with the ability of the Jewish wealthy class to
maintain its status in England. Consequently, Jewish solidarity was
presented as a vital interest of the wealthy Jewish class:

> What has been done by you for the elevation of your brethren? But let all
> that is practicable in this respect be attained, and you will ascend with
> them, as the majority become refined in their manners. Honour will
> emanate from the people and be reflected upon the leaders. Every onward
> movement of the middle and lower orders, must press you, the more
> advanced into higher eminence and it is therefore necessary on your parts
> to procure . . . the means of making its members of every class useful and
> excellent citizens. The aristocratic class of the Jews is formed of men of
> wealth . . . of wealth honourably acquired . . . but unless the strictest regard
> be had to the education . . . we shall have this class noted only for its
> money. (Faudel 1844: 14)

With regard to the obstacles that prevented co-ordination of Jewish
charities some additional criticism and exhortations were directed at the
wealthy; they, in Faudel's opinion, suffered from pride and mutual jeal-
ousy. 'Every charity is encountered by another for similar purposes . . .
both contend with all the force and feelings of competitors for public
favour . . . sink for once the mere desire to be a chairman, committee
men, and managers. Act with others and not as if you only were *patrons*
and *founders*' (Faudel 1844: 6, 12; emphasis is Faudel's).

Faudel was aware of the Colquhoun and van Oven scheme (Faudel
1848: 4) and reproposed many of their ideas. Like them, he believed that
'unity of purpose and management' would be achieved by 'providing a
building adapted to the whole' (p. 10). All the non-ecclesiastical matters
of the community were to be included in the scheme and superintended
by

> a General Committee or Council, consisting in the first instance, of those
> who are disposed to give their personal or pecuniary assistance . . . and

afterwards, during the operation of the project also of members selected by the public and popular election of the Jews . . . They should possess the confidence of the community from their members, education, wealth and footing in the society. (Faudel 1844: 18)

The Council was to be empowered in several ways:

1 To propose and carry out laws and regulations.
2 To enact a registration of all the Jews in England in order to obtain 'a large amount of statistical information, and the concentration of the community facilitated – no claimant for any purpose of education or charity could or would be recognized, unless upon the register' (Faudel 1844: 20).
3 To charge a small registration fee – 'very trifling to the poorest when considered as giving them defined claims as recognized members of the community' (Faudel 1844: 20). This fee was intended to produce an annual amount to be added to the general funds. 'The Society of Friends has a general register, and every member contributes to the local funds, these again to the general, thus sufficient sums are obtained. A somewhat similar modus operandi I would advocate for our adoption' (Faudel 1844: 29).
4 To receive and administer funds, grants, gifts and loans from synagogues and individuals including those that were reserved to cater for the synagogues' pensioners.
5 To reorganize existing charities which Faudel believed 'would result in great savings and make it possible to provide more adequate relief. Also through an efficient check of all persons relieved and preventing tradesman to offer help to the unknown and frequently unworthy' (Faudel 1844: 12).
6 To instruct all Jewish children and 'taking charge of all the offspring of the poor. I take from them all the claim generally resorted to for the charitable interference of the Synagogues as the poor will have very little difficulty in maintaining themselves if we maintain all their children to do which, it would be necessary to remove them to a suitable establishment . . . in connection with a school of industry' (Faudel 1844: 21). Faudel believed that 'the removal of the young from the old, at an early age very desirable for the contamination of evil example . . . tends to undo the instruction they receive and is the cause of so small a number attending the places already provided' (Faudel 1844: 22–3). By taking responsibility for the children of the poor, the economic causes that prevented their parents

from sending them to school could be more justifiably ignored. This too was a Benthamite idea according to which, in houses of industry the infant mortality would be considerably reduced, parents would be relieved of an economic burden, and children and society would greatly benefit from their training (Bentham, Pauper System Compared, Bentham Papers CLII b: 454–9, 509–15 quoted by Poynter 1969: 123). The adult poor generation was regarded by Faudel as socially dysfunctional and uneducable, therefore unable to furnish its children with the instrumental values and skills needed. The exclusive separation of the children of the poor from older members of their families during their formative years was, of course, opposed to Jewish tradition.

7 To establish a superior school for a limited number of the most talented boys in the vicinity of London University, to be trained for the professions of law, medicine, clergy, etc. Cutting off the most able boys with a potential for natural leadership could be detrimental to the poor from many aspects.

To amalgamate all the Jewish charities 'not to be understood the depriving of any of their funds, nor do I wish to divert legacies but to secure an efficient centralization with wholesome and necessary control' (Faudel 1844: 24).

8 To establish a well regulated system of relief under checks and controls to stop mendacity and all indiscriminate charity, regarded by Faudel 'as an evil encouraging consumers instead of helping producers, assisting idlers and beggars rather than artisans'.

9 One of Faudel's preoccupations was his desire to control mendacity. He regarded 'every beggar . . . employed in seeking the entire day whom to devour, considering himself entirely at liberty, morally and physically, to devote his entire time to the readiest way of getting money' (Faudel 1844: 25). To combat indiscriminate charity Faudel quoted Tacitus' concept of 'false compassion', defined as an injury to industry and community. It is worth noting that no *hallachic* injunctions with respect to charity were cited in Faudel's work, in sharp contrast to his other booklet, *A Few Words on the Jewish Disabilities Addressed to Sir Robert Harry Inglis, Bart., MP* (1848: 12–14). In his zeal to prevent the Jewish public from what he termed indiscriminate charity, Faudel deliberately omitted pertinent Jewish injunctions with regard to immediate, non means-test-based provisions he was aware of, substituting them with laissez-faire economic slogans. As other non-Jewish representatives of the wealthy class, Faudel ignored Benthamite writings

that did not support laissez-faire doctrine. Nor did he relate specifically to problems of unemployment, sickness, and so on, basically assuming that personal endeavour can counterbalance all predicaments facing the Jewish poor. In this sense Benthamite theory presented a double bind approach to social reform, promoting and at the same time obstructing it, but always providing justification for sharp social differentiation.

10 To build a House for the aged, decayed and temporarily destitute. It was proposed to divide the building into wards, 'each separate ward to be under control'. Some arrangements in the wards for the aged were comparable to those of the Greenwich Hospital (Faudel 1844: 28).

11 To appoint proper officers for the distribution of charity (Faudel 1844: 27).

12 To provide for an Anglo-Jewish press (p. 10). As far as social reform was concerned, 'a journal . . . placed on independent footing might be made a vehicle for affording a large amount of statistical information on the numbers, callings and education of the Jews – the incomes and expenditures of charitable societies and synagogues' (Faudel 1844: 31).

At the request of the *Voice of Jacob* (29 October 1841), some detailed statistical reports and investigations were preliminarily prepared. According to the editorial, the main aim was not their publication but rather 'to convene a meeting of all managers of the Jewish charities or a special meeting of the Board of Deputies for the consideration of the data so prepared'. The weekly *Voice of Jacob* and then the *Jewish Chronicle* reflected the aspirations of the rising middle-classes. Through frequent reporting of philanthropic disorganization in the Jewish press and with its support, Faudel hoped 'to shake off that terrible apathy and coldness, which have hitherto left them the sport and passive creatures of circumstances' (Faudel 1844: 31–2), and to create an atmosphere conducive to the implementation of his comprehensive plan.

The overwhelming measures of control included in the scheme were directed at the poor but Faudel was not sure of their willingness to accept his accusations and the changes he engineered:

> but how can their condition be improved unless with an earnest disposition on their own part towards it. Is obtaining occasional charity that relieves them only for a short period the sole aims of their lives? Is not the welfare of their children an all powerful feeling with them? Does the desti-

tution of old age never occur to their thoughts until the moment that it
commences, when helpless infirmity assails them? Is not the thought of
an hereafter sometimes present to their minds? If their answers, their
opinions upon these subjects are what they should be, and what must
naturally be expected, I am sure they will add, that they are prepared to
go with me in the scheme for their improvement and welfare. (Faudel
1844: 17)

Personal virtues such as parsimony, hard work, and ambition to get
ahead, were considered necessary in order to prevent any dependence
on public funds. The social philosophy in which Faudel had been
nurtured, prevented him from relating to the meagre income of the
Jewish poor, their inability to save and provide for old age and, in the
final analysis, their sufferings. Within the limitations of his social and
economic theory, Faudel can be regarded as an important exponent of
part of the Anglo-Jewish élite that viewed the disorganization of the
community as a serious threat to its status in the host society. This part
of the Jewish élite, characterized by some self-criticism was however,
marginal and not representative of the whole.

The conscience of the Jewish middle-class, like its non-Jewish counterpart, was influenced by the literary work of Charles Dickens. It is
worth noting that following the protest of a certain 'Jewish lady',
Dickens had counterbalanced the avaricious and corrupt character of
Fagin by creating Riah in *Our Mutual Friend*. Riah is a submissive Jew
who cared for his poor fellows, but his remains a rather neutral portrait
and the Jewish middle and upper classes appeared to have felt pres-
sured by the stereotyped figure of the Jews. At the end of his stage play,
'The Jew' (1794), Richard Cumberland elevated Sheva, his principal
character, as the widow's friend, the orphan's father, the poor man's
protector and universal philanthropist, but the negative description of
the Jewish moneylender persisted throughout the period. However,
during this period the efforts of the élite to rehabilitate its image through
philanthropic channels were limited. Some of the mechanisms of social
control suggested by Faudel in the 1840s were subsequently adopted
and implemented by the London Jewish Board of Guardians established
in 1859.

Generally, the Jewish charities failed to cooperate in setting up the
suggested superstructure and even to establish more modest modes of
cooperation in terms of fundraising and distribution of benefits.
Parochialism was deeply rooted. The personal needs of the leaders were
carried over as ever into public matters. The most important charities

were dominated by the Cousinhood and were managed in the same paternalistic and autocratic ways, not dissimilar to family banks. These charities, however, were limited in terms of the numbers and the needs of the poor they could relieve. As such, they were not the first resort of many distressed poor. Resentment towards the patronizing moralism of the charities probably deterred many potential applicants in severe situations. The feelings of the lower middle-class towards the attitude of the élite with respect to charity was described by Morris Lissack, an immigrant from Posen, in *Jewish Perseverance or the Jew at Home and Abroad: A Biography* (1851). Lissak started as a pedlar after being advised by another Jew to pawn his gold watch and some of his clothes and with the money to obtain some goods for sale, 'Oh! if the rich could see the struggle which their less fortunate, but honest, brethren have to endure, they would frequently be much more charitable and would feel much livelier sympathies with their sufferings; but sympathy is rarely strong where there is a great inequality of condition'.

In the late 1840s, Benjamin Gompertz outlined a plan for 'the suppression of mendicancy and the substitution of casual relief by self-help arrangements in an open letter to the secretary of the Hambro Synagogue (Hyamson 1908). Benjamin Gompertz (1779–1865) was the son of a wealthy merchant. He started his career as a stockbroker. As a distinguished mathematician he became the actuary of the Insurance Company established by his two brothers-in-law, Moses Montefiore and Nathan Rothschild. In 1822, Gompertz drew up the details of the abortive plan of a savings bank advanced by Nathan Rothschild. According to the *Memoir of the late Benjamin Gompertz FRS etc.* by M. Adler in 1927, his plan included the establishment of a Board of Guardians to be empowered to investigate the claims of the Jewish poor, to keep a register of all applicants for relief, to dispense charity and procure employment. This plan was influenced by the establishment of the Liverpool Hebrew Philanthropic Society and Jewish Ladies' Benevolent Institution in the 1840s initiatives continuously echoed in London. Gompertz's plan, which included proposals for amalgamating the Jewish charities lacked the backing of the most wealthy financiers within the Ashkenazic élite and failed a short time after its proposal (Margolionth 1851: 118). More than fourteen years elapsed until the Jewish élite was ready to support the amalgamation of the inadequate arrangements of the three City Synagogues by establishing the Jewish Board of Guardians for the Relief of the Jewish 'Foreign' Poor.

In this chapter it has been shown that the Jewish philanthropists were unable at this time to overcome some of their individualistic and competitive inclinations which resulted in a proliferation of small services, each one caring for a very limited number of the poor. As will be shown in chapter 4, the establishment of the Board of Guardians implemented many of the ideas included in the Faudel Scheme, possibly in a harsher manner than those intended by Faudel.

4

The Jewish Board of Guardians

IDEOLOGIES AND POLICY

This chapter relates to the establishment of the Jewish Board as a turning point in Anglo-Jewish philanthropy and its effects of deterring immigration and disciplining the population of the Jewish poor. The documents examined indicate that from its foundation, the Board reflected a good comprehension of the class interests of the wealthiest members of the élite. The Board gave its relief with great care, deliberation and self-consciousness, being aware of the manipulative value of its controlling activities in the economic, social and moral life of the poor.

The establishment of the Board in March 1859 can be explained by a number of cumulative factors. Possibly, the trigger was the trade depression of 1857–8 and the hard winter of 1858 that caused severe hardship amongst the poor; such calamities are often known to create greater social awareness. An important contributing factor steering public opinion was a series of strong, enduring articles that appeared in the *Jewish Chronicle* during 1857–8 on the subject of Jewish poverty and charities. The articles stressed that the problems, especially those of the 'foreign' poor, could no longer be shelved. The articles were probably written by Abraham Benisch, the editor of the *Jewish Chronicle*, who estimated the total yearly expenditure of the Jewish community on organized and private charity at £15,000. Benisch strongly advocated the coordination of all the communities' charities through a central Board of Guardians (*Jewish Chronicle*, 25 September 1857). Benisch's proposal in his editorial incorporated previous ideas for the organization of Jewish philanthropies made by Colquhoun and van Oven in 1802; indeed, the first *Half Yearly Report* of the Board presented its establishment as a belated realization of their scheme. Other plans that influenced the establishment of the Board were those of Walter Joseph

(1841), Henry Faudel and Benjamin Gompertz (1844), as well as that of Abraham Benisch influenced by the model of the Jewish *Comité de Bienfaisance* established in Paris by Napoleon I.

Expressing dissatisfaction with the system of charity, Benisch suggested copying 'some features as might easily be transferred' from the French-Jewry model. However, he realized that 'Our Saxon love of independence would render the amalgamation of all charities under one . . . impracticable . . . and repugnant to our national character' (*Jewish Chronicle*, 25 September 1857). His proposed Board of Guardians was to have an efficient paid secretary who was to make 'strict enquiry precede relief'. Another influential model was that of the Society for the Relief of Distressed Persons: 'Let such Society be formed . . . let one great charitable engine display its power' (*Jewish Chronicle*, 4 February 1859). The *Jewish Chronicle* reported a project brought before the community for the foundation of a Jewish workhouse with a labour test for able-bodied paupers to be established without delay. By the middle of the nineteenth century the Jews had accumulated considerable experience with regard to workhouses; for instance, the *Jewish Chronicle* of 25 September 1857 reports the election of a co-religionist, John Symons, as guardian at Hull. Such guardians took their work seriously. According to the *Hull Packet*, quoted by the *Jewish Chronicle*, he gave a lecture – the first one delivered by a guardian of Hull's union to the inmates and children of the workhouse: 'his subject was "The Way to Succeed in Life", the rules given were exemplified by sketches of the lives of eminent men who had risen from the ranks' (*Jewish Chronicle*, 18 March 1859). The involvement of Jews in the Poor Law arrangements can explain why the Board was constituted very much after the fashion of a Parochial Relief Board.

The Ephraim Alex proposal, in 1857, to establish the Jewish Board of Guardians, made on behalf of the Great Synagogue, was opposed by the other two synagogues. His plan was modest in comparison with the scheme proposed not long before by Benisch. Benisch, however, fully and continuously supported the scheme of Alex in the *Jewish Chronicle*, during the years 1858 and 1859.

The Board represented a large-scale implementation of elements of social control proposed in the various schemes from the very beginning of the century. It also coincided with the heydays of the capitalist economy which enabled the three synagogues to vote on an initial, although modest, amount for the function of the Board and to undertake the responsibility for its continuous financial support. The responsibility to finance the Board emanated from the doctrinal (*hallachic*) and constitutional obligations of the synagogues to assist the *orchim* (guests and wayfarers). At the same time, the Board appealed to the community at large for financial contributions. Another contributing factor was the immigration which, from the middle of the nineteenth century, had become increasingly noticeable. The Board was preceded by the Conjoint Board of Relief, established in 1834 by the major Ashkenazic synagogues in London, based on established cooperation between them with regard to the *orchim*, 'strange' poor – each individual synagogue being considered too limited as a unit of organization. The Board raised expectations, promising further advantages in amalgamation and cooperation with other charities in order to prevent the *orchim* 'over-running all our existing institutions' (Simon Waley, quoted in *Jewish Chronicle*, 1 July 1887, in a historical essay on the Board).

The seventeen members who founded the Board were delegates (of German, Polish and Dutch origin) of the Ashkenazic synagogues and were financiers, businessmen and professionals. In their respective synagogues they were electors with voting and office-holding privileges (as differentiated from seat holders and non-electors). Ephraim Alex, who was the elected president, was a successful middle-class dentist born in Cheltenham in 1800, Overseer of the Poor of the Great Synagogue. He served as president for ten years. These delegates of the synagogues met on 16 March 1859 in Black Horse Yard, Aldgate, and established the Board according to the decisions of the authorities of their respective synagogues. Empowered to deal with the 'foreign' poor only, the Board started its operation without delay using the amount of £440 contributed by the three synagogues.

Lionel Louis Cohen was a foreign banker and member of the Stock Exchange who, at twenty-seven, became the honorary secretary, until 1869 when he succeeded Alex as president. Cohen was a member of one of the most important families of the Cousinhood. The two daughters of Levi Barnet Cohen, Lionel's grandfather, were married to Nathan Rothschild and Moses Montefiore. Cohen, possessing significant executive abilities, personally assumed control over the Board's activities; his management style was characterized by careful scrutiny of details. Lionel established a dynasty that maintained its hegemony as Presidents of the Board until 1947 (with an interruption from 1920 to 1930). In this way, the Board evolved into a family enterprise – a Cousinhood within the Cousinhood.

The most important members of the Board were related by family ties and brought in other relatives to serve on the Board for more than two generations. Most of the important families of the Cousinhood were well represented on the Board and largely accepted the policies delineated by the Cohens and the even more important contributors, the Rothschilds.

In 1860, the *Jewish Chronicle* published a plan of Lionel Cohen entitled '*A Scheme For The Better Management Of All The Jewish Poor*' (15 June 1860). In this scheme the defects of synagogal assistance were detailed as follows:

1   Want of proper and periodical investigation.
2   Continuance of money relief to able-bodied paupers.
3   Inefficient medical attendance.
4   Granting fixed allowances to so-called casual poor.
5   Capricious mode of relief.
6   The limitation of relief to very minute sums, when perhaps by doubling or trebling the sums given, which the overseer cannot do, the applicant might be made to support himself.
7   The light test imposed on persons attaching themselves to the Synagogue.
8   The impossibility of prompt attention to occasional wants by the Synagogue Secretary.

In his scheme, Cohen concluded that, in practice, there was no distinction between the 'casual poor' who had remained under the care of the synagogues and the 'foreign' poor who were transferred to the Board. Even when such differentiation was made, it was rather arbitrary and unsatisfactory. 'I believe the wants of the poor are so shifting, so multitudinous and withal so pressing, that a body having no other synagogal duties to perform and independent officials can alone adequately deal with them' (Cohen, *Jewish Chronicle*, 15 June 1860). Cohen continued to struggle for the inclusion of all poor under the responsibility of the Board for more than ten years (*Jewish Chronicle*, 2 October 1870). Lionel Cohen was also the founder and the first vice-president of the United Synagogue, established in 1870, which reflected the adoption of the organizational models of the Nonconformist and Anglican churches for creating a formally centralized Rabbinate under the tutelage of the élite. According to this model, the Ashkenazic synagogues were amalgamated, and the authority invested in the Chief Rabbinate was similar to the prerogative of the Archbishop of Canterbury.

The Jewish Chronicle regarded Lionel Cohen as the 'High Priest of the secular government of the community' (*Jewish Chronicle*, 10 January 1879). Later in the century, the Cohens were associated with the Conservative Party, and Lionel's parliamentary career was prematurely terminated by his death in 1887 at the age of fifty-five. Among the founding members of the Board was also Jacob Waley (1819–73), called to the Bar at Lincoln's Inn, 1842, a Professor of Political Economy at the University College (1853–65) and, subsequently, Professor Emeritus Algernon Sydney, who came from a family of lawyers, and was appointed Honorary Solicitor. His appointment emphasized the importance the Board placed on legal procedure.

The establishment of the Board manifested the élite's recognition that the problem of the 'strange' poor could no longer continue to be entirely evaded. It also showed some sensitivity on the part of the élite to what non-Jews might think of the lower standards of the synagogal relief and an awareness that severe social problems among Jewish poor might hamper relations with the host society. The Board was to fill the vacuum created by the westward migration of the wealthy classes from the East End, which aggravated the situation of the East End poor. The extravagant lifestyle of the middle classes, characterized by large and conspicuous expenditure, further dissociated them from the poor. The Board also lamented the lost control of the rich over the poor caused by this migration:

> Formerly, when rich and poor lived in close proximity, the association of locality afforded some kind of intercourse, imperfect though it was. The rich and the poor were not as now estranged and apart. The worthless and the beggar were at least partially known as such to the donor; and in the instance of the worthy and respectable – when suffering became too keen, the wealthy then knew personally their respectable neighbours, and relieved them as such; but with the westward emigration both these conditions changed, and to the advantage of the beggar. (First BGHYR 1859: 10, 11)

In the West End, much of what can be termed the direct public responsibility of the wealthy could be discarded. The new congregations established there, linked together middle-class members of different places in Europe and elsewhere. While maintaining some aspects of Jewish tradition, their philanthropy was prone to be inspired primarily by the laissez-faire concepts of the corresponding non-Jewish community. Those concepts were not lacking in feelings of contempt for the weak. As the representative of the élite, the Board attempted to convince the poor Jewish public that the detrimental impact of the geographical distance 'has not altered the donor's heart' and its possible corollary 'that relief will soon be forthcoming' (First BGHYR 1859: 11). Consequently, the Board regarded its responsibility as being a channel, through which the donations of the middle and upper-classes could be distributed to the poor. In this way, the Board was to release the upper-classes from the direct pressure of the insistent poor, of the duty to relieve them personally, thus legitimizing a direct avoidance of the poor: 'let but the sums heretofore given to clamorous mendicants who beset our Synagogue gates and the doors of our private residences, be placed at the disposal of the Board, and ample funds will be the result' (Second *BGHYR* 1860: 13). The Board was also to discharge the members of the élite engaged in financial and overseas trade in the City of London, from the need to assume responsibility for the poor who were no more than a few minutes' walk or ride from their City offices. In this way they were exempted from seeing the poverty and degradation which, according to Pollins (1981), increased significantly during the period when the Board was established (pp. 3–4). (The first Office of the Board was on Black Horse Yard, Aldgate East; by the beginning of 1860, premises were rented on 13 Devonshire Square.)

From its commencement, the Board tried to apply an efficient administration based on models provided by English social organization. The élite attributed to itself the inclination and talent for sound administration and the ability to apply it persistently to the institutions of the community, as required in their business activities. As paternalism was often a wealthy amateur privilege, it was important for the élite to make this distinction. The original scheme of Ephraim Alex included a centrally organized, administrative apparatus purposely designed for rationalized control of the poor. This control was to be as encompassing as possible, for example: 'Clerk to keep a register of all the foreign and other poor applying for relief, their addresses and trades, where natives of, how long they have been in this country . . . and he shall also investigate all cases brought under his notice by the Board' (*A Scheme, &, 1859, 6, revised and enacted in 1867, Law 48*, p. 21). According to the scheme, the Board could obtain from various institutions the names of its recipients (p. 7). The intention of the élite in establishing the Board was to segregate the treatment of the 'foreign' poor from the other 'stipendiary' poor who were attached to the three city synagogues, or had a right to claim relief from them. In this way, the Board was to deal with them in differential ways influenced by the Poor Law Amendment Act of 1834. The possibility of cooperation with the Poor Law authorities made the problems that faced the élite more complex, and incompatible with the old-fashioned administration of the synagogues and necessitated the setting in place of the Board's machinery.

The Board was founded with the intention of functioning as a quasi-official statutory agency for the Jewish 'confirmed paupers', especially immigrants, within the community, and to operate alongside the local and central authorities of the Poor Law.

It was more than ten years before George Goschen attempted to find an answer to the minuted question 'how far it is possible to mark out the separate limits of the Poor Law and of charity respectively, and how is it possible to secure joint action between the two' (quoted in de Schweinitz 1961: 151). This minute was, according to de Schweinitz, the first recognition by the government in England of philanthropy as an organized force. References throughout the history of the Poor Law had been made to private charity, but never as an organized activity with which to negotiate and arrive at mutual understandings about policy and programme (1961: 151). The Charity Organization Society, and later the Board, regarded cooperation with the Poor Law as an important means to eliminate expenditure for the relief of what they considered 'undeserving poor', using rather heavy-handed procedures against them. The founding of the Board and its location in Aldgate was intended to deal with the poor in a separate place, at a distance from the synagogues and their religious, social and cultural activities.

The Board was to be named the Board of Guardians for the Relief of the Necessitous Foreign Poor. However, from the beginning, the leaders of the Board were interested in expanding their control over all the poor of the community and adopted the name of the Jewish Board of Guardians for the Relief of the Jewish Poor. Because of the stigma attached to the Board in the eyes of the poor of the synagogue, only in 1871, after prolonged efforts, did the Board succeed in taking over the responsibility for their poor from the three city synagogues. In this way the Board occupied an increasingly central place in the community. The establishment of the Board had been a belated development of the grouping of parishes and the shifting of responsibility from the parish vestries to the elected boards of Guardians and the supervisory central body of Poor Law Commissioners, and, later, the Poor Law Board, following the report of 1834.

With respect to the Jewish poor, the Board also attempted to fulfil the parallel function of a central body connecting other 'more voluntary' Jewish charities. This similarity to the host society's authorities facili-tated the Board's communication with other organizations for the relief of poverty. In establishing the Board, the élite took as its combined model the British statutory and voluntary philanthropies, as well as business patterns. One of the manifestations of this influence was the very name of the Jewish Board of Guardians with its strong controlling

connotations, which does not have a counterpart in the Hebrew nomen-
clature related to *tzedakah*. The influence of contemporary social
philosophy and arrangements was already evident in the administration of charities by the three main city synagogues before the
establishment of the Board. They used the term Overseer of the Poor –
defined as one who keeps watch over or directs, supervises or superin-
tends others. This term replaced the Hebrew charity term of *gabai
tzedakah* – meaning collector of charity and implying also the combined
functions of assessor of the income of the community's members and
distributor of the charity per se (Maimonides, *Mishneh Torah* VII, Gifts
for the Poor, chapter 9, para 1 [see Appendix I]). Some of the Jewish
traditional terms of charity used by the synagogues and by the Board at
the very beginning of its activities were gradually abandoned by the
Board with consequent detrimental implications for the poor. The less
segregated and more traditional Hebrew term, *orchim*, meaning guests
– not necessarily poor – was still printed in Hebrew at the bottom of the
page of the original *Laws and Regulations of the Board*, 1859. In the *First
Half Yearly Report* the term, *orchim*, was printed in Hebrew adjacent to
'foreign' or unattached poor (p. 17). It was still used in Hebrew in the
statistical tables of the *Annual Reports* of the 1860s for residents of less
than seven years in England (Seventh BGAR 1864: 8, pp. 30–1). The
diminution in the status of the poor was reflected in the use of a more
humiliating terminology. The Board was able to enhance the reputation
of its wealthiest members by publishing their conspicuous munificent
contributions in order to attract their support and retain their loyalty:

> From the first day of its existence when the munificent sum of £100 as a
> first donation was generously presented by Messrs N. M. Rothschild and
> Sons, the Board has been favoured by a continuous flow of liberality,
> reaching to an aggregate of upwards of £800, all spontaneously offered,
> without any other stimulus than the benevolence of the donors and the
> publication of the Board's monthly reports. (First *BGHYR* 1859: 22)

The wealthy members were described by the Board 'as the few
possessed by the indomitable and commanding genius, managed to win
their way to wealth and fame, despite every obstacle' (First *BGHYR*
1859: 6).

Some of the methods used by the Board were not new. They had been
previously used for considerable periods of time by the Overseer of the
Poor of the Synagogues and by the smaller Jewish philanthropies,
strongly influenced by the English models during the first half of the

nineteenth century. However, from the beginning, the Board was characterized by the extensive scale of its operations and its efforts of investigation.

A deep dislike for the poor as a group was reflected in the approach of the élite to the poor's long-neglected, cumulative and pressing needs:

> True it is that the Board did not feel justified in relaxing all investigations and in throwing open its doors to the promiscuous crowd of necessitous persons who might besiege them. (Third *BGHYR* Dec. 1860: 13–14)

It should be noted that the three ornate city synagogues forced the poor into a catch-as-catch-can situation, according to which the beadles of those synagogues weekly distributed small amounts in coins, frequently throwing them over a group of poor people waiting outside, barred by the gates. This cruel tactic gave an advantage to the strong and the young over the weak, and encouraged violence. The Board, however, blamed the distressed and aggravated poor for adjusting themselves to the haphazard arrangements that prevailed prior to the Board's establishment, as well as for the delay in the investigation process of its own system. The total disorder and confusion to which the poor were exposed by the three city synagogues was caused by internal frictions within the wealthy class, resulting in inadequate relief. Kokosalakis points out that the exclusion of some members from the power structure of the congregations, rather than religious or ideological issues, motivated the establishment of new synagogues (1982). As he shows, the superfluous organizational rift was an obstacle to the dynamic development of the community (Kokosalakis 1982: 69, 74). It is possible that some business rivalries jeopardized philanthropic actions.

The measures of control over the Jewish poor were in some ways a continuation of those used by the synagogues with regard to their poor. The financial dependency of communal institutions on voluntary contributions brought about a disinclination to use disciplinary measures against non-contributing wealthy members of the synagogues. However, as far as the poor were concerned, their livelihood depended on the ways in which the élite interpreted and implemented Jewish traditions, that is, whether it did so in the light of the interests of the poor. The Board's controls had been intended as much more comprehensive.

In the Board's formative years, the process of social control of the 'foreign' poor was increasingly differentiated and specialized by the

application of rules and sanctions and the work of designated functionaries (whether salaried personnel or volunteers). The intention of
the Board had been to rely on clear and articulated principles. Control
was exercised by minimizing, as far as possible, cash contributions,
especially until 1870. Instead, help in kind was given to prevent 'misuse
of relief' (except for loans). Significant proportions of the value of food
and coal were lost by the poor who, under distressing circumstances,
were forced to exchange food tickets for goods or sell tickets on the black
market for cash. Applications for relief – including the rejected ones –
were minutely recorded. To be relieved, the applicant was subjected to
visitants and different scrutinizing and controlling intrusions into the
family. Controlling and disciplinary measures included the use of bath
tickets as a prerequisite for relief (applicants had to bathe regularly).
These measures were intensified for those requiring prolonged relief.

The philosophy and practice of the Board contradicts statements
according to which, it 'functioned on the assumption that their
constituents wished to be moral, to improve themselves and regain
independence' (Black 1988: 79). Once the Board was established, it
tended to include an increasing number of departments directed by
committees. Those departments acted cooperatively, forming a deliberate network of social control and sometimes blaming the victims. As
an example, the Work Committee had 'refused the loan of sewing
machines to those applicants whose houses were reported by sanitary
visitors to be either dirty or overcrowded' (Ninth BGAR 1866–67: 47). In
the same *Annual Report*, the Visiting Committee recognized 'that the
mass of our poor, especially the foreign portion of it, are constantly, and
almost hopelessly, struggling in a chronic state of want and wretched-
ness', also that 'excessive slackness of work of almost every description
coupled with the high price of provisions' increased the hardships of the
poor (p. 55).

The élite's exclusionist policy was carried out by the Board from its
commencement:

> The allowance made by the Synagogues was far too small, and one of the
> reasons given for this parsimony was that an influx of foreigners was to
> be feared if too much relief were given. The experience of this Board has
> shown that the number of new cases it receives every month, of parties
> who have resided here less than a year, is very small, and the regulation
> stringently enforced that no person be relieved, unless resident here more
> than six months, will tend greatly to check the arrival of fresh paupers.
> (First *BGHYR* 1859: 18–19)

Continuous efforts to discourage immigration were, however, largely ineffective, taking into consideration the geopolitical factors which have a more significant influence on immigration. For instance, the American Civil War considerably decreased the number of immigrants that journeyed onwards to America; consequently, these immigrants remained in England (*Manchester Guardian*, 3 July 1861, quoted in Williams 1976: 268). The leaders of the Board regarded it, however, as their primary duty to protect the Anglo-Jewish establishment from the problems involved in immigration.

The Cohens were especially known for their antipathy towards immigration. Their conservative tendencies, with some variations, became the official policy of the Board and were accepted to some extent by the most important families of the élite. In designing and implementing its restrictionist policy, the élite was strongly supported by the professional and clerical middle class. Reacting to the proposal of Alex not to relieve any person who had been in Britain less than six months (Scheme and attached Laws 1859, 11: 5), Simon Waley and Sir Francis Goldsmid had suggested that no person be relieved until they had been resident for three to five years. Professor D. W. Marks, the Minister of the Reform Synagogue, had proposed that immigration of the poor should be checked only by repatriation (*Jewish Chronicle*, 1 July 1887, essay on Board's history by A. I. Mayers).

One of the ways by which the Board attempted to reverse immigration was the limitation of relief. In 1861, the Board announced that 'invariably refusing any other relief then [immigrant's] return passage has materially checked their arrivals' (Fourth BGAR 1861: 10). The policy of transmigration and repatriation was based on safeguards against costs of absorption. Characterized by pragmatic activism, the Board acted sharply to export the problem of the immigrants and possibly, the poor who had been in the country longer:

> The item of £46. 17s. 3d., for persons proceeding abroad, is regarded as a most economical and prudent outlay; for by means of this sum upwards of sixty persons, and mostly those of the poorest class, have left the country. (Second *BGHYR* 1860: 9)

The selection of the poor for transmigration and repatriation became the general policy of the Board. While the Board asserted that its purpose was to help the poor become self-supporting and retain their self-respect, applicants did not feel this way. The Board's claim was in practice, in conflict with its social philosophy and practical strategy, summarized as being 'to heed them off by demonstrative refusals of any appreciable relief to newly arrived immigrants' (Lipman 1990: 33). In turn, this practice was contradicted by the statistics of the Board, according to which the overall refusal rate was only approximately 5 per cent of the total number of applications. In addition to deterring immigrants and conveying its restrictionist policies to potential immigrants abroad, the Board was interested in lowering its expenses as much as possible (Lipman 1990: 33).

During the 1860s and 1870s, a restricted but steady flow of immigration continued but it did not reach the proportions of the 1880s, nor was the entrenched restrictionism an important or controversial issue. In the 1870s, the Board viewed the problem of severe poverty caused by immigration as more or less finite. In view of such expectations the Board was not prepared for the large influx of immigration.

A declared and important principle of the Board was 'that proper and deserving objects only would be relieved' (Lipman 1959: 26, based on the memoirs of A. I. Mayers, in the *Jewish Chronicle*, 1 July 1887). The application of this principle meant preferential considerations and concern for the 'deserving' poor, evident from the commencement of the Board's activities with regard to this category which originally had belonged to the middle classes, or was much closer to them. The Board was prepared to make more significant efforts in ameliorating their problems. The control of the Board was not always overt and was not recognized as such by some of the users of its services or by the Board. This was attributed to the paternalistic nature of some of the Board's controls, such as the advancing of loans and other services predominantly used by the 'deserving' poor. For instance, the Board's effort to stop the 'begging letters' written by the poor to different parts of the power structure in the community, was a recognition that continuation of this system was detrimental 'to the really deserving poor' (Fourth BGAR 1861: 12). This dichotomy implied an oversimplified and moralistic approach, especially as so many applicants to the Board were new immigrants and, as such, unknown to the community. Later, the Board followed the Charity Organization Society differentiation between 'helpable' and 'unhelpable' (Lipman 1959: 237) – a largely rhetorical change of stance. Moreover, the former entrenched terminology continued to be used by the Board throughout the nineteenth century and beyond.

The criteria of 'good' character and virtue, as proven by economic success and thrift, which were considered by the Board as preconditions for assistance, were sometimes especially cruel to the immigrants because of their inability to produce the required evidence. The painful investigations to detect 'undeserving' claims in the immigrant communities were resented as being repugnant. Rather than kinlike obligation, a reciprocal mistrust was created by the Board. Such an atmosphere was conducive to over-reactions, and callousness; claimants were penalized for infringing regulations. The Board continuously strived 'to influence the community in withholding relief until due inquiry be made' (Fourth BGAR 1861: 12).

From its inception, the Board was preoccupied with attempting to differentiate between 'deserving' and 'undeserving' poor. Reinvestigations of the poor on relief were made every six months (Scheme 1859: 7). The Mendicity Department was one of the first to be established by the Board, six months after the commencement of its operations (First *BGHYR* 1859: 15). This department invited the Board's subscribers 'to apply to it for information as to the merit of any applications they might individually receive for relief', however, only 'a few gentlemen, pre-eminent for their liberal and judicious charity, systematically refer to the Board for information.' The Board could not but 'greatly regret the limited use which has been made of this department' (First *BGHYR* 1859: 15). According to the *Jewish Chronicle*, 'since the formation of the Board the poor are forbidden to solicit from individuals, should they do so they are referred to the Board' (25 January 1861). The mistrust was directed to the group of 'imposters and self-selected paupers'. The report did not give information about the social and economical situation of this group. In the first six months of the Board's activities, 11 per cent of the applications were refused as compared to 7.5 per cent in the second part of the first year:

> As the register of the Board becomes more and more complete, the percentage of undeserving persons who venture to appear before it, will no doubt continue to decrease. (Second *BGHYR* 1860: 8)

It is clear that a large proportion of the efforts of the Board were dedicated to prevent what it regarded as abuse.

In compiling statistical summaries, the Board used the models required by the Poor Law Board from every union in England and Wales. In 1860, on the basis of such returns, the Board reached the conclusion that for 150 persons a 'test of labour should be applied and hope that in some future time means may be devised by which this test may be enforced' (Third *BGHYR* 1860: 9). In summarizing such data the Board did not consider the social and economic implications of the situation of the 'foreign' poor or the appropriateness of the use of the 'less eligibility' principle. In its efforts to deter immigration, the Board alternately ignored the fact that the problems that faced most of the users of its services at this time stemmed, to a great extent, from the crises they had undergone as immigrants, aggravated by recurrent trade depressions, low salaries, fluctuations of seasonal demands for labour and some hard winters – for instance, at the beginning of the 1860s. (During this period the immigrants were predominantly Russians and Poles, rather than Germans and Dutch).

The principles according to which the Board made some use of the unions' workhouses as disciplinary measures for resistant or recalcitrant persons were not published. With regard to this more sensitive issue, details were selectively omitted in contrast to the widely advertised quantification of other interventions. The local Poor Law unions' returns also are not informative about the number of their Jewish inmates. Black writes: 'The Board unquestionably used and could always consider employing the "workhouse threat"' (Black 1988: 79).

Generally, the Board claimed to be in a financial crisis as each new wave of immigrants arrived, such as at the beginning of the 1860s when the Board had a deficit of approximately £50. Given the importance that the Board accorded to such deficits, it tried to reduce the relief allotment, the principal item of expenditure.

Concomitantly, despite being far from generous, the leaders of the Board feared being regarded as such and, in this way, encouraging immigration and, therefore, general pauperism. In the distribution of relief, the Board was backed also by the influence of contemporary social philosophy; Mill declared that 'no locality has a moral right to make itself by mismanagement a nest of pauperism, necessarily overflowing into other localities, and impairing the moral and physical conditions of the whole labouring community' (Mill 1859: 117, 1870). The Board reduced the fixed allotments to the elderly (and later in the century to the native elderly as well as to new immigrants) to an inadequate level (Lipman 1990: 34).

Impressive and exacting as the charity work was (as described in the Board's publications), it was exposed to the critique of the laissez-faire middle-class doctrinarians:

> Conclusive contradiction to the assertions repeatedly made that its [the Board's] efforts are not sufficiently directed to help the poor to help themselves, and that the poor are pauperised instead of being stimulated by the benefactions which it affords them. (Thirteenth BGAR 1871: 14)

The Board continuously underwent such criticism from a part of the Jewish élite and the middle class imbued with a fear of pauperization. It is worth mentioning that the Board was sometimes urged directly by the Charity Organization Society, then known as the Society for Organizing Charitable Relief and Repressing Mendicity (with C. B. P. Bosanquet as secretary) to adjust the Board along with 'some at least' of the other charities' more progressive' policies, along the lines propagated by the Society. In a letter to the Board sent on 27 November 1871, C. J. Ribton Turner, secretary, suggested, a 'thorough investigation into the *antecedents* of every applicant for charity and the application of a provident test to candidates for pensions, admission to asylums, etc' (Thirteenth BGAR 1871: 78–80). In order to create 'further concentration and invigorated action', Turner also suggested 'that a Central Body should be formed consisting of representatives of all the Jewish charities' (p. 79). In the comments that followed, the leaders of the Board expressed their readiness to assume similar roles and functions to the Charity Organization Society *vis-à-vis* the Jewish charities which had restrictive aspects. The Board wrote that a 'considerable part of its expenditure is already incurred in investigations recorded for the use of other charities' (80). However, the actual power of the Board to control and coordinate other Jewish charities under the auspices of the middle and working classes was limited, and was increasingly so after the mass immigration of the 1880s. Already in 1871, the Board bitterly complained about the 'multifarious distributors of Jewish charity. Their investigation, as yet incomplete, discloses the existence of many institutions almost unknown, and working with apparently identical objects in similar directions' (p. 77).

By the end of the nineteenth century the Board was increasingly regarded as an entrenched institution, characterized by conservative resistance to change and unable to overcome the inertia which beset its structure and functions. The Board had difficulty in renouncing the arrangements developed during the first thirty years of its existence which became obsolete in the evolving collectivist approach. A conventional and high-minded moralizing paternalism was reflected, amongst other things, by the continuation of the arrangement, according to which imploring and humiliated applicants were interviewed by the seated 'rota' – Relief Committee – standing behind a brass rail. Towards the end of the century, only the aged and ailing women were allowed to sit. This arrangement was continued in spite of criticism, and had been justified by F. D. Mocatta as intended to facilitate business rather than motivated by fear of infection, in view of repeated epidemics

(*Jewish Chronicle*, 14 April 1893). During the 1890s, the Board was requested to improve the recording of visitation, and to introduce case conferences at which investigators were to be present. Such professionalization was regarded, however, as expensive in the light of the growing numbers of immigrants who remained in England for more than six months and were entitled to apply to the Board. During the twentieth century, control was exercised also by social workers. From its establishment, the paid officer status was socially and functionally inferior to that of the unpaid management and they were titled Esquire as opposed to Mister. An additional impetus that had caused the Board to intensify some of its activities and to improve the more visible and sanitary conditions in the East End were the unfavorable critiques that had appeared intermittently in the non-Jewish press and that were sometimes expressed in different official, high-standing forums, including Parliament.

In 1859, while the establishment of the Board was being seriously contemplated, Sir Joseph Sebag-Montefiore and Sampson Samuel envisaged its prospective provisions for all poor – irrespective of their synagogal rights or length of residence in England – as a visible consequence of the Board's foundation. The synagogues, however, feared that such a step could greatly harm the feelings of their attached poor, some of them 'decayed' merchants and other previously middle-class members. This persistence of the three city synagogues which established the Board and supported it financially, continued for about eleven years and is *ipso facto* evidence of the harsh manner in which the Board dealt with the poor.

The Board, however, assumed a professional air. Paid clerks, relieving and investigating officers were introduced from its inception. It was confident of its ability to ensure differential approaches to various categories of poverty. The leaders of the Board feared that the resistance of the three city synagogues to the transfer of their attached poor to the relief of the Board could degrade the Board and reduce its support. 'The restriction of relief to any one section of the poor would materially check the flow of benevolence which the knowledge of the charitable feelings of the community led the Board to believe might otherwise speedily rekindle evils of the old system and the synagogues' initial reluctance to transfer to the Board the supervision of their medical officers' (p. 19). In 1861, the Board regarded the increasing tendency of the synagogues to use its services as an evidence of:

the groundlessness of the assumption entertained at the establishment of the Board that the poor of the synagogues would regard the Board with disfavour and feel that the delicacy and hesitation in presenting themselves for relief at its doors. (Fourth BGAR 1861: 9)

In 1871, the investigation of the synagogues' poor requesting m*atzot* (unleavened Passover bread) was entrusted to the Board (Thirteenth BGAR 1870: 28), preceding the transfer of the responsibilities for all their needs to the Board during the same year.

According to Alex's scheme, the visitations of the poor were to be undertaken by Ministers of the Metropolitan Synagogues in cooperation with the Board. In order to implement this arrangement, London was to be divided into districts, each minister having a locality to himself. It is possible that Alex had been inspired by the district-based visitation at Elberfeld, and other towns in Germany, which concept had had some influence in England, combined with models of pastoral involvement of British charity-givers in charitable institutions. There is no indication as to the causes of the relinquishment of Alex's proposal in this area. The abandonment of the idea can be explained by the reluctance of British administrators and legislators to adopt a systematic community organization (de Schweinitz 1961: 98). An additional factor that could have contributed to the absence of rabbis from the membership of the Board during the whole nineteenth century, was the secularistic tendency of Lionel Cohen and the Jewish tradition of lay, rather than religious government.

According to the 1861 *Annual Report*, visiting the poor in their own homes entailed heavy sacrifices; however, no difficulty was found in staffing the visiting committee (BGAR 1861: 17). In the same year each visitor was given responsibility for a certain number of 'cases' (p. 18). The frequent reorganization of the work of this committee throughout the history of the Board can be explained, *inter alia*, by the cleavage which already existed in the structure of the community:

> The modest report of the Visiting Committee describes the results of the reorganization of that committee which took place early in the year. Its advantages are clearly stated in the report as being shared between rich and poor, in the intercourse which it induces between them. The ever-increasing distance to which the community expands, east and west, renders it essential that the sympathy which keeps it together should be aroused by frequent personal intercourse between all classes. (Twelfth BGAR 1870: 15)

The influence of the philanthropic thoughts of Octavia Hill and Edward Denison towards the end of the 1860s, can be traced here. In her history of the London Charity Organization Society, Mrs Bosanquet quotes the views of Sir Charles E. Trevelyan:

> Since the beginning of this century the gulf between rich and poor has become fearfully wide. The rich have become richer and the poor poorer. The proposal is to close this gulf and to bring back the rich into such close relation with the poor as cannot fail to have a civilizing and healing influence, and to knit all classes together in the bonds of mutual help and good will. (de Schweinitz 1961: 187, 258)

However, the influence of the Charity Organization Society and other allied movements of the Jewish élite and the Board, had its limits. The life of Edward Denison, son of a bishop of the Church of England who went to live in Stepney in the East End, to teach at night in informal working-class adult education, had no parallel at this time in the Anglo-Jewish élite's milieu. Nor was there a Jewish counterpart to Octavia Hill who, during this period, became convinced of the importance of improved housing for the poor. With the help of John Ruskin, she began a project of slum-dwelling improvement (de Schweinitz, pp. 43–6). While Octavia Hill came under the influence of Christian socialism (as the movement was denoted by John Frederick Denison Maurice), the Jewish élite that led the Board was moving in the opposite direction. It was in a process of transition from association with the Liberal Party to the Conservative/Unionist. It is worth noting that the Jewish wealthy classes and intelligentsia and, of course, the working class in western countries, have traditionally been identified with Liberalism. The unprecedented social conservativism of the Jewish élite is related to its increasingly immense wealth during this period. While the Christian Socialists still regarded the poor as largely responsible for their own social situation, the housing project of Octavia Hill and the movement for personal service amongst the poor, represented a turning point towards collectivism. Almost thirty years elapsed until the full impact of these movements reached the Jewish élite and influenced a more direct and concrete social involvement for the amelioration of the condition of the Jewish poor in the East End (see chapter 5 for discussions of housing and acculturation).

A system of checks and controls was built into the structure of the Board from its foundation and was enlarged gradually as the Board expanded its direct activities. The Board also activated its control mechanism through its satellite specialist institutions. The Board regarded its controlling intervention as being especially necessary when cooperation with the mandatory authorities was required:

> In 1870 the few persons of the Jewish faith in Governmental gaols have been collected into a single prison . . . thus the policy of wise administration encourages even prisoners to practise self-restraints prompted by a sense of religious obligation; surely mere indigence otherwise blameless should be safe from violation of conscience. (Twelfth BGAR 1870: 30)

The differentiation between 'culpable' and 'blameless' poverty reflects the feelings of the leaders of the Board that some of the poor were responsible for their neediness. As for Jewish lunatics, the Board had hoped that no legislative impediment could prevent the grouping of such persons in one asylum. The responsibility for achieving such arrangements was assumed by the Jewish Ministry of the United Synagogue which organized the supervision and visitation of Jewish inmates in asylums, prisons and reformatories. The reports of the United Synagogue in this matter were, however, to be sent regularly to the Board (Thirteenth BGAR 1871: 27–9). The administrative machinery of the Board was considered by some contemporary social observers as an exemplary and pioneering institution, highly organized and able to experiment more easily and rapidly (for example, J. H. Stallard, in *London Pauperism amongst Jews and Christians* 1867).

Compared with the Poor Law Guardians, the Board has been considered by some modern historians as largely generous (Young and Ashton 1956: 83). There were, however, no comparative historical studies done to prove that, in terms of quality and degree, the Board had performed at a level higher than that of other contemporary British philanthropists who had embraced Victorian philanthropic approaches. Despite the eagerness of the Board to excel in contemporary modern patterns and to be more British than the British, many of the superlatives characterizing its activities are rather impressionistic. The preferential assistance that the Board offered to the 'deserving', including former middle-class members, was not peculiar to the Board alone.

The London Board continued to exercise a strong influence on the organization of Jewish philanthropists in the provinces and in London. Amongst others, the Jewish Manchester Board of Guardians was modelled upon that of London 'almost in every respect' (*Jewish Chronicle* 37, 1868, quoted in Williams 1876: 284).

The immigrants generally did not perceive the élite to be motivated by the religious obligations of *tzedakah* or 'true charity'. The ways in which the Board administered its assistance heightened antagonism.

Immigrants felt they were looked down upon by judgmental individuals lacking a 'Jewish heart'. The Guardians, as the Board was familiarly called in the East End, was not a likeable body and was regarded by the poor with apprehension and fear (Green 1991: 198–9). To many who sought its help, the judgement of the Board as to their eligibility for relief seemed harsh.

The Board was conscious of the fact that some of its arrangements and services were considered by the poor as humiliating, however, it had continued them deliberately. In 1866 the Board reported that:

> borrowers, who are generally a respectable and industrious class, would also be relieved from the humiliation of attending the relief committees indiscriminately with the crowd of general applicants. (Ninth BGAR 1866: 20)

In 1868, only sixteen persons were exempted from attending the Relief Committee every month (Tenth BGAR 1868: 14). The report of 1868 added 'that the self respect of the lessees [of sewing machines] is thus maintained by keeping them aloof from the general recipients of relief and the large class of poor probably now amounting to a thousand persons' (p. 19). The registers, including the names of the applicants to the Board and the users of its services, were 'unreservedly placed at the disposal of the community for inspection and reference as a means of ascertaining the merits of persons applying to them for relief' (Ninth BGAR 1866–7: 26).

The systematic monitoring of applicants in an open register had been one of the more non-confidential and humiliating procedures of the Board (the open register was set in operation in 1859, First BGHYR 1859: 15). In 1871, the Annual Report announced that 'any persons . . . availed themselves daily of the registers of the Board and of the intimate knowledge of the poor by its officers to test the merits of the applications which they received' (Thirteenth BGAR 1871: 17). It is possible that the register included the sums of relief received. The monitoring of the applicants probably frightened away many poor, creating additional abhorrence of receiving charity and the humiliating approach to those who were actually assisted. How many poor in distress avoided becoming beneficiaries of the Board and the other Jewish philanthropies, because they knew that this would place them at the bottom of the social pyramid?

How many others applied for charity only in extreme need and tried their utmost endeavour to get along without the interference of the Board? The suspicions and charges of the Board with regard to imposture and the difficulties of the beneficiaries to defend themselves against such claims, created an additional lack of self respect. The severe loss of status of the recipient can be implied from the short duration of dependence of those who became recipients, as mentioned in several annual reports of the Board. Humiliation continued unabated for decades. The official opprobrium towards the poor in its official publications, is evidence that the poor were made to feel the indignity of their position by the practice of the Board. The Jewish poor felt that at least some of their needs had legitimate institutional roots, and that the context of the rules of the Board were unJewish and insufficiently responsive, and that as such 'do not belong to them'. The services offered by the assimilated native members of the Board in their modern highly stereotyped forms and content – dissimilar to their religious customs and social conventions – were unfamiliar to the poor and regarded by them with deep distaste. Moreover, they lacked many of the Jewish symbols to which they were accustomed. Whatever the motives of the élite (for instance, limiting immigration), relief was given in a patronizing, superior manner, depressing the dignity of the recipients. Green (1991) writes:

> Many Jews, even at the time, thought the Board's leaders were more conscious of their role in protecting the image of Anglo-Jewry than in satisfying the needs of the poor. The Board's attitude to the problem of mass immigration during the 1880s was hardly enlightened . . . Its proposals to deal with the plight of the immigrants seemed to smack more of the old Poor Laws than the Bible. (Green 1991: 202)

The Jewish poor remained free men and women; poverty did not generally break their spirit to the extent that they could accept apathetically the approach of the Board. Binenstock (1951) concludes, on the basis of his study, that different values, beliefs and practices predominant in the *shtetel*, appeared to be conducive to non-authoritarian or anti-authoritarian patterns of behaviour in adult life. In his research, he deals with different factors, such as education, that sustained moral autonomy of the individual, his critical reaction and independence of authority (1951: 150).

Evidence of the power of the poor, other than their ability to uproot themselves and emigrate, was their motivation to 'play the system', for instance, applying to several charities at the same time to acquire the barest of necessities, selling or pawning relief in kind, such as clothes, to get money for food, etc. The doctrine that emphasized the deficiencies of the poor as the cause of their situation was 'as much a political ideology as an explanation of behaviour' (Bailey 1975: xxviii). The class distinctions coincided with the culturally alleged juxtapositions in which the poor were presented by the élite: decent, worthy and useful versus immoral, useless and degenerate.

Considering poverty as a moral rather than social condition, the élite was horrified by the apparent lack of industry, thrift, cleanliness and all other middle-class Victorian virtues. The élite presented an increasing desire to teach the poor habits of industry and self reliance. Such measures have been often declared by the Board as designed to increase the power and autonomy of the poor, however, the work of the large majority of the Jewish poor in the sweatshop system was, *ipso facto*, evidence that the immigrants were more than willing to do any kind of work to provide a bare living under terrible exploitation. (To compete for contracts, workshop masters lowered the piecework rates and wages of their workers to a cruel extent.) It is worth mentioning that sometimes the élite presented the Jewish poor to the host community as sober, hardworking, family men – Smilesian types par excellence. Possibly the motivation to defend the Jewish poor stemmed partly from self-interest rather than altruism, for the Jewish élite realized that some of the opponents to the Jewish poor were also expressing their feelings against their wealthy patrons.

One of the main conclusions of this discussion is that even before the great immigration, which began in 1882, and which is dealt with in the next section, the Board only extended its 'scientific philanthropy' to a limited number of those considered to be deserving poor.

CONTROLLING THE IMMIGRATION OF THE POOR

This section gives evidence that the policy of the Board on immigration was dictated by its custodians, the Cohen family, known for their opposition to mass immigration and sometimes for restrictive legislation. This was also the policy which characterized the Anglo-Jewish élite as a whole; the Board represented class rather than personal or group interests.

The rule by which relief was refused to those who had been in the country less than six months was proposed by Ephraim Alex, the first president of the Board (1859–69), in *A Scheme for a Board of Guardians, to be formed for the relief of the necessitous foreign poor*, published as a pamphlet. It became an integral part of the Board's original *Laws and Regulations* (Law 11: 5), published by the committee composed from various representatives of the city's three synagogues. By this rule the

Board excluded from vital relief the new immigrants who were obviously in greatest distress, in order to press them to agree to transmigration or to be repatriated. However, according to the *Resolutions* of the Board (p. 3), added to the *Laws and Regulations*, the Relief Committee (rota) had been 'invested with discretionary power in cases of emergency, to relieve any applicants, even if they have been domiciled in this country for a less period than six months'. (Laws and Regulations, 8 [n.d., c.1859]) According to the First *Half Yearly Report* of 1859, the application of this rule was a continuation of the policy that existed before the establishment of the Board:

> The allowance made by the Synagogues was far too small, and one of the reasons given for this parsimony was that an influx of foreigners was to be feared if too much relief were given. The experience of this Board has shown that this evil may be met by other means. For it gives the Board the greatest satisfaction to state that the number of new cases it receives every month, of parties who have resided here less than a year, is very small, and the regulation stringently enforced that no person be relieved, unless resident here more than six months, will tend greatly to check the arrival of fresh paupers. (pp. 18–19)

This is evidence that the situation of the newly arrived immigrants was worsened by the centralized control brought about by the advent of the Board, and the haphazard assistance given by the Synagogues was, in some limited aspect, more humane and closer to the Jewish tradition of charity.

The prerogative of the Relief Committee to disregard the Six Month Rule in special cases or situations, brought about a direct correlation between the increase in immigration and the severity of the enforcement of the rule. This implies that in its general restrictive practice, the Board showed from time to time, a certain flexibility towards the newly arrived immigrants (Eighth BGAR 1865: 8). Lipman mentions that in October-November 1865 the rule was applied 'more stringently' when the Board was faced with increasing flows of immigrants (1959: 32-3). In another instance, Lipman writes that a more flexible application of the Six Month Rule could expose the Board to the nativist critique, for example, being accused of attracting immigration (p. 101). However, significant restrictionist movement did not develop until the mass immigration of the 1880s.

Evidence of the leaders of the Board adhering to their tenets in applying the rule of Six Months appeared in the *Jewish Chronicle* of 7 December 1866 and 19 June 1868. The persistence of this rule was backed indirectly by the philosophy of Herbert Spencer, according to whom, it would be socially preferable to abandon the poor to nature's intended fate. The rule represented a bizarre exclusion for an institution manifestly created for the betterment of the 'foreign poor'; however, the immediate introduction of this rule and its application is evidence of the deliberate intention of the founders to use the Board as an instrument for controlling immigration. The persistent use of this rule by the Board reflected its commitment to deterrence. In applying it intensively, the Board felt sustained and legitimized by the contemporary Poor Law approach and, later in the period discussed, the Majority Report of the Royal Commission on the Poor Law.

This rule must have caused deep bewilderment and anger to newly arrived immigrants considering their traditional background. In several places the *Talmud* suggests that it is the Covenant between God and Israel that makes 'All Israel responsible for one another' (Talmud B. Sota, 376). The Hebrew term for 'responsible' used in the passage is *arevim* (guarantors), and has a strong contractual connotation, therefore the injunction is a synthesis between kinship and consent. According to another basic injunction, it is severely prohibited to postpone a request of a poor person for food, and its provision is to precede investigation of the request (Maimonides, *Mishneh Torah* VII, *Injunctions* concerning Gifts for the Poor, chapter 7, para 6 [see Appendix I]). In fact, the application for relief prior to the six month deadline was regarded by the Board as an unfitness to survive the life struggle. In the framework of Social Darwinism, the Six Month Rule was a type of test that the Board instituted to determine those who could not be regarded as fit for the struggle of survival.

As most of the immigrants were penniless, the application of this rule caused tremendous suffering. The immigrants were, in fact, thrown on the more limited private resources of the middle classes and/or other poor, whether relatives, kin, *landsleit* (a fellow from the same town in eastern Europe) or other working-class members who supported the minor Jewish charities in the East End. By refusing help to the immigrants, the Board constantly reduced the already limited means of the Jewish working-class and poor. (Subsequent waves of immigrants pouring into the East End made the burden of assistance a continuous one.) However, as a result of this rule, alternative institutions were established by the Jewish middle and working class in order to help the immigrants upon their arrival. The Board continuously attempted to eradicate such institutions or at least to limit their activity or otherwise bring them under its own control. The Six Month Rule was widely and continuously advertised in the European Jewish press at the Board's expense.

It is interesting that the Franco-Jewish establishment discussed the possibility of adopting the Anglo-Jewish six month waiting period before immigrants could request relief but, in practice, this rule was not applied. It is possible that the leeway given by the French élite to immigrants can account for the more independent institutions of the latter. The application of this rule legitimized the neglect of the needs of the newly arrived poor as individuals and families and as a specific group within the community in such vital areas as health, education and housing.

There are no statistics pertaining to the social situation of the newly arrived immigrants during the first six months of their stay while they were not eligible for the help of the Board (except for transmigration or repatriation). However, the situation of the Jewish poor and working class is reflected in the existing evidence of the mortality of their children. In 1896, a committee was designated to investigate mortality of Jewish children (following a general study on this subject published in *The Hospital*). It was discovered that among the Jewish poor, the death rate for children under ten approached 82 per cent compared to 20 per cent among the children of the wealthy Jews.

The total number of deaths of children under ten was more than double in comparison to the national level for this category. By 1893, the death rate increased by almost 6 per cent reaching 60.25 per cent (Black 1988: 230). The Investigation Committee appointed by the Jewish establishment claimed that three-fifths of the Jewish population were immigrants of less than ten years in England, blaming improvident young Jewish parents for the death of their children (Black 1988: 230). The lack of basic provisions faced by the poor was not presented by the Investigation Committee as problematic.

This is evidence that even the needs of the more established immigrants who were in London for up to ten years were addressed only on a small scale, especially if they were not included in the category of the deserving poor. The austerity reflected in the conclusions of this investigation can be explained by the doctrinal frame of reference of the élite combined with class superiority which, to a significant extent, eliminated sentiments of compassion from the 'rational' organization of philanthropy.

During the six month waiting period, many new immigrants succeeded – albeit with tremendous difficulty that could have been averted – to remain in London. In the process of adjustment those immigrants were helped by relatives, kinsmen, *landsleit* and alternative, smaller and more flexible institutions, such as the *hevras*.

The more new immigrants were informed about the limitations of the authority of the Board, the weaker was the control the Board was able to exercise over them. The inconsistency in the policy of the élite stemmed from the discrepancy between its various goals: excluding the immigrants from relief for a period of six months facilitated the process of re-emigration and repatriation as well as the deterrence of other potential immigrants. In this sense, the Six Month Rule functioned as a control by inaction. On the other hand, this policy increased and developed the alternative services that were established to help the immigrants. Those services were offered more quickly through a more unconditional eligibility for relief. It was a taxing dilemma for the Board, because despite its policy after the 1880s, immigration continued on a large scale.

In the 1880s, it became apparent to the élite that it would be faced with a prolonged and irreversible mass immigration from eastern Europe. Most of the immigrants aspired to reach America. Some, however, remained in England as a temporary stopping point when their cash ran out. For different reasons, some of which did not depend on the immigrants themselves, the temporary settlement in England became permanent. The proportions of immigrants who moved on, versus those who stayed, is unknown as the intervals between arrival in Britain and departure varied between days and years. The Board was the most significant institution dealing with immigration, despite its opposition to it. Unable to prevent mass immigration, the sponsors and the leaders of the Board were preoccupied with several alternative courses of action. Some recommended legal restriction of immigration by the state, provided that a distinction between refugees and immigrants per se was operable. However, taking into consideration the complicated, diversified and dynamic conditions in such a vast country as Russia and other parts of Eastern Europe, it was difficult to differentiate between those whose survival depended upon escape, and mere immigrants who made their way to the frontiers because of other reasons. Those members of the Board, and of the élite in general, who favoured such a distinction and, from time to time accused the immigrants of coming to Britain in order to become rich, were very much interested in applying to the immigrants, who were not victims of direct persecution, the principle of 'less eligibility' in order to exclude them from relief, whatever their means.

Other members who implemented *de facto* the restrictionist policies of the Board, were opposed to the willing transfer to the state of the legal prerogatives in limiting immigration; rather, they favoured a continuation of the intensive voluntary restrictions on immigration long exercised by the Board. This part of the élite emphasized the ability of the Board to deal with all the economic and social aspects of immigration including the expulsion of their paupers. In doing this, they relied on their accumulated experience in dealing with transmigration, dispersion and repatriation.

In 1902, Sir Leonard Cohen, President of the Board, (1900–20), stated that 'it is not for legislation to determine if immigration was needed or not' (*Jewish Chronicle*, 28 March 1902). The Cohens, the official almoners of the élite responsible for the policy and function of the Board, were long known for their restrictionist conservatism. At times they recommended the enforcement of legal limitations on immigration. With regard to repatriation, the weightiest issue, the Cohens were supported morally and financially by the wealthy class as a whole.

A somewhat different approach was presented by Alfred Cohen, a brother of Leonard, in an appearance before the Council of the Jewish Colonization Association, of which he was a board member, declared that he regarded the alien Jews as 'dirty, squalid and unpleasant', and the Yiddish jargon as a cancer causing anti-Semitism (*Jewish Chronicle*, 15 November 1901). However, he was not in favour of restrictive legislation. He claimed that it would be dangerous from an economic perspective to limit the flow of cheap labour and, therefore, the immigrants should be allowed to come freely into Britain. Some of the members of the élite and more members of the Jewish middle class, were directly interested in cheap immigrant labour, especially enterprising manufacturers and merchants in consumer trades such as ready made clothing, shoes and boots, furniture, cigars, and so on. One such example was the firm of Moses, Son and Davis, substantial wholesale clothiers (Finestein 1992: 104).

After the 1900s, as a consequence of the increased trend towards restrictionism, different attempts were made by the Board to find practical modalities for a selective immigration. By 1893, a screening system denoted 'triage', was proposed by Nathan S. Joseph who, at this time, had already accumulated more than twenty-five years of experience, having been responsible for the policy of the Board in different areas. In 1893, Joseph became chairman of the Executive of Russo-Jewish Committee and Conjoint Committee of the Russo-Jewish Committee and Board of Guardians, 1893–1909. He advocated restrictions against the 'helpless' immigrants as differentiated from the able-bodied:

This class constitutes a grave danger to the community. Its members were always paupers and useless parasites in their own country. Many of them were never persecuted but came with the paupers and parasites and live or starve on the pittance that the Russo-Jewish Committee and the Board of Guardians successively bestow on them, to the detriment of the more deserving because more improvable cases. The lifeboat is well-nigh full. If we can admit any more passengers, they must be such as can lend a hand to the oars. To admit an unlimited number of helpless souls, who are mere dead weight, would not be mercy, but homicide. (*Jewish Chronicle*, 7 June 1892)

Joseph proposed a tripartite classification of immigrants based on 'industrial fitness':

1   Skilled artisans, victims of persecution to be assisted by loans etc., to become economically independent. These were supposed to be fit from the moral and physical points of view: 'vigorous, robust, healthy'.
2   'Fit' to transmigrate.
3   The poor, the weak, the adventurer and mendicant. (*Jewish Chronicle*, 12 March 1893)

An editorial of the *Jewish Chronicle* compared such 'nice exemplars' with the 'feeble and stunted tailors of Whitechapel' (*Jewish Chronicle*, 15 November 1889). Social Darwinism was combined with the terminology taken from the élite occupational background. In his testimonial before the Royal Commission on Alien Immigration, Nathan Joseph declared 'We should never dream of sending a bad specimen on to America because we should say "before we spend thirty to forty pounds on this case, will it prove a good investment?" Most Jews . . . look upon charity as a piece of business (Royal Commission on Alien Immigration Min. No. 15948). In his testimony, he also proposed to the anti-alien leader 'an Alien Expulsion Act', according to which the Home Secretary could expel anarchists, criminal aliens, idiots, the insane, the diseased, prostitutes and procurers; also immigrants of less than three years who became a public burden for three to four months, other than recipients of outdoor medical relief. An additional category included long-resident aliens who had more than once been fined, prosecuted, and adjudicated as bankrupt. Their families were to be expelled as well.

Joseph further suggested to permit aliens to come on probation. He regarded expulsion as more efficient than restriction by which, it was difficult to determine 'what class the alien belonged to'. Joseph asserted before the Commission that 'we are doing it every day in large numbers and they go willingly' (Royal Commission on Alien Immigration, 1742, Min. No. 15811–900). It is possible that due to the impact of Joseph's testimony, the Aliens' Bill was introduced in February 1904, which barred from landing immigrants without an evident source of support, those convicted for a crime and those convicted for a crime in their countries of origin, and those of notorious bad character (such powers were granted to the Home Secretary).

Joseph's suggestions with regard to probation and expulsion, rather than *a priori* restriction, were implicitly based on the Benthamite test of unprecedented severity. It was, in fact, as a continuation of such a test that the Board created and applied the six month waiting period. During the suggested probation period, the immigrants were to prove their ability to survive the most harsh conditions without any help from the institutions sponsored by the élite.

Joseph's views reflected an approach of non-interference in accordance with laissez-faire capitalism influenced by the philosophy of Adam Smith and J. S. Mill. (Clark 1985: 71). Joseph published his anti-humanitarian ideas in the *Jewish Chronicle*: 'The days had passed when people allowed their hearts to run away with their heads and were led mainly by sentiment in the administration of their charity' (*Jewish Chronicle*, 8 May 1901). Emphasizing the contradictions between altruistic feelings and what he regarded as a rational approach to the poor, Joseph suggested an abrogation of the charitable element of charity.

The effort of the Board to restrict the 'nursing' by the Visiting Committee of the Russo-Jewish Committee is reflected in the instructions of the Board from 28 December 1892:

> We entirely concur in this restriction, no 'first' visiting should be entrusted to visitors; no house-to-house should be permitted; and protracted 'nursing' of cases should be discouraged in every way. (Board of Guardians Minutes Book 3: 79)

Sir Julian Goldsmid, the Chairman of the Russo-Jewish Committee, attempted to persuade the Board to adopt a more lenient policy by writing to Benjamin Cohen, the President of the Board:

> It is inevitable in consequence that in the good sense of the word there must be more 'nursing' of such cases than of the ordinary cases of paupers with which the Board of Guardians Visiting committee has to deal. (Letter of 17 January 1893, Board of Guardians Letter Box)

However, the Board succeeded in imposing its hard line. According to the 'Suggestions of Mr Lionel L. Alexander as to the necessary conditions as to which the work of the Russian Conjoint Committee can usefully be continued' he stipulated:

> that Visitors be required to abstain from all unnecessary and undesirable 'nursing' of cases, and to cease their ministrations to cases when requested by the Committee to do so. (Board of Guardians Minutes Book 23 April 1893, Book 3: 97d,e)

Allowing for the subordination to the Rothschilds and Cohens, Joseph and Alexander were involved in the highest and most crucial policy making and implementation of the Board. Alexander suggested:

> That all Russian cases which left home in consequence of conditions in Russia making it difficult for them to maintain themselves and their families there, be considered as indirect victims of persecution. That helpless and hopeless cases which need not have left Russia, be, whenever possible, sent back to their homes so soon as they can be persuaded to return; and that other relief be refused them with a view of inducing departure. (BGMB 23 April 1893, Book 3: 97d)

The Board was, and remained throughout the period, the main instrument of the élite concerned with immigration control. As for the Russian refugees, the Board cooperated with the Mansion House Committee and its successor, the Russo-Jewish Committee, founded in 1882 and directed until 1894 by Sir Julian Godsmid, a Liberal MP and member of the Visiting Committee of the Board. The functions of this organization were parallel to those of the Board. Black writes that the Russo-Jewish Committee conducted its activities,

> on a somewhat more enlightened and generous line. Board executives felt not merrily their philosophy but their honour impugned, a contretemps that threatened to divide Anglo-Jewry into warring camps. Sir Julian's political tact patched over differences. (Black 1988: 13)

However, the differences between Sir Julian Goldsmid and the leaders of the Board were not significant and the discrepancies in their views were settled by compromises based on the common interests of the élite as a whole.

As the systems proposed for classification of the immigrants were largely ineffective in practice, the Board applied vague and blurred criteria for screening. Generally, only the youngest and most promising were offered help to transmigrate. One of the factors that weighed heavily for repatriation, rather than transmigration, was the cheaper cost of the former and, therefore, more immigrants were repatriated than were helped to reach America or South Africa. Repatriation was obviously less expensive than the assistance needed by the immigrants for remaining in Britain.

In spite of having no statutory power, the Board used the exasperation of the immigrants in order to force them to repatriate by the very refusal of relief. Lipman apologetically argues that it had been the traditional practice of the synagogues' overseers of the poor 'to give applicants enough to get them on to the next town and the next overseer' (Lipman 1959: 54). Such practice, however, can be denoted in modern terms, as transmigration rather than repatriation. Lipman prefers the term emigration to the Continent, rather than repatriation. According to Lipman, the Board continued the policy of repatriation that existed in England before its establishment (Lipman 1959: 54). Lipman estimates that the approximate number of repatriated Jews between 1880 and 1914 was 50,000 individuals (17,500 cases). Most of the emigrants had been in Britain for less than seven years (Lipman 1959: 94–6). He notes further:

> The repatriation to Eastern Europe, leaves one with the tragic thought that some at least of those thus returned must have become victims of persecution once they were back, it would have been far better had it been possible for them to emigrate to the U.S. or to the Colonies. (Lipman 1959: 96)

It is evident that repatriation of such a large number of people to the territories from which they had escaped could not have been done without the tremendous pressure created by the Board. The Board placed great importance on the deterring impact of repatriation and to the other checks and controls that were harshly applied, in order to prevent the newly arrived immigrants from finding shelter beyond that offered for a short period by the Jews' Temporary Shelter and other elementary assistance.

Repatriation caused many tragedies and tremendous distress. In many instances it actually endangered the lives of the repatriatees. After being uprooted from their *shtetls*, selling all their belongings, endangering themselves on the way to Britain, and failing to make a start in England (lacking the much-needed assistance of the Board), the repatriation was a terrible blow. Most probably, standing behind a copper rail before the 'rota' (the Relief Committee) was much like standing before the feared Tzarist officials. As bad as the situation of the settled immigrant in England had been, it was considered by most poor immigrants as generally better than the life they had left behind them in Russia or Romania, considering the low standard of living of the majority of the Jewish population in those countries.

Until the 1870s, immigration was regarded by the Jewish élite as wholly determined by economic conditions. The emphasis on the motivation of the immigrants to improve their economic situation continued in different degrees until beyond the turn of the century. Obviously, economic and religious tolerance in Britain and its 'strategic' geographical position on the way to America were some of the important pulling factors for immigrants. Additional economic motivations were also related to the extensive poverty of the Jewish population in Russia, which sometimes compared unfavorably with the worst conditions in the East End. At the same time, the élite deliberately attempted as much as possible to disregard the severe discrimination in Eastern Europe as a pushing factor. This was sometimes accomplished by excluding such factors from the general context of the situation of the Jews there. An announcement that Jews were to be expelled from Moscow and elsewhere outside the Pale of Settlement at Passover 1891, affected the lives of 400,000 Jews in Imperial Russia. Such events continually influenced the tempo of immigration. A considerable time elapsed until the Jewish élite was compelled to acknowledge the plight of the Russian Jewry caused by severe political problems of religious hatred and discrimination. After the pogrom of Kishinev Bassarabia, it was more difficult for the élite to claim that the social problems of the Russian Jewry were caused mainly by a surplus of Jewish population. Holmes (1988) writes:

> The Jewish public all over the world was only too familiar with poverty which occurred through no fault of the poor, with discriminatory acts that instantly reduced many well-to-do Jews to paupers. Certainly, often persecutions coincided with the deterioration of economic conditions. (Holmes 1988: 11)

Holmes considers the repressive policy of the Tzarist regime towards the Jews, as a key influence to the mass emigration from Russia (p. 27). In an effort to justify its restrictionist policy, the Jewish élite continuously advanced the liberal hope that persecution in Eastern Europe would cease and the economic situation would improve. Representing the social situation of the immigrants to the host community, the Jewish élite showed their conflicting attitudes of shame and contempt for the immigrant. Hannah Arendt writes:

> They were rapidly assimilating themselves to those elements of society in which all political passions are smothered beneath the dead weight of social snobbery, big business, and hitherto unknown opportunities for profit. They hoped to get rid of the antipathy which this tendency had called forth by diverting it against their poor and as yet unassimilated immigrant brethren. ('On Humanity in Dark Times: Thoughts about Lessing' in *Man in Dark Times*, 1968)

Interventions on behalf of Jews facing discrimination in other countries, through British diplomatic channels, were undertaken by members of the Jewish élite, and especially, Sir Moses Montefiore. The Jewish élite was expected to make such interventions, being one of the wealthier and more influential Jewish élites in one of the most powerful empires of the world at the time. In the latter part of the nineteenth century, such intervention was also used to prevent forces pushing towards immigration by reducing persecutions in the country from which the immigrants came.

During the nineteenth century, organized worldwide Jewry consisted mainly of alliances of Jewish aristocracies in different western countries, who had taken it upon themselves to protect Jewish interests. Such attempts were partially successful. Such international Jewish cooperation also dealt with limiting Jewish immigration in general towards western countries and transferring the responsibilities of supporting them to different countries. Obviously, the Anglo-Jewish élite was instrumental in diverting the stream of immigrants (especially Romanian) away from England.

The Jewish élite also attempted to reduce immigration by excluding poor immigrants, and to confine immigration to the middle class (considered much more helpable, and in the long term, less burdening on the budget of the Board). The Jewish élite promulgated the theory that it could do nothing for the *luftmenschen* (literally, people living on air). It asked the European Jewish organizations to cooperate in this matter, preventing many poor from emigrating. However, under the heavy pressure of immigrants from Eastern Europe, those organizations were either unable or unwilling to live up to the understanding they had with the Anglo-Jewish élite. After the 1880s, refugees poured out of Russia and other countries in large numbers, in spite of all the efforts to stop them.

In the early 1880s, there were mutual recriminations between the English and American leaders with regard to the classification and absorption of immigrants, reflecting the expectations of the American-Jewish leaders for 'better material' (Panitz 1964: 112, 120). The American-Jewish establishment suggested that the English élite was not making as much effort as it could (Black 1988: 264). This is understandable, considering that by the end of the nineteenth century, more than 20 per cent of all British millionaires were members of the Cousinhood. (Rubinstein 1982: 13)

From the 1890s, the American-Jewish establishment expected the élite in Britain, as well as in other western European countries, to support the families of the poor immigrants in their countries, in order to allow their breadwinners who reached America to establish themselves (Black 1988: 264). However, the Board regarded such families as deserted and made many intensive efforts to prevent the enlargement of this arrangement. It attempted to punish and deter such wives and children by making use of the workhouses. The policy of the Board on deserted wives and their children was formulated in a letter presented by Lionel Cohen, the President of the Board, to the other members of the Executive Committee on 4 May 1880:

> In accordance with the regulation laid down by the Board, no case in which the children were old enough to require educational supervision was to be sent to the workhouse. Eleven cases came under this category . . . in all the four admissible cases the proffered workhouse relief was refused. In vain I explained to the women the arrangements which had been made, and the care which would be taken of their infant children. Each refused to go to the workhouse, although I was, of course, compelled, in consequence, to abstain from relieving them. To this end I venture to submit -
>
> 1st. That the workhouse test must be inflexibly adhered to in all cases in which the children are under 7 to 9 years of age, and that any deviation from the enforcement of this test must be reported to the Board.
>
> 2nd. That public notice should be given that after a certain date no relief (unless under exceptional circumstances) will be given to women whose husbands desert them . . . (Board of Guardians Minutes Book 4 May 1880, Book 2: 269–70)

In America, repatriation to Europe of immigrants requiring welfare assistance was practised mainly by New York City philanthropists, where most of the immigrants disembarked. There too, there was a deep antipathy of the established middle classes, whose parents or grandparents came from Germany, against the *ostjuden* (eastern Jews). They developed a vocal nativism, regarding the Easterners as unproductive, lazy and filthy. Such feelings towards the immigrants facilitated in some ways communication between the different western élites. However, the specific interests of the élite in each particular country to prevent immigration or, at least, to get *bessere menschen* (better people) created continuous difficulties

In spite of this friction, communication between the Jewish leaders was maintained in the hope that international cooperation would prevent, redirect and control immigration. The classifications developed by the élites for the selection of those whom they regarded as the most preferred immigrants, were based on rigid anti-alien and prejudiced feelings. Basically, the immigrants were seen as coming from countries considered unenlightened and backwards, an inferior species of lower morality and technological development. The immigrants' well-developed religious education and *Yiddishkeit* (Jewishness, including Jewish culture) compared to native Anglo-Jewry, was disregarded as largely obsolete and irrelevant.

The mass repatriation to Eastern Europe implemented by the Board between 1882 and 1914 (54,000 individuals, one in every two immigrants) reflects the great efficiency of these harsh methods. Beyond the six month period the Board enabled large numbers of poor to maintain themselves at a minimal level of subsistence during periods of unemployment and sickness. Some punitive aspects of the policy of the Board and its position with respect to the developing state's intervention will now be dealt with.

DISCIPLINING THE POOR:
JEWISH PHILANTHROPY AND THE POOR LAW

The discussion will now focus on the policy of the Board with regard to the use of workhouses for those who were defined as 'incorrigible cases' or as a deterrent to particular groups of Jewish poor, including immigrants. The resentment of at least a part of the middle classes and, of course, of the poor to this policy was reflected in the establishment of a Jewish Workhouse with large public financial and moral support, in spite of fierce opposition from the Board. The Board's policy in enlarging the rights of the Jewish poor, including immigrants, to the mandatory services offered by the Government and/or parochial authorities will also be investigated. The Board regarded itself as the representative of Jewish taxpayers and ratepayers and, as such, as having the discretionary power to place the responsibility for the relief of the poor on to the unions as a matter of principle. (The poor rate paid by the London Jewish population was estimated by the Board as approximately one per cent of that of the total Metropolitan population of three and a half million souls.) The law formulated at the establishment of the Board stated, 'Applications may be made to the different parishes in which paupers reside to obtain outdoor relief for them' (Board's Law 19, *Laws and Regulations* 1859: 7). The adjustment requested from the unions for the special arrangements needed for avoiding infringement of dietary laws of the poor placed in the workhouses, reflected the sense of security that the Jewish élite felt in the 1860s. The idea of passing 'confirmed paupers' to the Poor Law was envisaged by Alex in his Scheme and intended by other members as a deterrent measure to special groups of immigrants (*A Scheme* 1859: 7).

The Board preferred to make use of the parochial workhouses where the poor resided – a much cheaper arrangement than establishing and maintaining its own workhouse. To implement this policy, the Board attempted to convince the Poor Law authorities to permit Jewish inmates certain religious observances through special provisions. This policy was a continuation of the effort made in this respect by the Board of Deputies since the Poor Law Amendment Bill of 1834. In 1861, Sir Moses Montefiore, as President of the Jewish Board of Deputies, applied to the Poor Law Board in order to expedite the arrangements requested by the Board (Letter of City of London Union to the Editor of the *Jewish Chronicle*, 15 November 1861).

The Board of Guardians continued to cooperate with the Board of Deputies in this matter making joint representations to the Poor Law Commissioners. Encountering difficulties in convincing the Poor Law authorities to make the dietary arrangements for Jewish inmates, the Board proposed to substitute the Workhouse Test with a Labour Test:

> It is therefore respectfully urged that, as regards the able-bodied poor, an order in the form of instructions, laying down the principles on which guardians are to act, when Jewish able-bodied paupers apply for relief, relaxing in their case the provisions of the 'out-door relief orders', and recommending the substitution, as far as practicable, of the labour test for the workhouse test, would seem a proper foundation for an improved practice. (*Jewish Chronicle*, 4 October 1861)

The outdoor relief could be given according to this proposal either in cash or in tickets to tradesmen. The test, itself, was to be carried out in the workhouse yard, possibly chopping wood or breaking stones. The purpose of the proposal was to show that 'no impediment need exist to the able-bodied Jewish pauper complying with the regulations of the union, save and except residence in the house' (*Jewish Chronicle*, 4 October 1861).

The Board regarded the lack of concerted action in the framework of the Poor Law as an obsolete and unnecessary policy especially after the publication in 1869 of the Minute and Circular of George Goschen, President of the Poor Law Board, defining the appropriate functions of the Poor Law and charity and requesting increased cooperation between the Poor Law's arrangements and public and private philanthropies. In 1859 the Board contemplated the establishment of its own workhouse:

> The Board proposes, or rather hopes at some period however remote, to aid in the formation of an institution in which those poor who receive relief, and know trades, may be compelled to practise them, and even instruct others in their pursuit. The public would probably soon supply sufficient work for the inmates, who would thus be in a great measure maintained by the produce of their labour, instead of being an absolute burden.
>
> An accumulation of funds for many years will be wanting to carry out any such scheme as this, and it is merely mentioned as proving, with other contemplated measures, that it is not the intention of the Board to confine itself to its present limited sphere of operations. (First *Board of Guardians Half Yearly Report* 1859: 20)

However, this plan was abandoned in favour of the use of the existing statutory provisions. In 1861, a subcommittee of the Board was appointed to study the implications of the Poor Law legislature, with the assistance of Alderman Salomons, MP and Sampson Samuel, Solicitor and Secretary of the Board of Deputies

During the same year the subcommittee had an interview with the highest authority of the Poor Law. The several unions in the East End regarded the requests of the Board, mainly for special dietary arrangements, as prone 'to fetter their discretion' and promised to relate favourably to each case submitted on an individual basis. The unions claimed that they

> had never found any reluctance on the part of the Jewish poor to enter the workhouses. The reply [of the Board] was obvious that application was

never made until the applicant had been brought to the verge of starvation. (Fifth *Board of Guardians Annual Report* 1862: 24)

Indeed, the struggle for the use of the Poor Law's services was largely
carried on at the expense of the tremendous suffering of the poor, especially those selected by the Board as test cases. A proposal for a bill
according to which the Jewish Boards of Guardians were to be vested
with official powers by the Poor Law Boards appeared in the *Jewish
Chronicle* of 21 March 1862. According to this proposal the Board had to
have 'the right of parochial authorities, so far as concerned the Jewish
poor, that might voluntarily seek relief from it'. The Jewish Boards were
to send to the central authorities detailed accounts of the relief given to
each of the applicants, naming the parish to which the applicants
belonged.

The unions were to recover 'not the amount of relief given for it, but
the amount that it would have cost the union had its guardians themselves relieved the applicant' (*Jewish Chronicle*, 21 March 1862). The
Board did not expect opposition to this proposal from the Liberals nor
from the Conservatives:

> The Liberals would see no reason for opposing the measure as it would
> not at all affect the existing poor law system, lay any new burden upon
> the ratepayers, or do violence to the conscience of anybody, since the
> Jewish poor would after, as before the passing of such a Bill, be still at
> liberty to repair direct to the union for relief. Nor would the Conservatives
> oppose such a measure; for, although many of them ardently seek the
> conversion of the Jews to Christianity, yet it is admitted that, whilst they
> remain Jews, they ought neither directly nor indirectly be impeded in the
> exercise of their religion. (*Jewish Chronicle*, 21 March 1862)

In 1870, the Board, even more apprehensive of the expenditure that
could be involved in founding its own workhouses, strongly rejected
the idea of establishing such an institution: 'to found separate workhouses or separate hospitals at a time when the State seems about to
make [those] that exist available to Jews seems an unnecessary and
unjustified step and one which the good sense of the community will
surely disown and repudiate' (Twelfth BGAR 1870: 21). This was a
message from the Board to those members of the Jewish middle class
and working class intelligentsia who were horrified by the idea of
placing Jewish poor in workhouses and about a year or so later were
involved in establishing an alternative Jewish workhouse outside the
Board's orbit. Voices against the Poor Law system had been intermit-

tently echoed in the *Jewish Chronicle* since its foundation (see for instance the issue of 25 February 1842). This was recognized by the Board:

> the Jewish public, to their credit be it said have an instinctive and deep-seated natural aversion to allow their poor to become inmates of a workhouse. Apart from the disregard to Jewish dietary laws, which a residence in the workhouse entails, the community have felt it an outrage on that feeling of charity which is interwoven with every precept of their religion, not to allow the poor Jew free support and assistance among his own brethren. (Eighth BGAR 1865: 19)

In 1870, the Board acknowledged again 'that considerable doubt is entertained in some quarters as to the policy of claiming parochial aid on behalf of the Jewish poor. But surely this is a prejudice which a little investigation will dissipate. Jews are unfairly prejudiced by being excluded in participation in funds to which they are equally bound with others to contribute' (Twelfth *Board of Guardians Annual Report* 1870: 21). During this period the infringement of the principle of 'Jews take care of their own' was repulsive to a part of the Jewish middle class which opposed even more the idea of placing Jewish poor in parochial workhouses. Therefore, addressing itself to the Jewish public the Board omitted the arguments presented to the Poor Law Authorities (such as the instigation of a deterrent workhouse test and so on).

A Jewish workhouse was established by Solomon A. Green, a shopkeeper in Goulston Street, E1, near Wentworth Street, in 1871. The founder became the president of the institution. According to the *Jewish Chronicle* his initiative was supported by 'a few worthy men of the working class'. There were 1,400 initial subscribers, a figure which rose a few weeks later to 1,900. The inmates were fourteen aged destitute Jews. In May 1871 James Stansfeld, the president of the Poor Law Board, agreed to the request of a deputation of the Jewish Workhouse to allow the transfer of local rates from the parishes where the Jewish inmates lived (*Jewish Chronicle*, 5 May 1871).

A report on the first general meeting of the subscribers and donors of the Jewish Workhouse was held in Spitalfields in November 1871. At this meeting the plight of Jewish persons who suffered and died in the workhouses without being removed therefrom by Jewish philanthropic organizations, which knew of their existence, was raised as a reproach to the Jewish community (*Jewish Chronicle*, 24 November 1871).

The founding of such an alternative institution was seen by the Board as a clear opposition to its policy and position within the community:

It appeared that while the Board had been negotiating with the Unions and with the Government Board to run the workhouses available to Jews without violation of their religious scruples, and to obtain parochial subventions for inmates removed from the workhouse to denominational institutions, a new association had been started at once to remove and take charge of any Jew who happened to be in a workhouse. It became, therefore, useless for the Board to trouble the constituted authorities with arrangements for the benefit of Jews of the charge of whom, while this association exists, the community may be supposed willing to relieve them; and, although convinced of the good policy and advantage of the course which it advocated, that of rendering the parochial system generally available to Jews, the Board was reluctantly compelled to pause just on the brink of success. (Thirteenth *Board of Guardians Annual Report*, 1871: 26)

In 1874, there were negotiations between the committee of the Jewish Workhouse, chaired by S. A. Green, and representatives of the Executive Committee of the Board, F. D. Mocatta, Lionel L. Cohen and the Secretary of the Board, S. Landeshut. At the meeting that took place on 15 June 1874 the representatives of the Board insisted that:

With respect to the provision inserted by the Committee of the Workhouse as to applications on behalf of persons in a Christian workhouse, it was unanimously decided that special reference to persons so circumstanced was undesirable, as affording an inducement to applicants to go to a Christian workhouse, and use their stay there as a leverage wherewith to open to themselves the doors of a Jewish Institution. (Board of Guardians Minutes Book of Executive Committee 1874: 63b)

It was proposed also, that:

It shall not in future be necessary for intended inmates to pass through a Christian workhouse, but that all deserving cases should be admissible. (BGMBEC 1874: 62)

The suggestion of the Board reflected its tactics to override the purpose of the Jewish Workhouse to release Jewish poor from the unions' workhouses. This way, the Board was able to control the admission of inmates according to its own policies, that is, instituting a preference for the 'deserving' poor. The Board suggested that 'applications for admission be made to the office of the Board, and a report of the same be submitted to the Committee every week' (BGMBEC 1874: 63). This Management Committee was intended to include three members of the Board of Guardians. F. D. Mocatta, and Lionel Cohen, the President of the Board, also suggested that 'children shall not be admitted into the Jewish Workhouse', again in this way preventing the Jewish Workhouse from removing Jewish children from union work-houses, one of the main concerns of the Jewish middle-class members who established the Jewish Workhouse.

The Jewish Workhouse was closed in 1877, six years after its foun-dation, having been consistently opposed by the Board (*Jewish Chronicle*, 21 April 1871). In order to terminate this middle-class project, the élite blocked vital financial support and used its power to persuade the larger, disinterested middle class of the rationale of its own policy.

To facilitate special provisions such as kosher food, exempting Jewish inmates from work on the Sabbath and Jewish holidays, the Board initiated the concentration of Jewish inmates in a particular parochial workhouse, and in 1861, Sir David Salomons, MP was instru-mental in legalizing this arrangement by introducing in the Metropolitan Poor Law amendment a particular section (no. 17), which enabled the poor of any one religious denomination to be put together in a selected workhouse. However, the request of such a concession was contradictory to the tendency of the English legislation to prohibit a predominance of any one religious grouping. In 1871, after meeting Mr Corbett, the Poor Law Inspector, the delegation of the Board requested an interview with the Right Honourable James Stansfeld, the President of the Local Government Board. While conferring with him, the dele-gation was informed however, 'that the Local Government had no power to compel any parish to send any denominational class of poor to another parish where special provisions could be made for them' (Thirteenth BGAR 1871: 25). Stansfeld was, however, ready to consider 'any clause which the Board might desire to introduce in the next Poor Law Bill'. This meant that the Poor Law Board was not ready to burden the ratepayers of one parish with the maintenance of Jewish poor from other parishes.

The struggle of the Board to reach a modus operandi with the Poor Law Authorities in order to have use of the unions' workhouses continued into the 1880s. Apparently the Manchester Jewish Board of Guardians, which cooperated in this matter with the London Board, was more successful in obtaining concessions in being allowed to lapse in favour of out-relief for the Jewish poor (Williams 1976: 287–9). The importance of this struggle by the London and Manchester Boards is evident in the personal involvement of David Salomons (1797–1873), who received his knighthood in 1855 following his election as Lord

Mayor of London, and his Baronetcy in 1869. In the light of the resistance of the Poor Law authorities the general optimism of the Board was unwarranted. However, during the 1860s and 1870s the Board was encouraged to continue its struggle by small concessions made by the unions mistaken by the Board as 'substantial boons' and important precedents, such as the agreement of the parish of St George in the East End to pay a subvention of 3s. 6d. a week for the maintenance of a poor widow removed to the Jewish Widows' Home Asylum (Thirteenth BGAR 1871: 26). The Board had regarded itself as disadvantaged by its inability to impose the workhouse test enforced by the parochial authorities. The Board complained about the necessity to relieve the able-bodied through outdoor arrangements. In 1861, two hundred people were assisted 'for whom some labour test could have been imposed' (Fourth BGAR 1861: 14). In 1861, the Board was much more firm in this matter and regarded the workhouse test as an essential element for avoiding fraud and mendicity: 'The Board will never tire of reiterating, that some means should be found either through the instrumentality of the general parochial system or by the independent exertions of the community of providing work or labour test for the able-bodied Jewish poor' (Fifth BGAR 1862: 13). (The Mendicity Committee had been in operation since the commencement of the activities of the Board.) The Board also regarded itself as incapacitated in its efforts to prevent or at least to curb immigration because of its inability to use the deterring impact of the labour test. This situation was presented to the Whitechapel Union in 1870 as an important argument (Twelfth BGAR 1870: 37–8).

The right of the Jewish poor to make use of the unions' workhouses was presented to the Poor Law authorities as a matter of principle rather than a primarily financial arrangement:

> The Jewish Board of Guardians applies for a share of parochial relief to be administered without violation to the conscientious scruples of Jews, not so much because any funds which it could raise would be inadequate to the discharge of the burdens cast upon it, as because it feels that an irresponsible system of relief acting without concert with parochial administration, is prejudicial alike to the poor themselves, and to the district in which they reside. (Twelfth BGAR 1870: 37)

For intra-community purposes, however, the financial problems involved in the issue of using statutory services was fully acknowledged:

it may be fairly assumed that these cases were left to shift in some measure for themselves, dependent to some extent on the uncertain distributions of the Synagogues, on the casual alms of the public, or still more on the charity and sympathy of their own poor neighbours, while many, if not the majority of them, gradually found their way to the workhouses, and became by degrees lost and forgotten . . . The Board itself feels, that it would certainly lose the confidence of the public, as well as its own self-esteem, if it permitted a single case of a Jewish pauper to sink into the oblivion of the Workhouse, while the funds at its disposal remained unexhausted, and its power to influence the community unabated. (Emphasis added. Fourth BGAR 1861: 19)

In this statement the Board presented its best face to those members of the community who sympathized with the underdog, but it also paved the way for an eventual change in its policy caused by budgetary problems. In line with its disclaimer (in the last sentence of the quote above), the Board was increasingly preoccupied with efforts to make use of the provision of the Poor Law. In fact, a large proportion of the Annual Reports of the Board and its other published documents were dedicated to the struggle for statutory provisions.

In this struggle the Board presented the poor as though they were interested in entering the unions' workhouses 'the disability under which the Jewish Board practically laboured, from their being unable on religious grounds to enter the workhouse . . . '. (Seventh BGAR 1864: 22)

In 1870, the statistician Joseph Jacobs found few Jewish inmates in workhouses (Alderman 1989). Obviously, this relatively small number can be explained by the reluctance of the Poor Law authorities to make the concessions that the Board requested, and the unpopularity amongst the Jewish middle and poor classes of placing the poor in a system known for its brutality. It is possible that at least some of the Jews that had been 'lost and forgotten' in the workhouses mentioned by the Board's Fourth Annual Report, 1861 – previously mentioned – preferred not to identify themselves as Jews for different reasons, including the low standard of assistance provided by the Board to those considered the undeserving poor.

With respect to the aged and sick poor, the élite could not completely evade making provisions for them. In its effort to shift this burden to the statutory services, some concessions were obtained by the Board for outdoor parochial relief without the imposition of the workhouse test (Ninth BGAR 1866–7: 26). Further attempts of the Board to receive such support had been unsuccessful, coinciding with the state policy in the 1870s to restrict outdoor relief in the East London parishes (Lipman

1990: 34). Additional attempts were made by the Board in 1874 to prevent the intended 'deserving' elderly poor from passing through a Christian workhouse prior to being admitted to a Jewish old-age home. In the case of 'deserving' children, the Board faced a dilemma:

> Jewish children, deserted by their parents, were either left in the parochial schools and lost to the community, or if the Board assumed the care and charge of them, it not only undertook a duty for which its machinery was completely unfitted, but it absolutely secured immunity for the worthless parents who, under the law, are only liable to prosecution by a parish officer, which prosecution cannot not be initiated till the children had become chargeable to the Union. (Tenth BGAR 1868: 22)

In 1868, Nathan M. Rothschild, MP, the first Lord Rothschild, assumed the chairmanship of the Poor Law Subcommittee, the other members being Professor Jacob Waley, member of the Royal Commission on Law and Transfer of Real Property, and Jacob Franklin, founder and editor of the *Voice of Jacob* (1841–6). This committee was instrumental in establishing a new law (*Act 25 and 26 Vic., Cap. 43*) according to which the guardians of any parish or union could send any poor child to any school certified by the Poor Law Board. The *Act 29 and 30 Vic., Cap. 113*, made provisions for educating children in the religion to which they belonged. This arrangement permitted the removal of Jewish children from the unions' workhouses at the expense of the respective unions. In 1869, the Jews' Hospital was registered as a certified school under the new act, and application was made to remove a Jewish child from the Whitechapel Union to the Jews' Hospital. The subvention of the Poor Law was assessed at 6s. per week for each child, with the Board paying 2s. 6d. per week to make up the difference in cost (Eleventh BGAR 1869: 21). Further orders for the removal of the children became a matter of routine. In the meantime, the Jews' Orphan Asylum became a certified school. Some children removed from the workhouse whose fathers' residence had been detected by the Board, were returned to them. No comments relating to the social and emotional aspect of the problem involved in such desertion were added to the detailed descriptions of the legal and procedural aspects. The Board concluded 'Thus and thus alone, could desertion of children by their parents be legally prevented or punished' (Eleventh BGAR 1869: 21).

Encouraged by this achievement, the Board continued its negotiations with the Poor Law authorities without being able (in 1869) to disclose their nature in the Annual Report of the same year (p. 22).

Under the less expensive arrangement, the Board expedited the process of removal of deserted and other Jewish children from the workhouses, in this way preventing the previous pressures of the more sensitive members of the middle classes and workers' élite. In parallel, the Board tried to obtain parochial subventions for doubly orphaned children without having to go through the workhouse.

Amongst the groups for which the Board intended to use the workhouse, were the families whose breadwinners emigrated to America in search of work and accommodation in order to bring their families over. The Board denoted wives of such emigrants and their children as 'deserted'. The Board did not hesitate to send deserted wives to local workhouses as an additional means of deterrence, punishment and detection of their deserting husbands. In 1865, the Visiting Committee, chaired by F. D. Mocatta, requested the Executive Committee to 'grant no other aid than toward sending the families so deserted back to the place whence they originally came'. The Visiting Committee regarded this measure as preventing 'unworthy heads . . . to throw the wife and children on the community for support or to entail upon it the expense of sending the whole family after him' (Eighth BGAR 1865: 59). However, the Executive Committee felt that, at that time, the Visiting Committee went too far and that it 'could only in very exceptional cases assume the responsibility suggested by the Visiting Committee . . . thereby widening the gulf which exists among them' (Eighth BGAR 1865: 13–14). Sometimes the Board expressed an understanding for the plight of those families. Notwithstanding this fact, the Board was determined to deal with them sharply: 'It is greatly to be feared that unless some severe and stringent measures of dealing with the unfortunate families thus deserted by their natural protectors, be adopted this wicked and mischievous practice will continue to increase' (Report of the Visiting Committee, Thirteenth BGAR 1871: 57–8).

This practice was in line with the policy of the Charity Organization Society which was not to offer assistance to deserted wives and to recommend the workhouse as a solution for them (Fido 1977: 26).* Kosher food had been supplied as part of an 'organized system' within the East London Union in 1869, to accommodate six destitute women and their children whose husbands emigrated directly to America: 'the Board was greatly embarrassed by their presence and it was impossible

*In spite of significant common denominators and opinions, there were differences between the polices of the Charity Organization Society and the Board with regard to the State interventions in terms of income, maintenance and so on. These issues were discussed by Jones (1977: 92, 275 n21).

to find lodgings where they could be received' (Eleventh BGAR 1869: 22). The extra cost of those rations were defrayed by the Board. A special ward was provided for those Jewish inmates so that they might not be exposed to the possible hostility of other inmates. This concession proved to be an ad hoc arrangement rather than a permanent one, similar to those sometimes made by the unions for the Jewish holidays.

The Board attempted to make those women chargeable upon parish aid with the hope that the parochial authorities would agree to make representations to the country from which they came to assume responsibility for their maintenance (Eleventh BGAR 1869: 22). In this the Board overestimated the willingness of the unions to embark on the precedent-setting intervention the Board proposed. Finally, the Board assumed responsibility for transferring the six women and their children to America. This proposal of the Board represented an emerging trend to request the interference of the state with respect to the immigration of Jewish poor, which had developed into a fully fledged restrictionism by the turn of the century.

From the end of the eighteenth century the Poor Law was interpreted as applying to people of whatever nation or religion who lived in Britain. The Poor Law Amendment Act of 1834 did not interfere with this interpretation. This policy was thought necessary in order to ensure the comprehensive application of the principle of 'less eligibility' and was in line with the larger laissez-faire laissez-passer doctrine that prevailed in immigration policy. In spite of this general policy, the unions in the East End, overburdened by a poor population, feared to make additional concessions that could, in their opinion, attract Jewish immigration from the Continent. In its reply to a Memorial of the Board, the Whitechapel Union stated:

> It thus becomes not only a serious question whether any material modification of the workhouse dietary can be effected in the case of Jewish inmates . . . will not thereby be held out to foreigners to migrate to London, where a legal provision is made for their maintenance without violence to their religious feelings . . . in view of this, the Guardians are bound to raise the question how far they would be justified, in the interest of the ratepayers, in offering a religious asylum to the destitute Jews of all nations . . . arriving from lands where little or no legal provision is made for the destitute poor . . . it is evident that once the existing 'difficulty' is removed, an English workhouse will be regarded as a most desirable asylum which no internal discipline will induce its foreign occupants to leave. (Reply of Whitechapel Union, 7 December 1870, quoted in the Twelfth BGAR 1870: 33)

While the Board was eager to use the discipline of the workhouses in order to minimize outdoor relief, the Whitechapel Union feared that the modification of workhouse dietary arrangements could not be made 'without prejudicing the discipline and arrangements of a mixed workhouse' (Twelfth BGAR 1870: 34).

The approach of the parochial authorities to the question of immigration was very careful and ambiguous. The *Annual Reports* of the Board do not reflect consideration of the standard of the workhouse intended for the placement of the Jewish poor, in view of the contemporary awareness that few workhouses had functioned satisfactorily for a considerable period of time (Marshall 1968: 14–15).

In 1870, the Board 'induced' a number of Jewish women and children suffering from relapsing fever to enter temporarily into the East London Union, apparently to prevent contamination (Twelfth BGAR 1870: 30). At this time the Board found that

> the best mode to arrest pauperism, or to mitigate it, is to temper the administration of stipendiaries (Bound to spare the rates) by the action of charitable associations impelled by sympathy . . . for if all conscientious scruples that now operate to prevent their entry into the Workhouse were removed, the special grievance which restricts them, at present to application for out relief only, would disappear. (Memorial of the Board to the Guardians of the City of London and Whitechapel Unions attached to a letter to the Right Hon. G. J. Goschen, MP, President, Poor Law Board of 12 January 1871: 26, 31)

In its effort to establish comprehensive control of the poor, the Board criticized the community for encouraging the "begging letter" writing system 'which has recently been largely on the increase'. The Board requested such letters to be referred 'for investigation and when desirable for relief, that the mischievous practice can effectually be suppressed' (Thirteenth BGAR 1871: 58). According to the Jewish tradition of charity, it is prohibited to ban begging from door-to-door or in any other form.

While the arrangements for maintaining Jewish religious observances in the workhouses were continuously sought by the Board – the splitting of families in the workhouses and their *hallachic* implications were ignored, as were the feelings of the Jewish immigrants with regard to the workhouse as a non-Jewish institution.

In accordance with the *shtetl* tradition brought over by immigrants from Eastern Europe, it was unusual for a Jew to apply to a non-Jewish institution. Such applications were viewed by all Jewish classes as a sign of relegation and/or depreciation of Jewish service and as a stigmatization.

The motivation of the Board to continue the struggle can be explained by the deterring power attributed to the workhouse. It can also be viewed as an integral part of the Board's policy to reduce sectarianism as much as possible. While some of the contributors resented the consequences of the policy of the Board on the Jewish poor, the Board itself remained unmoved. In view of the sensitivity of some parts of the middle class, the deterrent elements were sometimes disguised by the Board, denoting those placed in workhouses as appropriate or special cases. Lipman interprets the characteristic of such poor as 'undesirable immigrants such as those who tried unreasonably to avoid the responsibility of maintaining their families' (Lipman 1990: 34). In fact, however, the workhouse was intended (Lipman 1959: 29) and used for, amongst others, special groups of immigrants rather than problematic individuals.

From the beginning of the nineteenth century, the Jewish élite, like its host counterpart, wanted to be left alone – a standpoint compatible with 'Jews take care of their own' to which Jewish élites in the Diaspora have long been accustomed. The standpoint was also consolidated as a consequence of their business interests and due to the ineffectiveness of the domestic government. During the nineteenth century, however, this stance began to conflict with the increasing efficiency of central and municipal government interventions. The validity of public intervention, on the other hand, was attractive to the wealthy classes, and the Jewish élite was ready, at this stage, to use any opportunity offered to cut the costs of 'Jews take care of their own' caused by Jewish poverty and the influx of poor immigrants (the 'importation' of whom had seemed boundless and uncontrollable).

Other important factors that can explain the metamorphosis in the specific position of the Jewish élite to state interference, were its relatively rapid political emancipation and interests in the sound functioning of central and local government, especially in domestic issues. For different reasons, the members of the Jewish élite were official participants in internal politics rather than foreign affairs. Their increased security as members of the wider British upper classes increasingly motivated them to claim rights of Anglo-Jewry to be equal taxpayers. The interests of the Jewish élite, primarily for its own sake, were to have a close control on the social problems created by the Jewish immigration and poverty in order to prevent and overcome the rising anti-Jewish feelings (which had long existed in Britain but which were not as severe as on the Continent), which became more pronounced after the start of mass immigration. Until this time the Jewish élite had felt that the predicaments of the Jewish poor were under its relative control and no mandatory restrictions were suggested by its leading members.

The social services established by the Jewish élite and the middle and working classes prevented an active test of the capacities of the host community to solve problems related to the relief of the immigrants and the education of their children. However, in the field of housing, sanitation and medical care, Jewish immigration significantly increased the demands upon local facilities, especially in the East End parishes where the Jews resided.

The use of the workhouses alone was perceived by the poor and other groups within the Jewish community as a malevolent abuse of power, serving the interests of the élite. This discussion has indicated that the Board, from its very foundation, was highly alert to the increasing involvement of the state and made intensive and continuous efforts to obtain financial support for Jewish poor without their having to pass the Workhouse Test, and to persuade the unions' authorities to make special arrangements which were supposed to enable Jews to remain in their workhouses. This policy of the Board to cooperate with the developing Welfare State was based on the increasing security of the wealthy class. The problems connected with financing the Board's activities are related in the next chapter.

5

Social, Economic and Cultural Policy of the Board

FINANCE: CHECKS AND BALANCES

The limitations of funds available to the Jewish philanthropies and to the Board for their main activities will now be analyzed. It is argued that the motivation to finance proposed and existing philanthropic services, was permanently influenced by the élite's constant fear of becoming a victim of its own generosity, by providing incentives for new immigrants and even the settled poor to remain in London.

The wealth of the Jewish élite became proverbial. 'Some few hundred families among them possess enormous wealth, so much so, that they appeared to have given rise to the proverb "as rich as a Jew"' (*Jewish Chronicle*, 9 December 1864). The luxury that those families permitted themselves is reflected in a sermon of the Chief Rabbi of the New Synagogue, quoted in a letter to the editor of the *Jewish Chronicle*: 'the destructive consequences of over-indulgence in luxuries and especially the extravagance in dress which in late years has become conspicuous among us to a fearful extent'. The rabbi believed that the outward show prevented the inward joy required for rejoicing the Festival of Tabernacles (*Jewish Chronicle*, 9 October 1887).

The willingness of the élite to contribute to the Jewish philanthropies was limited. The existence of distress was, however, to a considerable extent admitted by the Jewish wealthy and middle classes at the end of the 1850s, as reflected in the *Jewish Chronicle*. The small charities such as the Jewish Ladies' Benevolent Loan Society, for instance, were overwhelmed by the number of applicants in comparison with their restricted resources. A son of one of the committee's ladies wrote to the editor of the *Jewish Chronicle*:

For how is it possible that a small band of ladies can devote, or even find, sufficient leisure or opportunity to visit the dwellings of ten thousand poor, as frequently as their unavoidable destitution demands . . . If funds were placed more liberally than at present at their disposal, their visits would be more frequent; for they would then possess something more substantial than mere advice to offer for the consolation of the starving. (*Jewish Chronicle*, 25 February 1859)

A meeting was held at Sussex Hall in March 1859 in response to Jewish distress and a series of articles entitled, 'Appalling Distress Among the Jewish Poor', which appeared in the *Jewish Chronicle* (for example, *Jewish Chronicle*, 15 February 1859).

This distress continued well after the Board was established. A letter to the editor of 1861 ran: 'what a squalidness exists in those places! How dirty and loathsome is everything you see! How noisome are the effluvia you inhale! What miserable objects claim your sympathy at every turn! Here nothing seems to live but poverty.'

In its formative years, the Board was supported by the subventions of the three city synagogues (£220 from the Great Synagogue, being its average annual expenditure for the 'strange' poor, and £110 voted as quota by each of the other synagogues (First *BGHYR* 1859: 13). The *Jewish Chronicle* editorial commented with regard to those contributions:

Incidentally we learn that the three city congregations annually spent in the relief of the strange poor £440. At the smallness of this sum we are truly astonished. When we recollect the constant complaint of the influx of the foreign poor which incessantly re-echoed in our ears, we cannot help expressing our surprise at the hollowness, we should almost say hypocrisy, that lay at the bottom of this outcry. Three of the leading congregations in Europe, in the largest and wealthiest city, the thorough-fare of the world, constantly lamenting the enormous expenditure entailed upon them by foreign poor, when the total amount of the annual relief did not exceed £440! (*Jewish Chronicle*, 2 March 1860)

In the same editorial it became clear that the 'magnificent sum' which the Conjoint Board of Synagogues distributed on special recommendation only and to the most honourable applicant was a five shilling piece (*Jewish Chronicle*, 2 March 1860).

These subventions increased to almost £1,300 in 1872 and subsequently remained at almost the same level. In view of the large expenditure incurred at the very commencement of the Board's activities, the Board increasingly depended upon the willingness of the wealthy members of the élite for support outside of the synagogal framework. Its main resources were yearly gifts, trust funds, legacies and special donations such as memorial offerings. The activities of the Loan and Work Departments were increasingly based on trust funds.

The Board lacked a system of budgetary planning. Expenditure depended to a large extent on the number of immigrants, and unemployment as a result of trade depressions and the severity of the winters. One of the main mechanisms by which the Board had reduced its expenditure, was the variation in the amounts of relief given, such as decreasing allotments and grants. Money relief casually given by the rota – Relief Committee – was 'restricted within the narrowest possible limits' (Fourth BGAR 1861: 15). In this way, the Board ensured that it would not become 'a magnet attracting both the unfortunates and the enterprising' (Fifth BGAR 1862: 10).

The Board had been backed by the unanimous consensus among the governing classes that provisions for the destitute should be of a quality that was 'less eligible' when compared with the poorest independent labourer. This consensus influenced the philosophy and practice of the Board. According to a series of letters published in the *Jewish Chronicle* the resources and the apparatus of the Board were far too limited to deal with the problem of Jewish poverty:

> The staff of relieving officers is too small, and the time allowed to receive applications is not sufficient for every case to be thoroughly investigated. How many, unable to obtain admission, go away hopeless and discomfited, and obliged to seek relief from house to house. This is not what it should be, nor will the public be satisfied with such an administration of their money. (*Jewish Chronicle*, 26 April 1861)

In 1867, the number of fixed allowances of the Board was twenty eight at a weekly cost of £5.16s.6d. The number of periodical allowances was twenty seven at the cost of £5.2s.6d. per week. This expenditure absorbed nearly one-fifth of the entire amount of general relief at this time. It was regarded by the Board as very 'serious', requiring a more careful decision of the Relief Committee (Ninth BGAR 1866–7: 16). The Board found 'no alternative' but to support those poor until they eventually found places in one of the communal institutions rather than send them to the workhouses. The way in which the Board regarded this expenditure explains its struggle for obtaining concessions in the use of the workhouses and outdoor relief subventions (Ninth BGAR 1866–7: 16). The amount the Board received from the Poor Law authorities was, at this time, still insignificant when compared with the total annual expenditure of the Board. It was, however, important to the Board in light of the prospective potential increase of mandatory contributions. In the next year – 1868 – the amount of parochial relief which was received by the Board for the poor collecting fixed periodical allowances, was 15s. and seventeen loaves per week. The Board reported that:

> it would be to a great extent unjust to blame the various Unions for the inadequacy of this sum for the greatest difficulties arise in overcoming objections of the recipients to apply for it at all, and whatever has been obtained, has generally been through the interposition of the Board. (Tenth BGAR 1868: 14)

The avoidance of the Poor Law authorities by the Jewish poor, despite their extreme poverty, is evidence of their dependence on the Board's inadequate allotments. The Board, however, reported that 'the greatest care is taken to restrict, as far as is consistent with humanity, an expenditure so serious' [£9.16s. per week in 1868] (Tenth BGAR 1868: 14). Obviously, this permanent policy towards the well-known incapacitated poor, contradicts the myth of the élite's generosity. Moreover, during the late 1860s, the wealth of the Jewish élite reached a very high point in its progressive accumulation.

According to the scheme, the Board was to function also in the contemporary arrangement of voting charities: 'Contributors to the Board were to be furnished with tickets of recommendation' (1859: 7). The tickets represented relief in kind, usually bread, grocery, meat and coal provided to the protegés of the donors through the Board. It is possible that the Board attempted to convince some donors to place the tickets under its responsibility, for distribution based on investigation. The Board was, however, ready to comply with the wishes of the donors, which contradicted its declared principle of indiscriminate relief.

In 1870, the grand total of the expenditure of the various departments of the Board was £5,067 – compared with £4,244 in 1869. The great part of this increase was attributed

> to the augmentation of the amount of disbursements made by various benefactors to specific cases indicated by them but which they preferred to disburse through the Board. (Twelfth BGAR 1870: 2)

Such direct grants to specific persons – for the distribution of which the Board acted as intermediator – increased to £693 in 1869 compared with £121 two years previously. Still the Board regarded its technical intermediacy in this sort of voting charity as 'conclusive evidence of the hold it has acquired on the confidence of the public' (Twelfth BGAR 1870: 2). This arrangement reflects the dependency of the Board on the middle-class and wealthy private benefactions. During a later period, F. D. Mocatta, vice president of the Charity Organization Society also became Chairman of the Charity Voting Association which had opposed the voting charity system and advanced more egalitarian concepts of philanthropic administration.

The revenue income in the 1870s was approximately £6,400, the revenue expenditure was £5,200 and the expenditure for administration £1,100. The revenue expenditure was used as follows:

Relief in kind	loaves and bread tickets, meat, grocery and coal – approx. £1,125.
Money relief	fixed weekly and periodical allowances, special orders of the Hon. Officers, emigration and other allotments, mourners in the week of mourning, childbirth, etc. – approx. £1,400.
Special relief	blankets, rugs, flannel, bedding, clothing, prayer books, tools purchase – approx. £200.
Medical relief	surgical fees, drugs, maternity charity, midwifery cases, port, wine, brandy, gin, milk, bath tickets – including salaries to medical officers and apothecaries – approx. £1,250.
Loans, Work and Work rooms	sewing machines and other implements, salaries of supervisors – approx. £1,050.
Administration	Rent, salaries of secretary, clerk, relieving and investigating officers and other administrative staff, sanitary inspector – approx. £1,100.

(Based on Twelfth BGAR 1870, Analysis of Expenditure signed by Baron Ferdinand de Rothschild, Treasurer.)

In 1890, the revenue income and revenue expenditure were about £17,500 and the cost of administration almost £1,850. Yearly deficits were incurred by the Board in the early 1860s of about £50 and reached an accumulated deficit of almost £12,000 in the 1900s. At this time, suggestions were made to suspend the law with regard to the funding of legacies and donations in memoriam, in order to increase the capital. Such arrangements reduced the deficit. Fears were continuously expressed by the élite that the 'importation' of the needy would force the Board to transcend its financial possibilities and cut into the endowment and exhaust all the resources available to it and to other institutions dealing with the immigrants, thereby largely pauperizing the community. The purpose of such statements was *inter alia* to justify the restrictionist policy of the Board.

Between 1851 and 1881 the Jewish population in London increased considerably, then dramatically until the First World War. During the years between 1869 and 1882, the Board dealt with seven to eight thousand persons yearly (two thousand cases of individuals and families), 20 to 30 per cent of whom were assisted by some form of Jewish philanthropy – including that of the Board. The total number of persons the Board dealt with represented 20 to 25 per cent of the total Jewish population (Lipman 1990: 33). The number of applications to the Board increased between 1894 and 1900 to more than five thousand per annum (Lipman 1959: 81). To function in this period of mass immigration, the Board needed much larger resources.

The continuous activities of the Board depended mainly on the large subscriptions of a small number of the wealthy members of the élite, consequently increasing their authority and control (*Jewish Chronicle*, 5 June 1885). The list of contributors at the end of each annual report symbolized the respectability and generosity of the wealthy and middle classes. However, it was very important to the Board to show that it was supported by the community as a whole and efforts were made in this direction. In 1902 the Board formed the East End Aid Society for the purpose of enabling the poor to assist the Board by weekly contributions of one penny. In this way, solidarity incentives were provided to middle-class adherents.

The Board was able to maintain itself financially because of the shift of the larger expenditure connected with health and education to the state and other sources depending on public revenues, following the implementation of more collectivist policies. At the same time, the Board avoided the responsibility for maintaining institutions where residents lived on the premises which could have been very expensive to support. The Board remained responsible for other aspects of relief. However, the élite and the Board continued to claim that they were taking care of the Jewish poor from their own resources, largely disregarding subsidies from public taxpayers and ratepayers. The main services that the Board continued to provide, partly on a voluntary basis, were for children and the elderly.

The expenditure by members of the Jewish élite on philanthropic causes also included those they incurred as wealthy and aristocratic British people who lived by the principle of *noblesse oblige* as well as owners of country houses. In the House of Commons, in supporting the opening of Parliament to Jews (in a bill of 1841), Lord John Russell praised the families of Rothschild, Salomons, Montefiore and others which 'have long been established in the country and well known to be deeply interested in the prosperity of the country, have a great stake in it . . . ' (quoted in Finestein 1993: 25). According to Finestein, when extended to churches, such Jewish philanthropy was perplexing to some Christians and David Salomons' donations as High Sheriff of Kent for building churches were severely criticized by Sir Robert Inglis (House of Commons, 10 March 1841, quoted in Finestein 1993: 48n, 49). It is evidence of the extent to which the élite wished to please the host society and the greater implications of these wishes and interests. The contributions of the Jewish élite were an integral part of the way in which acceptance into the broader context of the English wealthy class was achieved. It can also be explained as a result of the situation of the wealthy Jewish class that moved away from the Jewish residential concentration in the East End and into a non-Jewish environment:

> Nathan Mayer Rothschild was somewhat apprehensive at the prospect of taking a villa [in Standford Hill] in 1816. His prosperity had been much commented upon, not always favourably, and Herries, the Commissary-in-Chief, warned him that possession of a villa would only encourage backbiting . . . Nathan found time to serve as a vice-president of the newly established local dispensary, besides making various improvements to his own estate. The family stayed on until 1835, when they bought Gunnersbury. (Brown 1990: 81)

Obviously, the élite donated large amounts of money. The question can be asked, however, did the élite give until it hurt or were they rather spending from a super abundance of wealth? Could they not have given more to ensure a fairer distribution of resources? Was the élite's motivation, what can be described as altruistic behaviour (pleasure at another's pleasure, and pain at another's pain, this is, based mainly on sympathy) that combined with the élite's utilitarianism – or rather philanthropic choices that contributed to the élite's collective security and welfare, but did actually counter their sympathy, that is, interested commitment? Whatever the historians' opinion was in respect of the Anglo-Jewish élite's generosity, it seems that they donated a large amount of money in spite of their antipathy towards the poor in England. Philanthropy enabled the Jewish élite to deny its stereotypical representation as acquisitive, thrusting and aggressive, and to prove that it was not selfishly preoccupied only with material success. The Jewish élite developed the Board as a voluntary, powerful organization with elaborate checks and balances able to prevent commitment beyond what the élite itself desired.

According to the concept of *tzedakah* (defined in chapter 1), Jews who by their own efforts are unable to support themselves and provide their elementary needs, as well as other components of their social and religious life, have positive rights to some of the resources of other Jews. This means that the wealthy are required by Jewish law to share their resources to an extent necessary to fulfil the basic requirements of the needy.

How much should one give a poor person? – 'sufficient to provide him with what he is lacking' (Deuteronomy 15: 8); 'You are thus obliged to fill his want you are not, however, obliged to restore his wealth' (Maimonides, *Mishneh Torah* VII, The Book of Agriculture, chapter 7, paras 3–8; see Appendix I for an explanation of how this is fulfilled). As to the amount of the *tzedakah* that an individual has to give and its relation to his earnings, there are upper and lower limits. With regard to the lower limit:

> a man is obliged to give his own sustenance priority over that of any other person. He is not obliged to give charity until his own sustenance is met, since scripture states that your brother should live together with you – your own life takes precedence over that of your brother. (*Tur Yore Deah*, 251, based on Saadia Gaon)

However, Rabbi Yechiel Michal Epstein wrote that this injunction applied only to the very poor who can provide only bread and water for themselves, and persons who eat meat and cooked dishes and are able to clothe themselves are obliged to give charity in a normal manner. Otherwise, only the very rich would be obliged to give charity (Aruch Hashulchan, 251; 4, 5, according to Domb 1980: 38). Rabbi S. Z. Auerbach – a contemporary authority – points out that 'if a person earns sufficient for his needs, the *maaser* [monetary tithes] obligation applies to his full income and not only toward what is left after paying for his personal subsistence' (Chapters 3 and 4).

With respect to the upper limit, there are differences of opinion among the *hallachic* authorities as to whether the upper limit of one fifth is to be interpreted strictly. More recent authorities proposed that this limit is relevant only to persons who might jeopardize their own financial security by giving more; 'A very wealthy person may distribute more than one fifth of his possessions' (R. Abraham Danzig, *Chayyei Adam*, 144: 10).

The standpoint of the *hallachah* on the issue of the upper limit which is relevant to the wealthy can be concluded as follows:

1   Where there is pressing need and the donor can afford one fifth without difficulty, one fifth is obligatory, and more than one fifth is commendable or obligatory, according to circumstances.
2   Where there is pressing need and the donor can afford one fifth only with difficulty, giving one-fifth is 'the choicest way of fulfilling the *mitzvah*' (a commandment of Jewish law), that is for the person who is prepared to cause himself a certain amount of hardship in order to fulfil a *mitzvah* in the best possible way; one tenth constitutes an 'average fulfillment', and less than one tenth an ungenerous attitude. (quoted in Domb 1980: 37–8)

It should be noted that the concept of equality in its present meaning cannot be found directly in the Bible and the *hallachic* traditions. Apparently, the *hallachah* does not support the more radical redistribution which could reduce the wealthy to a level close to that of the impoverished.

> A person should not distribute more than one fifth so that he should not himself need the support of others. (R. Moshe Isserles, *Yoreh Deah*, 249, p. 1)

If such a situation is not envisaged, a wealthy man has the obligation to contribute the greatest possible amount.

Taking into consideration that in pre-welfare states Jews had to 'take care of their own', the retention of the economic power of the wealthy 'big donors' was regarded as a guarantee of continuous provision of the community's needs.

The preceding description and analysis has indicated that according to the Judaic concepts of the *tzedakah* there are meaningful limits on the rights of the wealthy to dispose of their wealth according to their personal preferences.

The empirically based assumption of the wealthy Jewish élite in England was that no justification existed for limiting the rights of Jewish philanthropists over their wealth by referring to the basic needs of the London Jewish poor and more so with respect to the new immigrants. This assumption was based on the liberalist trend of the period and its emphasis on the right to freedom which had involved exclusive possessions. Indeed, Herbert Spencer denounced state intervention and regarded private charity as detrimental to social advance, but allowed it in order not to interfere with the liberties of the potential donors.

The paternalistic structure of the relationship between the élite and the poor was characterized by an overwhelming control of funds enabling the élite to play an 'imperialistic' role in developing services, defining and determining need, and imposing restrictions upon the relief of urban Jewish poverty.

RESTRICTED POLICY ARRANGEMENTS

The discussion now turns to the activities of the Board in related areas of work and loans as well as medical relief and housing. These areas provide examples of the policy and practice of the Board when it was confronted with substantial social problems. The late and reluctant recognition it gave to the collective needs of the poor, as against a narrow concentration on a personal or individualistic approach, varied from area to area. The departments of work, loans and medical relief, among others, cooperated amongst themselves, acting as a network of social control. The sanitary inspections provided by the Board were intended to prevent epidemics sometimes caused by severe housing conditions.

Work

My contention is that the laissez-faire orientation of the élite was detrimental to a more positive and significant intervention that could have been made to counteract unemployment and lack of vocational skills.

The Work Committee was one of the first to be established. Continuous efforts were made by the Board in the teaching of trades to apprentices. With regard to girls, the Board emphasized the inculcation of habits which it considered to be lacking, such as cleanliness, regularity and industry. In 1869, however, it became obvious to the members of the Work Committee responsible for the Work Rooms, that it lacked sufficient involvement and intimate knowledge of the dynamic developments in the work market, to train young women effectively:

> Notwithstanding some pressure put by the Board of Guardians upon applicants for relief, the highest number of apprentices obtained was 46 – the Work Rooms being able to accommodate 60 – they endeavoured to trace the cause which actuated the poor in exhibiting so paradoxical an indifference to an establishment which bid fair to confer upon them a very substantial boon. From various enquiries made upon the subject it appeared that the making of dresses, underclothing, and shirts was not sufficiently remunerative to offer to poor girls a prospect of obtaining a livelihood, and that the great majority of them preferred to become tailoresses, which, during six or seven months of the year, proves to them more lucrative. (Eleventh BGAR 1869: 9)

The distance between the classes was further complicated by Victorian middle-class moral paternalism: 'But one of the objects contemplated by the Board in calling the establishment into life, was to obviate, if possible, the constant intercourse of Jewish girls with uneducated men which is rendered necessary in the tailoring trade, and cannot fail frequently to lead to immorality' (Eleventh BGAR 1869: 9).

The Work Committee included some pioneering women volunteers. A sense of social obligation combined with a deep conviction caused those women, members of the élite, to devote a considerable amount of time in attempting to improve the conditions of the 'girls of the industrial class'. Women were active in the conjoint visiting work and participated in activities for the Board's Work Rooms, apprenticeships and clothing. Towards the end of the century, wives of the leading male members of the Board were involved in prestigious British associations dealing with conditions of maltreated children and prisoners. However, as a whole, women members of the Board identified themselves with the prevalent philanthropic concepts of the male members, accepting them without the more profound questioning that could arise from a more feminist frame of reference.

In 1869 the Work Committee resolved to diversify its operations by introducing several other trades. The immigrants and the poor presented the perceived threat of poverty and displacement to some non-Jewish workers in competing branches and thus created anti-Jewish feelings. However, the attempts to prevent further Jewish concentration in the garment industries were not very successful.

Moreover, the Board's intensive lending of sewing machines and advancing of loans for their purchase, increased the massive Jewish concentration in tailoring, countervailing the attempts to vary Jewish occupational structure. The Board itself recognized its inability to take positive action with regard to the great majority of the unskilled Jewish poor:

> The number of cases which can be materially assisted by being visited, forms but a small proportion of the aggregate relieved by the Board, the great majority of which is naturally composed of helpless persons, – either the aged or infirm, or those who are without any regular means of subsistence, or the knowledge of any remunerative trade. Very many of such cases are of the class which under ordinary circumstances would be handed over to the workhouse; but at present the Board is forced to devote a large portion of its aid towards their relief. Nevertheless, the comparatively few persons who appear likely to be permanently helped by a well-directed, and well-timed effort, by a somewhat liberal grant in money, and by intelligent advice, form precisely the class which the Board would most cheerfully and liberally relieve. (Report of the Visiting Committee signed by F. D. Mocatta, Chairman. Eleventh BGAR 1869: 52)

By opting for strict preferential assistance of certain categories of applicants, the Board excluded the largest part of the poor, reflecting a pessimistic view of their capabilities and potentials.

The Work Committee encountered serious difficulties in placing young men and women from 'our working classes'. The Board appealed to potential Jewish employers, such as heads of firms in the various departments of trade and commerce. The complaints about the unwillingness of the Jewish wealthy class to employ Jewish persons were mentioned several times in the *Jewish Chronicle*, for instance in the issue of 26 April 1861. Later that year, in a letter to the editor, 'Henricus' complained:

> Our richer brethren, such as merchants and business men, have a great objection to employ their co-religionists, because these are not able to work on Saturdays and holidays; these, therefore have no chance of procuring a livelihood among their own people, but are driven to our neighbours . . . But charity, sir, is not what we want: we are a proud people. More good would be done by employing us than by giving us charity; we wish to work for our livelihood, and make a position of our own; by which means our condition as a people would be greatly elevated. It is a stigma on our community that the rich do not employ the poor. (*Jewish Chronicle*, 18 September 1863)

The period from the middle of the nineteenth century was characterized by significant growth of the Jewish middle class, strongly dominated by its economic interests which, apparently, were not compatible with the employment of Jewish workers and labourers.

The Jewish poor, on the other hand, including the immigrants, dovetailed into the existing economic scene. Therefore, there was no need for a productivization of the Jewish poor as was sometimes suggested by the Jewish wealthy and middle classes.

The immigrants developed the cheap British trade in clothing and footwear, increasing exports and creating the mobility for themselves in the host society. Despite the low wages and difficult living conditions, the Jewish poor proved their remarkable ability to adjust to the hardship of the labour market.

On 8 February 1892 a subcommittee of the Jewish Board of Guardians was appointed 'to enquire into the present system of relief to the able-bodied unemployed'. Mr L. L. Alexander, the Hon. Secretary of the Board 'was good enough to attend' on the two meetings of this subcommittee (Board of Guardians Minutes Book, 16 March 1892, Book 3: 59). In its report the subcommittee reacted to a proposal made by Mr Herman Landau, a member of the nouveau riche group of the élite. Landau's proposal was that 'a Wood-Chopping Yard should be established by the Board, with the object of decreasing the number of applicants for recurrent relief" (Board of Guardians Minutes Book, 16 March 1892, Book 3: 59). However, Landau's proposal was rejected by the subcommittee, one of the main reasons being:

> The Sub-Committee believe that the number of persons belonging to this class [able-bodied unemployed], who, under the existing arrangements of the Board succeeded in obtaining relief from the Board is *extremely small*. (BGMB, 16 March 1892, Book 3: 59; emphasis mine)

The limited help offered to the Jewish unemployed by the Board proves the correctness of the thesis of Piven and Cloward (1971) with respect to the extensive role of relief offered by different institutions to the temporarily unemployed in the regulation of the labour market.

The structure of Jewish employment necessitated the continuous assistance of the Jewish philanthropists to 'carry' the Jewish workers through the long months of unemployment until the market was ready to absorb them, again intermittently. However, this assistance was provided at a very minimal level. The avoidance of the workhouses by the Jewish poor, for instance, is explained by Jones, *inter alia*, in terms of 'greater self-sufficiency' and as evidence of Bentham's prediction that 'the truly rational, economic man would turn to the Poor Law only as his very last resort' (Jones 1977: 89).

Philanthropy was certainly not the solution to the basic problem of Jewish poverty nor could philanthropy change the forces of the capitalist mode of production. On 12 July 1894, a deputation on behalf of the Committee of the Jewish Unemployed visited the Board's premises and presented the following suggestions to the Executive Committee of the Board:

1   That the Jewish Board of Guardians should immediately relieve those cases of the Jewish Unemployed which are now in distress.
2   That a Bureau should be established for the registration of the Unemployed.
3   That the Jewish Board of Guardians should supply work in lieu of charity.
4   That a Conference be called together of Employers of Jewish labour, with a view to take some action to reduce the hours of labour, and by that means to reduce the number of Unemployed.
5   That the Jewish Board of Guardians should approach Jewish Members of Parliament, with the view of urging the matter of the restriction of shorter hours of work, upon the House of Commons.
6   That an Inspector of Factories and Workshops, who is able to speak 'Yiddish', should be appointed by the Government.
7   That a member of the Committee of the Unemployed should accompany the Investigating Officer of the Board, in the investigation of cases of the Unemployed in need of relief. (BGMB 12 July 1894, 3: 124–6)

The recommendations of the Executive Committee were as follows:

1   The first function of this Board is to relieve, after investigation, persons who are in distress, and especially those who are out of employment, which always has been done; and having regard to the distress now existing, they are applying the Funds at their disposal with as much liberality as they can.
2   That a Committee of the Board might be appointed for the purpose of considering this question.
3   The Executive are of the opinion that it is impossible to carry out this suggestion.
4   & 5   That this matter is outside the scope of the Board.
6   That this is a matter which requires some consideration, and we therefore refer it to the Board.
7   That we think such an arrangement undesirable. (BGMB 12 July 1894, 3: 124)

The Board's Minute Books include a resolution of the more detailed reply that was given to the delegates of the Jewish Unemployed

Committee. As they reflect the position of the Board with regard to the important problem of Jewish unemployment they are quoted almost in their entirety:

> The Board desires to express its deep sympathy with the unemployed in the privations that follow from the dearth of employment and hopes that the demand for labour will shortly increase and that the sufferings of the unemployed will be thereby alleviated.

> Resolved that the Delegates be informed:

1   See Recommendation (1) of the Executive Committee above.
2   That the Board is unable to concern itself with the establishment of Labour Registers, *which appear to the Board to come rather within the province of the workers themselves.*
3   That the Board adheres to its Resolution, if not impossible to establish a Labour Yard or other means of supplying work in lieu of charity.
4   & 5   That the Board is unable to concern itself with general economic labour questions that are absolutely outside its scope.
6   That it is inexpedient to ask the Government to reconsider its decision not to appoint a Yiddish-speaking Inspector of Factories & workshops.
7   That the Board, while always prepared to receive any information from all reliable powers, considers that it has in its own officers and a large band of visitors a sufficient means of investigation.
    I am, Sir, Your Obedient Servant (Signed) N. Stephany, Sec.

> A vote of thanks to the chair concluded the meeting.
>
> 12 July 1894   B. L. Cohen
> (BGMB 12 July 1894, 3: 125–6; emphasis mine)

As shown in the following chapter, such pressures of the Jewish working class had some long-range limited impact on the leaders of the Jewish philanthropists, however, its main tendency continued to be directed by a trend of paternalistic intervention on an *ad hoc* basis, however ineffective. Imbued with the laissez-faire spirit, the Jewish élite rejected the demands of the Jewish Unemployed Committee. Those demands were based on larger, collective arrangements against adversity and deficiencies caused by unemployment. The interventions required by the Jewish Unemployed Committee were possibly regarded by the Board as unwise and unscientific philanthropy, and as such, irrelevant and hazardous. According to the doctrines of self-help and a free-market economy, they had to help themselves.

It is evident from the foregoing that the limited apprenticeship and retraining programmes of the Board did not have any significant impact on the labour market, which was characterized by a very high rate of Jewish unemployment. The efforts made by the élite to disperse the Jewish working class from the East End in order to enlarge their occupational opportunities were largely unsuccessful.

Loans

In this section it is shown that the provision of loans was intended to help some of those considered to be deserving poor to become rapidly independent economically.

Free loans were supplied by the Board, amongst others, to artisans for purchasing tools necessary to their trades. In 1861, through donations by Charlotte Baroness Lionel de Rothschild (at first anonymously presented), an arrangement was established by the Board for hiring out sewing machines, on which the borrowers were given the option to buy on weekly reduced terms. By 1874 a few hundred sewing machines had been issued. All applicants for loans of tools and implements were to find sureties, however, sometimes they were advanced loans even if they were unable to find a surety (Ninth BGAR 1866–7: 19). The applicants were thoroughly investigated through personal visits of volunteers, their character and competence were considered and assessed.

Through loans and other types of relief the Board was able to maintain order and control. The regulation of the flow of labour in and out of the market was achieved by loans to the temporary unemployed during the slack seasons, a process that Mizruchi denotes as an 'abeyance device' (1983: 104). This system operated by the Board was particularly important, taking into consideration the pitifully low wages of the garment, shoe and boot makers, as well as other workshop trades. The earnings of those workers did not usually permit them an accumulation of savings and the seasonal precariousness forced the workers to live off loans from the Board, relatives and friends.

Lipman regards the procedures applied by the Loan Committee to able-bodied poor and other categories as much more humane in comparison with those of the Poor Law (1959: 59). While the Board fulfilled a parallel function to those of the parochial authorities with regard to the Jewish poor, a comparison with voluntary services is of greater relevance. In fact, the person assisted by the Loan Committee did not represent the majority of the applicants or users of the Board's services, as the loans were granted mainly to 'deserving' borrowers. The extended use of the term 'deserving' by the members of the Loan and Visiting Committee indicates a clear preferential policy towards those belonging in the past to the Jewish middle classes. It appeared that the members of those committees felt that the 'deserving' applicants were closer to their mentality.

Through such activities as advancing free loans, the Board influenced the structure of the community as well as its political orientation by increasing dependence upon the élite and the identification with its aims. The loans encouraged economic independence and to some extent improved the standards of life of those who became owners of small shops. However, they also strengthened social economic individualism and conservativism. At the same time this intervention by the Board curtailed the influences of the Jewish socialist movement. While it may be argued that this was unavoidable anyway, the Board certainly expedited the process. Consequently, the free loans, hiring and subsidizing of sewing machines and other work implements contributed to some splitting of the Jewish working class. This emerging division was also possible because of the tendency of many of those who, gaining upward mobility, turned away from their own groups. Obviously there were additional factors that can explain why the élite was able, to some extent, to divide the solidarity of the Jewish working classes.

Thus, the expansion of loans, hiring sewing machines and the provision of tools increased the social mobility of many poor people, but this arrangement conflicted with the policy of the Board to diversify the occupational structure of the Jewish poor.

Health

The Board was motivated both by recurrent epidemics and by the fear that the Jews, and especially the immigrants, would be accused of spreading infectious diseases. The medical care of the poor was traditionally assumed by the doctors employed by the three city synagogues. In 1824 the Society for Supporting the Destitute Sick, Mishenet Le-Holim (Support for the Poor) was established, supported by weekly one penny subscriptions. By 1835 the members of the society proposed a scheme to establish a Jewish Hospital. An article in favour of erecting this hospital was published in the *Hebrew Review and Magazine of Rabbinical Literature* (11 September 1835). In the 1840s twenty-four beds were allotted for Jewish patients with arrangements for dietary observances, such as in the Metropolitan Free Hospital in Devonshire Square (in which there were eight beds). Different proposals continued to appear in the *Jewish Chronicle* criticizing the insufficiency of existing arrangements. Those deficiencies were acknowledged by Dr D. H. Dite, Doctor to the Board (Medical Officer) (*Jewish Chronicle*, 13 September 1867, 20 September 1867).

In addition to the hospital treatment provided by the voluntary hospitals subsidized by public donations, the Jewish poor made use of the workhouse infirmaries supplied by the rates and the medical services of the Christian Missionary Society. Only the Sephardim possessed a hospital, Beitholim, established in 1748 at Leman Street and transferred to the Mile End Road in 1792. However, this institution soon ceased to function as a hospital, limiting acceptance to some maternity cases.

As an integral part of the expansion of its activity the Board took over, in 1862, the medical relief given by the three main synagogues. At this time the *Annual Report* showed more sensitivity to the medical needs of the poor in comparison with their other predicaments. The Board employed its own doctors and apothecary. In 1869, the Board reported that 'To the patient visited at his home, the attendance of a Jewish doctor who can understand his language and sympathise with his habits is doubtless a valuable boon.' However, 'doubts are beginning to be entertained whether it is necessary to maintain a surgery for the supply of medicines to Jewish poor, when hospitals and dispensaries are freely open to them and resorted to by them' (Eleventh BGAR 1869: 15).

The Gathorne Hardy's Act passed during this period, providing for the establishment and the extension of the parochial dispensaries for the sick poor, also influenced the decision of the Board to discontinue its medical services (Eleventh BGAR 1869: 15). However, the Board still hesitated. In 1869, the Medical Committee refuted the rumour that a relapsing fever epidemic had been imported by Jewish immigrants from Poland, following which the Board decided to employ temporarily, the services of a Sanitary Inspector as a preventive measure (p. 14).

In 1873, the Board discontinued the functions of its dispensary and in 1879 terminated the medical advice and the dispensing of drugs, port wine, gin and whiskey, which according to the records were widely prescribed throughout the period, and possibly may give some indication as to the level of medical care offered to the poor. Both discontinuations were made after trial periods. Lipman writes that 'the Medical Committee watched carefully for complaints but none were received . . . a careful watch was kept to see whether hardship was involved but the Medical Committee found none' (Lipman 1959: 62). No comments are made by Lipman with regard to the validity of the

Board's investigation of the effects of the discontinuations.

The number of attendances at the medical services of the Board (dispensary, surgery and urgent cases at home, etc.), according to the statistics of the Board, increased from 5,000 in 1863 to more than 40,000 in 1871 (p. 61). Allowing for the existence of alternative services that could satisfactorily substitute the existing Jewish one, the Board used pseudo-scientific methods of investigation to prove that none of the users were affected negatively by its discontinuation. The tendentious conclusions of the Board implies either that the service was not significant or that its extent was greatly exaggerated. This is an indication of the power of the élite over the poor and the working class as well as of its ability to manipulate the middle class, including the intelligentsia.

The ambitions of the Board to control different aspects connected with poverty, such as health, prompted it to expand its medical services for a period of nine to eleven years. However, in the light of the large expenditure involved, the élite decided to shift the burden of health onto the Metropolitan hospitals and the Poor Law Union's infirmaries. The formal justification for this step was that 'there was nothing of a specifically Jewish character' in medical relief. (Magnus 1909: 119).

The termination of free medical care by the Board was also in line with the policy of the Charity Organization Society according to which, poor people in receipt of wages were to contribute small amounts towards their medical care, and were encouraged to join provident societies which offered infirmary services. The continuous opposition of the élite to the establishment of a Jewish hospital was based on a trend which increasingly attempted to move away from a sectarian approach; financial considerations were possibly even more important (*Jewish Chronicle*, 10 July 1868). Instead, the élite preferred to enlarge the provision of kosher food in London hospitals. A renewed movement to establish a Jewish hospital in 1909 was again strongly opposed by the élite headed by Nathaniel (Natty) Rothschild. The policy and practice in the field of medical relief shows how significantly the Board was influenced by the contemporary expansion of the medical services at a local level through central intervention.

As most of the East End of London was populated by non-Jews, the increased demand for medical facilities caused by the termination of the Board's services was felt mainly in the few parishes in which the Jewish poor resided. For a discussion on the burden created by the immigration on the local non-Jewish arrangements, see Jones (Jones 1977: 4).

The general tendency of the Board to avail itself of the facilities that the state provided was particularly reflected in the field of medical relief, possibly more than in any other field. To the extent that the Board continued to be involved in medical relief, it was 'to supplement not to supersede which is common to all' (BGMB 26 May 1873, 1: 80).

The Board maintained that 'the State knows no creed in its provision for medical relief and it is the duty of the Board to avail itself of the facilities which the State provides' (80). However, the Board was still regarded as responsible for the prevention of the risk of the spread of cholera. In a letter sent by the Assistant Secretary of the Local Government Board in Whitehall on 31 August 1892 to Benjamin L. Cohen, the President of the Board, the thanks of the Local Government Board were expressed for the letter received from the Board [no longer in the Board's Letter Box]. The Local Government Board also wrote that:

> they will rely on your Board of Guardians to render Sanitary Authorities and other Officers every possible assistance in tracing and keeping under observation all Jewish immigrants recently arrived or arriving in this country under conditions which, in the judgement of the Authorities or of the Jewish 'Sanitary Committee', involve any risk of the introduction or spread of Cholera. (Letter of Local Government Board to the Board, 31 August 1892, Board of Guardians Letter Box)

The continuing increase in tax-supported facilities permitted the Board to rely on their services, reducing its own expenditure accordingly. On 23 October 1911, the Medical Sub-Committee of the Board decided:

> it is of the opinion that the Board would not be justified in incurring large additional expenditure for the purpose of sending tuberculous patients to sanatoria. That for the present all such patients as it shall be deemed proper to send for sanatorium treatment shall be sent to Daneswood or some other sanatorium where their reception will be free of cost to the Board. (London Jewish Board of Guardians' Minutes of Sanitary Committee, 1885–1911, A Report of the Medical Sub-Committee)

In the report of the Medical Committee of 26 May 1873 (Memorandum), it was

> further submitted to the Board as being worthy of consideration whether or not the system of provident medical relief could be introduced among the Jewish poor. At the Brewer Street (Clerkenwell) Dispensary, a charge of one penny is made for each supply of medicine, and during 1872 these pence amounted to the handsome sum of £101. 6s. 4d. The result produced is not to be measured altogether by the amount of money but it is rather

to be looked for in the feeling of independence and self-respect which the system is calculated to encourage and foster. (BGMB 26 May 1873, 1: 80)

Such tendencies were obviously in line with the contemporary policy of the Charity Organization Society which associated indigence with moral failure, social reform and punishment. The élite regarded the free provision of medical care to the poor as an erosion of the prudence and responsibility of the poor.

The inadequacy of medical help available to the Jewish poor, following the decisions of the Board to discontinue such services, is reflected in an extended letter sent to B. L. Cohen MP, by M. Hyamson, Honorable Secretary of the Jewish Dispensary, a philanthropic organization established by the Jewish middle class. The purpose of this letter was to obtain access to the Register of the Board, in order for the Dispensary to limit its philanthropic services to persons on relief. Some of the following views of the Committee of the Dispensary, expressed in the letter, are quoted at length, and they represent the problems encountered by the poor following the discontinuation of the Board's medical services:

> The aim of the promoters of the Jewish Dispensary is to benefit the Jewish Sick Poor who are so destitute that they are not even in a position to pay the moderate contributions required by the provident Medical Societies. Anyone conversant with the large number of cases permanently on the books of the Jewish Board of Guardians will not deny the existence of such a class, steeped to the lips in abject poverty and having every claim on our consideration and sympathy. Destitute Jews are prostrated by sickness they are referred to the parochial machinery. It is respectfully contended that there is no distinction in principle between medical relief and relief of any other kind, between a loaf of bread and a bottle of medicine. At present, between 700 and 800 cases of Foreign Jews apply for medical relief to the Parish Authorities. Sometimes, days elapse before they are attended to. The Parish Doctors whom they at length see do not understand Judisch. It is believed that many breadwinners will be saved from disablement and death . . . this class will be treated, in periods of illness, not like dumb brutes but like intelligent human beings – by medical men with whom they can freely converse. (Board of Guardians Letter Box, Letter of 30 November 1896)

The discontinuation of the medical services by the Board was explained and justified (Eleventh BGAR 1869: 15). Defending its policy, the Board used a pedagogical and rhetorical approach, emphasizing the alternatives of providential arrangements for the poor. However, some middle-class philanthropists speaking on behalf of the poor, sensed that the poor needed greater security, irrespective of their ability to provide against the adversity of disease and chronic illness. The medical services of the Board were discontinued prematurely, before alternative suffi-cient services were available, causing considerable suffering and hardship to the poor.

Here it has been shown that the Board retreated from the field of health, expecting the poor to apply to the statutory and voluntary non-Jewish services which became increasingly available. However, during the transition periods a great deal of suffering was caused to the poor.

Housing

Only a few almshouses and homes were built by Jewish philanthropists from the 1830s to the 1870s. These were intended to accommodate a very limited number of elderly members of the city synagogues' partly 'respectable' paying residents. Gradually, the Board assumed responsi-bility for some of them but did not engage in building new ones, considering the resources needed for such projects and maintaining them as beyond its scope and possibilities. The *First Half Yearly Report* of the Board in 1859 promised 'at no distant day a scheme for bettering the homes and dwellings of the poor' (Third *BGHYR* December 1860: 21). The urgent necessity to improve the dwellings of the poor was mentioned in the *Jewish Chronicle* of 2 March 1860 and of 25 January 1861 in which the establishment of a building society was suggested. A public meeting of the important members of the élite was held in May 1861 on the Model Lodging Houses for the Jewish poor; the chairman was Sir Francis Goldsmid, MP. The resolution taken at this meeting was the establishment of a Jewish and general Model Lodging House Association Limited, Jewish applicants to be given priority of place (*Jewish Chronicle*, 25 January 1861). However, this project was not imple-mented.

In 1865, Nathan S. Joseph, architect and one of the youngest members of the Board, drew the attention of the Executive Committee to the defects in the sanitary conditions of the dwellings of the poor. Amongst others: the absence of supplies of drinking water, defective or non-exis-tent drainage, poor ventilation and accumulation of refuse.

During this period there was a serious danger of epidemic which brought about some pressure on the Board to undertake some repairs of the tenements of the poor in lieu of the landlords. However,

Mr. Lionel L. Cohen was also averse to any work being undertaken by the Board; the sanitary defects he admitted to exist, but he considered that the Jewish poor were no worse off in this respect than their neighbours, and could not expect to be in a better position . . . On the other hand, it was argued by the President that the emergency with which it was intended to grapple called for a rigid sacrifice of a principle to expediency; that apart from the social view it would be a direct economy to undertake works of a limited nature, as by preventing disease the burden which illness in a poor family threw on the Board's relief funds would be spared. (*Jewish Chronicle*, 4 August 1865)

Following this report, the Board appointed its own sanitary inspector to detect such defects and to press the landlords and local authorities to improve the sanitary conditions (Eighth BGAR 1865: 21). In the same year the Board expressed its hope that the Jewish poor could somewhat improve their housing conditions following the munificent Peabody donation (p. 29). However, during 1867 no sanitary inspections were made on behalf of the Board. No explanation was given for this discontinuation and the fact that in the previous year the East End was affected by cholera, one of the recurrent epidemics in the East End of London during the nineteenth century. The annual report does not reflect the consequences of the epidemic for the inhabitants, however, the subsequent significant increase in the cost of medical services provided by the Board was specified (Tenth BGAR 1868: 13). In 1863 the Model Lodging Houses in Commercial Street were opened. The record hoped 'that they will prove to be sufficiently remunerative to induce the establishment of similar buildings on a larger scale' (Sixth BGAR 1863: 44). However, in 1865 the Board reported with regard to the 'dwelling of our lower classes':

Unfortunately the profits realized by these undertakings are not as yet inviting for financial investment; but it seems now to be an ascertained fact that 5 per cent, can be obtained by the erection of suitable dwellings for the labouring classes, if conducted with prudence and on a sufficiently large scale. (Eighth BGAR 1865: 61)

A request to the Montefiores, Rothschilds and Goldsmids to come forward and help the severe situation in the dwellings of the poor was published in the *Jewish Chronicle*.

The Jews in the East End were in the poor, or near poor, categories; the new immigrants moved to the cheapest, derelict accommodation with poor sanitation, usually those abandoned by previous poor working-class tenants. Small workshops were often located in the houses occupied by large immigrant families. Bedrooms too were used as work rooms. Sanctions were contemplated by the Board, to discontinue relief to the tenants of those houses. An attempt to punish the victims is reflected in the *Jewish Chronicle*'s editorial suggesting the refusal of relief to those who lived in overcrowded housing (12 August 1881). The dwellers of those houses had to pay exorbitant rent to landlords who, in the large part, neglected their properties, making only cosmetic reparations at the request of the Sanitary Inspector of the Board. The Sanitary Inspector demanded, without being challenged, that the tenants keep their rooms clean and whitewashed – evidence of the quasi-authority of the Board (Gartner 1973: 153).

Beginning with the mass immigration in the 1880s, housing conditions of the Jewish inhabitants in the East End worsened, the housing problem became more politicized as it became more visible. In 1885, the Four Per Cent Industrial Dwellings Company was established by the Rothschilds and shortly afterwards a model housing project was erected in the East End. The immediate impetus for action on this severe issue that had been neglected for decades, was the appointment of the Royal Commission on Housing, presided over by the Prince of Wales. The motivation of the élite was to appear in a more favourable light before the Commission. Also, the impact of immigration on the living conditions in the East End had been too severe to be ignored. Possibly, the Jewish élite feared that the Jewish immigrants would be accused of forcing the already resident gentile population to less adequate accommodation. The Four Per Cent Industrial Dwellings (called the Rothschild's Buildings by the population) comprised of 198 units. Additional tenement houses were built by the company in 1890 (285 units), 1893 and 1896. However, during this period of mass immigration those solutions were far from solving the severe housing problems. The model project of Rothschild was also a political gesture intended to defuse the severe housing problems. Rothschild's scheme combined a fair profit element to the investor with the education of the poor with regard to respectability, correctness and frugality.

By the end of the nineteenth century, resentment of the East End Jewish population over housing conditions grew considerably because of exploitative rents and landlords' abuses. Unsanitary houses were continuously bought by landlords who, after superficial repairs, rented out the tenements; some Jewish landlords and housing brokers were involved in such transactions. In order to pay the increasingly raised rents, many tenants had to sublet the already overcrowded apartments.

The resentment of the abused tenants was somewhat quieted by Samuel Montague who feared that a more assertive protest would endanger his interests in the East End. At the mass meeting on high rents which he chaired on December 19, 1898, Montague denied a personal ownership of property in the East End, expressed sympathy for the Jewish working class by accusing the exploitative landlords and stressed the need for modern housing projects. Finally, Montague announced the donation of twenty-six acres of land that he owned in Edmonton, to be used for building houses for three to four thousand people through the London County Council. Typically, the élite regained and maintained control by enhancing its virtue and creating an additional area of dependence of the poor on both existing and new institutions; in this instance the East London Tenants' and General Legal Protection Committees, both of which functioned in close cooperation with the Board and under Montague's tutelage (*Jewish Chronicle*, 20 January 1899).

During the nineteenth century the élite was not ready to provide alternatives to the security, social and religious advantages that the poor felt in the East End. Some incentives for deconcentration were offered by Montague to respectable working-class persons while, according to his policy, the *schlemiels* (bunglers, dolts) were to remain in the East End. The term emphasized the responsibility of this category for their situation, and as such they were not eligible for better working conditions or social mobility.* Montague rather preferred to keep them in the East End so they would maintain a low profile. Both Montague and the Board encountered difficulties in convincing candidates to move out of the East End and the East Enders were accused of resisting cooperation with the philanthropic institutions (*Jewish Chronicle*, 12 February 1904, 19 February 1904).

With regard to the solution of the severe housing problem in the East End, Samuel Montague anticipated the availability of local government resources. Alderman writes 'no matter how admirable the record of the Four Per Cent and other philanthropic ventures in this field, local people looked to the Council rather than to private enterprise to provide the necessary volume of new housing needed' (1989: 32). Notwithstanding, the standpoint of the majority of the élite represented by the Conservative Rothschilds and Cohens was different.

In 1898 the Progressives in the London County Council proposed to

---

*In the Yiddish language an alternative term *shlimazel* (an extremely unlucky person) whose failure is due more to having no *mazel* (luck)

take advantage of the 1890 Housing Act in order to erect working-class dwellings and to do the clearances involved at the sole cost of the Council. The Conservative MP, Sir Benjamin Cohen (brother of Lionel, stockbroker and President of the Board from 1887–1900), attacked the proposal of the Progressives as a restriction on private initiative, 'dwelling companies', he told the Council, 'could do the housing of the working classes in suitable tenements in refined quarters at reasonable rents and yet pay a fair return to their shareholders' (Alderman 1989: 36). With regard to the activities of the Board in this area, the Sanitary Committee was in close contact with the London County Council. The Board of Works of the Whitechapel District was in constant communication with the Board with regard to the sanitary conditions in areas where Jews resided (Board of Guardians Letter Box, Reply to the Report by Dr Haner, upon the Sanitary Condition of the Whitechapel District, December 1894).

Cooperating with the unions and Whitechapel District Board, the Board made efforts to pressure the Metropolitan Board of Works for improvements (Alderman 1989: 33). Using its sanitary inspector in the Jewish areas of Whitechapel, Bethnal Green, St George's and Mile End, the Board provided the London County Council with valuable information considered reliable by the latter. The Board also functioned as a pressure factor in the field of public health.

However, the primary policies of the Board with regard to the problem of overcrowding in the East End were based on transmigration and repatriation. Montague, and to some extent the Board, also attempted a policy of dispersion of the Jewish working class to the provinces. To facilitate this process, Montague considered the establishment there of alternative religious and other Jewish services. However, the need to find work within a narrow range of occupations compatible with their skills, made such prospective projects largely impracticable. Obviously there were other considerations in the 'social mind' of the poor and the immigrants, amongst others the security they felt living together with their families, kin and *landsleit*.

The mass immigration and the collectivistic trends forced the Jewish élite to adopt a more structuralist approach in terms of relating to the housing problem as a predominantly physical need for shelter. At the same time the élite continued to focus on a culturalist approach, reflected in Anglicization.

Under different pressures from below and those exercised indirectly by the Royal Commission on Housing, the élite had no choice but to regard housing needs in the Jewish East End as similar to those of the underprivileged English population of London. The Housing Project also signified some shift from a predominant pattern of helping the poor individually to a more comprehensive support of community needs. The problem-solving modality of the élite was based on a remunerative profit-making criteria.

The housing projects built by the Jewish élite are an example of complementary interests, but the implementation developed at a tempo set by the élite according to its particular benefits.

Only late in the nineteenth century was the problem of housing tackled to any degree by the Jewish philanthropies. This was done to a considerable extent under the influence of non-Jewish projects in this field. The housing problem involved a great deal of class antagonism, as many of the landlords were Jews. While there were some differences in the approach of the Board, regarding its various fields of practice stemming from historical precedents or the preferences of some large donors, the deployment of the Board's services was based on some unifying concepts of contemporary philanthropy (such as thorough economic and moral investigation). The emphasis on personal defects legitimized the neglect of broader social problems as significant political issues in the perpetuation of Jewish poverty.

ACCULTURATION: ANGLICIZATION

The discussion now turns to a consideration of the élite's activities in the acculturation and socialization of the poor. The Board itself supported such activities; for example, from the commencement of its activities in 1859, the Board required parents to provide proof of their children's attendance at school, as a precondition for receiving assistance. The Jewish Press, as will become clear, continuously supported the efforts of the élite to expedite the acceptance of the poor into the host society by forcing them into a rapid and sometimes mechanical process of acculturation.

The Jewish élite was at all times preoccupied with the fear that their acceptance by the corresponding stratum in the host community could be undermined by the strangeness of the new immigrants.

Acculturation: Patronage and Anglicization

In this section the influence of the Settlement Movement on the Jewish élite is described and analyzed.

Montague recognized the importance of sociocultural activities in the East End and was instrumental in founding the Jewish Working Mens' Club in 1874 under the auspices of the wealthy class, however, members of the workers' élite participated in the organization of the activities – an unprecedented phenomenon in the philanthropy of the establishment. According to Gutwein (1992), the collaboration of the workers was a deliberate attempt to create a more independent Jewish poor class; however, at the beginning of the nineteenth century, Montague's group did not envisage the Jewish community outside the framework of public control established by the élite (1992: 157). According to different sources the Club was not generally attended by unskilled labourers and newly arrived immigrants. Endelman (1983) writes:

> [the club's sponsors] hoped to attract the immigrants to the Club's extensive facilities in great Alie street, but the tone and character of the Club's activities did not appeal to the Yiddish-speaking newcomers, who could not be induced to join. Most of the Club's members continued to be drawn from the Anglicized workmen of the area until its closing in 1912. (Endelman 1983: 116)

This demonstrates the increasing differentiation within the Jewish working class *per se*. The establishment of the Jewish Working Men's Club was influenced by the British Working Men's Club movement from which it borrowed its name (Williams 1990: 22). The cultural and educational system set up by the élite was an important agent in persuading the working class and the poor to believe that the system was just, and to accept the constraints involved in the social structure of the community. The Club fulfilled an important role in creating the impression of a closer relationship between the working class and the élite.

The East End Scheme advanced in 1896 by Nathaniel Rothschild was a concession, made in order to defuse discontent, to prove that matters were dealt with and under control. By this process, allegiance was cultivated to the traditional élite. The Scheme was based on a combination of charity and paternalism. Some of its main elements were the acculturation and conservative Anglicization of the alien poor who, according to the *Jewish Chronicle,* were to be civilized. Most of the plans included in the Scheme were implemented. They included youth clubs where enthusiastic young members of the élite and some professional middle-class members were involved in different activities. The aims of the youth clubs were: lowering the visibility of the 'strange', moral uplifting, offering an alternative to radical leftist movements and counteracting delinquency. The aims of the club were dictated by the specific relations between the Jewish classes and the Jewish situation in England and as such differed in important aspects from their British counterparts.

The clubs' leaders acted also as guardians of poor boys, assisting in the apprenticing activities of the Board under the supervision of the Work Committee. There is a general agreement amongst historians with regard to the overall success of the youth clubs, which can be attributed to the enthusiasm amongst the middle classes created by the Settlement Movement. This movement also influenced the approach of the volunteers motivated by the Visiting Committee of the Board. The Scheme was largely based on contemporary models taken from the host society. The Chief Rabbi suggested an institution modelled on Toynbee Hall as a place where 'the indwellers of East and West could meet . . . and where our working classes could be taught correct conceptions of the relations of Capital and Labour, of employers and toilers' (*Jewish Chronicle*, 13 March 1896). This is an example of the use of religious authority – and by implication, of religious teachings – as a political doctrine and instrument of control over the lower classes, implying the divine origins of a static social structure. The young members of the élite were exhorted to move to the East End, a somewhat belated version of the Settlement Movement emanating from Toynbee Hall.

The Lads' Brigade – another feature of the East End Scheme – emphasized class discipline and knowing one's exact place in the social organization, always obeying and honouring superior ranks. Such aims were manifested in the sermons delivered by rabbis to the lads. In 1902, the preachings of discipline of the ancient Israélites were evoked as a model (*Jewish Chronicle*, 1 February 1902). In this way, ideas were identified with remote but diverting historical situations. This intent was to counteract what the Jewish élite perceived as the primitive disorderly Jewish mobs of Eastern Europe and manifested the fears that the concentration of the poor classes in the East End ghetto created amongst the members of the élite.

Given the scale of immigration and its accompanying need, the limited services established to acculturate the Jewish poor were restricted in their impact. But despite this, and their paternalistic and authoritarian character, their contribution was not insignificant.

Schooling

This section deals with the elementary schools established by the élite, which provided basic literacy and numeracy to Jewish children and deliberately promoted their Anglicization. From its commencement, the Board was characterized by a tendency for a comprehensive paternalistic control which included education of the young generation and Anglicization. According to the original Board's Laws and Regulations, 'Children of those receiving relief must attend a school, vouchers of which must be produced' (Law 12: 5, 1859; Scheme by Ephraim Alex: 7, 1859).

The reporter of the *Jewish Chronicle* who was present at the reception of the Relief Committee, gave a vivid description of how this policy was implemented:

> The next applicant was a man whose very countenance had starvation written on it. His tale was short and concise. He was a foreigner, with four children; he had no work, nor was there a prospect of any. While making the preliminary inquiries, we were much struck with the altered tone of the president; all his usual kindness seemed to have vanished, and had be been a relieving-officer of the 'Oliver Twist' school, it could not have been more harsh. 'Where have your children been today?' he enquired.
>
> 'They have remained at home with me, sir,' was the reply.
>
> 'I knew it, and they remained at home with you yesterday and the day before as well. Now, sir, let us clearly understand each other. Send your children to school tomorrow, and keep them there the whole of the week; if you do not, you will receive nothing more from us'. (*Jewish Chronicle*, 6 January 1865)

It is possible that the presence of the Jewish press reporters somewhat 'softened' the approach of the Relief Committee to the applicants for relief.

The financial support that the Rothschilds gave to the Board, for which they also fulfilled the role of treasurers for long periods of time, was paralleled by the enlargement and maintenance of the largest Jews' Free School. Opened in 1817, and moved to Bell Lane, Spitalfields in 1821, this school included some important elements of philanthropy such as clothing and apprenticing, characteristic of the other Jewish free schools. This endeavour considerably increased the prestige of the Rothschild family. It was considered important in providing religious education and in combatting the activities of the Christian missionaries. For a long time the school was maintained by the family only, as governmental grants for children's education through the Treasury were available only to Jewish schools which admitted children of all faiths and permitted the withdrawal of children of other denominations from Jewish religious instruction. The Jewish Free School was very much a multi-generational Rothschilds' project and their favourite charity. At the beginning of the twentieth century, school uniforms with the colours of the Rothschild family were provided yearly to approximately 4,000 pupils. In the framework of providing an elementary knowledge according to the contemporary standards for education of the poor, the school was the main instrument of Anglicization and for inculcating middle-class values. It also continuously propagated the mythos of the Rothschilds in the East End. As such, it was considered a stronghold vis-à-vis Montague's arriviste group.

The enlargement of the responsibilities of the state enabled the Jewish élite to minimize its expenses regarding the formal education of children. Few Jewish voluntary day schools were opened after the 1870s.

Jewish Press

This section presents evidence of the self-justification and legitimization by the élite, supported by the manipulation of communal opinion through the Jewish Chronicle, as the main organ of communication. It also deals with some of the alternative perspectives provided by the Jewish press.

The Jewish Chronicle and the Voice of Jacob were founded in 1841. In its revised form of 1844 the Jewish Chronicle was entitled the Jewish Chronicle and the Working Men's Friend. Joseph Mitchell, its owner (d. 1854), was a wealthy 'self made man' who regarded himself 'as a representative of the working classes'. Mitchell, however, campaigned for civil rather than social equality (Cesarani 1992: 261).

Abraham Benisch, editor of the Jewish Chronicle, contributed in the late 1850s to the establishment of the Board by its own scheme and the campaign advanced under his editorship. However, once it was founded, Benisch accepted the policies of the Board in an uncontested way. Jacob Franklin, the founder, editor and owner of the Voice of Jacob between 1841 and 1846, became a member of the Jewish Board of Guardians (1865–77) and Chairman of the Committee for Legislative and Parochial Affairs.

Lionel Louis Cohen, the dynamic Honorary Secretary of the Board and its President after 1869, was one of the three members of the consortium that nominated the editor of the Jewish Chronicle in 1868.

Becoming the community's leading weekly newspaper, the *Jewish Chronicle* generally supported the status quo in the application of the plutocratic principles of the élite. It reported on the meetings and developments of the Board and related to Jewish poverty in terms of the contemporary discussion.

During the mass immigration, the *Jewish Chronicle* most often supported the efforts of the élite in discouraging the immigrants from staying in England and acted as the Board's public relations organ expressing its official opinions. In this way the *Jewish Chronicle* created an inhospitable atmosphere stressing that immigration could be detrimental to the immigrants themselves. According to the *Jewish Chronicle*'s restrictionism, repatriation could prevent the formation of a 'pauper colony thrown upon the rates' causing anti-Semitism: 'For let there be no mistake the interests of the wealthy Hebrew are as much at stake as those of any other class' (*Jewish Chronicle*, 6 December 1901).

Here was an attempt to divert the immigrants already living in England from class consciousness and enlarge the number of the middle-class members who opposed immigration, especially artisans in the same occupational field as the immigrants. At the same time the *Jewish Chronicle* had tempted the 'better class of members' of the East End to join the West End synagogues. The *Jewish Chronicle* also suggested that the Board request a fair ability of speaking English as a condition for being given assistance (*Jewish Chronicle*, 22 July 1904).

The *Jewish Chronicle* welcomed any help offered by the élite to the poor, generally avoiding any condemnation of deficiencies. To the extent that concern about the situation of the poor was expressed, it was rather restrained and hesitant, and as such could not influence public expectations about the responsibilities of the wealthy. In the last quarter of the nineteenth century and in the early part of the twentieth century the Anglo-Jewish press was characterized by a lack of criticism of its élite and a lack of initiative needed to incite action, such as creating an East End movement for social reform.

Only at the beginning of this century is there more evidence of some attempt to shame the rich in order to provoke them into initiating and improving projects relating to the collective needs of the poor. The *Jewish Chronicle* accepted for publication some articles expressing opposition, largely by moralists, provided they did not challenge the balance of social forces within the contemporary structure or burden the middle-class conscience too much.

The more determined critics of the establishment were readily labeled 'extremists' and as such, were rejected. The Hebrew Socialist

Union was established in 1876 by Aron Lieberman, an immigrant from Lithuania. In August 1875, the socialist paper, *Arbeter Fraint* (the Workers' Friend), expressed the resentment of the radicals against the establishment. It was influenced by the revolutionary movement in Russia and the previous experiences of the Jewish proletariat of Eastern Europe in class clashes. This paper presented the opposition of the working class to the values imposed by the élite through its philanthropic activities of Anglicization. It had rejected the helplessness attributed to the Jewish working class and the way in which the institutions of the élite flaunted the élite's social superiority. Another paper which reflected the opinion of the immigrants, maintaining their identity, was the *Polishe Yidl-Die-Zukunft*.

Sometimes, critical voices could be heard, however they were generally limited by self-censorship and the propagation of conservative predilections to marginalize subversive ideas. The most bitter criticism of the orientation and policy of the Board and of the Jewish élite came from the immigrant press basically denouncing the lack of proper institutions for the absorption of immigrants, resulting from the fear of attracting them.

The efforts of the wealthy class to transform the poor immigrants in order to make them as similar as possible to their English counterparts, and invisible as a distinct group, stemmed from its fear of anti-Jewish feelings. This process of assimilation to the host society, which was to some degree inevitable and indeed necessary, assumed 'mechanical' characteristics. This was greatly encouraged and reinforced by the *Jewish Chronicle*, which represented the Jewish élite within the community to the other Jewish classes and, beyond, to the host community.

SOCIAL ORGANIZATION BEYOND THE JEWISH ELITE

This section deals with the institutions established by the poor themselves as they attempted to establish their independence from the domineering philanthropy of the élite. It describes areas in which the poor organized themselves independently, or with the help of middle-class members. The chapter also discusses philanthropic institutions that attempted to remain outside the orbit of the Board. Underlying these attempts was a growing consciousness on the part of the Jewish poor and working classes of their particular identity and interests within the Anglo-Jewish community.

A considerable number of Jewish philanthropies coexisted with charities associated with synagogues and with the services offered by the Board. Most of these institutions were established by the Jewish middle classes and often derived their name from their counterparts in the host society. While they differed in scope or specialization, the common denominator of those philanthropies was the differentiation between the 'deserving' and 'undeserving' poor. The manifest aims were generally to enable the recipient to reach or regain as soon as possible the ability to help himself and become economically and socially independent in the spirit of the period. The small philanthropies emphasized what they regarded as the need of the poor for moral support and adopted a rather educational and didactic approach to the immigrants' matters of daily living.

While different forms of assistance offered by these various philanthropies were often inadequate and unsystematic, their usefulness and comfort to the poor may have been generally underestimated. It is possible that those less centralized institutions were, despite their doctrinaire declarations in the spirit of the period, more flexible and sensitive to the needs of the poor. They were less formal and trusted the poor more, giving them the latitude necessary to benefit from charitable assistance.

Many philanthropic projects continued to operate on a voting system. The advertisements for forthcoming balloting published by the charity candidates to enhance their competitive probability, exposed them and increased the worth of the benefactors, legitimizing what was considered a *mitzvah*, (fulfillment of an important commandment of Jewish law), thus giving them a sense of power and pride. This random system effectively discriminated against those who could not afford an advertisement or could not obtain the protection of sponsors – naturally the persons in greatest need.

The Board made a continuous and intensive effort to incorporate such philanthropies or at least bring them into the orbit of its social philosophy. To the extent that the Board succeeded, those small philanthropies were used by the Board for specialized, auxiliary and supplementary services that it could not offer by itself. In the process of coordinating its own services with such satellite charities, the Board further instilled its philosophy and maintained its authority over them. Its 'imperialistic' tendencies meant that the Board regarded pluralism in the field of philanthropy as dangerous to the fulfillment of its own attempt at comprehensive control.

However, the Board encountered great difficulties in succeeding in this policy in the light of the strong motivations of the members of the commercial middle class to expose their own generosity apart from the élite. Black regards the attitude of the élite to the other philanthropies as hostile (Black 1988: 179). Black cites the accusation of a middle-class lady founder of a small charity in North London in 1891, who described the élite as 'insensitive, hiding humanity and equity behind the formalism of coldly Benthamite rules' (Black: 179). This charity founder did agree to means tests and investigations to avoid misapplied relief, but rejected the humiliation of the applicants by other procedures of the Board. However, while the charity that she administered was enlarged, she acted in full cooperation with the Board (Black 1988: 179).

By 1900 there were approximately 1,200 unemployed or underemployed breadwinners who needed the seasonal winter services of the Soup Kitchen in Spitalfields (established in 1854). According to the Board this institution refused to provide the names of its beneficiaries. However, their list was open to the scrutiny of all its subscribers. The Board insisted on the avoidance of duplication, emphasizing the criterion of the obligation of the community to relieve distress rather than poverty – again a concept which is not compatible with the traditional Jewish view of charity. The argument of the Soup Kitchen's sponsors in favour of avoiding stigmatization was disregarded by the Board. The leaders of the Board were firm in their decisions and dealt sharply with what they regarded as an inducement to pauperism. Coming under strong pressure, the Soup Kitchen had to compromise and provide the weekly list of the beneficiaries required by the Board (*Jewish Chronicle*, 6 October 1905).

Consequently, the philanthropies which strongly cooperated with the Board, were influenced by its 'hard line' policies. This is illustrated by the admission policy of the Jews' Hospital and Orphan Asylum at Norwood, which refused to accept single orphaned immigrant children whose parents had resided for less than two years in England (except for double orphans under special circumstances) even when the late parents had been killed in the Eastern European pogroms.

The initiatives of the poor were met with strong opposition from the Board. A shelter was founded by 'Simha Baker' (Simon Cohen) in an impoverished synagogue in Church Lane, East End, to fill the vacuum created by the Six Month Rule. The scope of this institution was to supply first aid to homeless poor immigrants and transmigrants, to provide temporary housing and clothing. Supplying such help to newly arrived immigrants, the shelter infringed on the policy of the Board. Determined to close Simha Baker's Shelter, a delegation headed by F. D. Mocatta visited the shelter and was instrumental in influencing the local authorities to close it on sanitary grounds (A. Mindy, Jews' Temporary Shelter, Transcript, Mocatta Library).

The popular resentment and oppositional reaction that this injunction raised in the East End, (which included a protest meeting), led to the establishment of a new Jews' Temporary Shelter in 1885, this time with the support of Samuel Montague, his business partner Franklin, and nouveau riche Hermann Landau (1844–1924). Landau was an immigrant who was a Hebrew teacher in Poland and had amassed considerable capital as a banker in London and was later to become a member of the élite. Only in 1900 did the Board finally consent to recognize the Jewish Temporary Shelter, again, in order to bring it under its control at least in matters that were vital to the interest of the élite. This process was 'facilitated' by a large donation from the Rothschilds.

However, the establishment of the shelter represented an unprecedented antagonistic alternative to the institutional policy of the Board, initiated 'from below' and with the support of the popular opinion in the East End. The working class and the poor lacked the resources and determination to act in an entirely independent way. Accepting the paternalism of Montague and of Landau proved in the long term, as we shall see, to be detrimental to the interests of the poor immigrants. Despite this, the establishment of the shelter strengthened the consciousness of the poor East End Jews, juxtaposing their interests with those of the élite.

Although Landau declared his intentions to operate the Jews' Temporary Shelter in an humanitarian spirit, after being accepted as the first Pole in the élite, as a stockbroker and banker, he adjusted the activities of the Jewish Temporary Shelter in line with policies dictated by the Board with which he continued to cooperate closely. In this spirit the Managing Committee announced its duty, which was to

> Remove any erroneous impressions that . . . this Institution is a mischievous innovation calculated to encourage, rather than to check, the unhappily continuous immigration of destitute foreign Jews . . . with a view to provide a further wholesome check to the immigration of any pauper adventurers who might be attracted hither . . . as well as in contemplation to institute a Labour Test of such a character as not to interfere with the already over stocked market. (A. Mindy, Jews' Temporary Shelter, Transcript, Mocatta Library)

The Spartan austerity of the Shelter made it as unattractive and repellent as possible, but was far from having any significant impact on the pushing and pulling forces which motivated immigration from the Continent.

In 1871, the Board estimated the amount distributed 'without registration, without concert and without system' at 'three or four times as great as that which the organized institution (the Board) is enabled to devote in the same period' (Thirteenth BGAR 1873: 18). The Board regarded the bulk of the community as indifferent to the 'evils' of profligate charity, and the number of Jewish philanthropies that resisted subordination to the Board increased after the mass immigration which started in the 1880s.

Influenced by the Charity Organization Society, the Board emphasized the need for rational organization, efficiency, and consolidation of Jewish philanthropies, in line with its search for order and control. However, such centralization could cause the loss of the specific identities of the smallest charities (some of them had their roots in the traditional Judaism). This, in turn, could decrease the total amount of money donated to the poor, taking into consideration the readiness of middle-class donors to frequently give small amounts of money. Many of the small charities were based on class protectionism and limited their help to middle-class persons. Others, however, helped the poor and the immigrants, functioning as an alternative to the control of the Board.

The Ashkenazic Jews in the East End felt a kinship for each other as they laboured in shops; few were able to leave the East End before a generation or two elapsed and those who did were exceptions to the general rule. They came to England possessing a culture and historical past in common. Though divided by regional backgrounds they managed to understand each other, in spite of differences in their native Yiddish dialect. On arrival they were generally Orthodox. In spite of obvious inter-class frictions due to diverging interests of workers, masters and landlords, the immigrants felt that they had much in common.

On this basis of social cohesiveness, a reciprocal form of help, partly philanthropic, shielded many of the poor from dependence on the élite's charity and the potential stigma involved. Much assistance in providing immediate help, temporary loans, accommodation and finding employment, was provided in the informal circle of family, friends and neighbours. Both this informal and the more formal assistance provided a strong sense of community and interdependence. The reciprocal help among this class can be understood in the light of their common background in Eastern Europe. Hannah Arendt (1968) writes:

> Humanity in the form of fraternity invariably appears historically among
> persecuted peoples and in the eighteenth century Europe it might have
> been quite natural to detect it among Jews. (Arendt 1968: 13)

Unfortunately, there is an absence of substantial records and specialized study on such *hevras* and the larger phenomena of important acts
of assistance which went quite unrecorded, although mentioned by
some observers.

In 1865, a *Jewish Chronicle* reporter was present at the reception of
applicants by the Relief Committee; he wrote about some of the cases
that appeared, for example:

> a Prussian Jew, was quite blind, and led into the room by a child of one of
> the lodgers of the house he lived in. It was his first appearance in
> Devonshire square, and he informed the Board that he had been some
> weeks in England, and was utterly destitute. On being asked how he had
> contrived to live, he replied that the poor Jews in Petticoat Lane had made
> a subscription for him, and he had received about eight shillings a week
> from the pence they had subscribed. (*Jewish Chronicle*, 6 January 1865)

The *hevras* were traditional Eastern European voluntary organizations in the East End. A *hevra* combined the function of a friendly society
with those of a religious fraternity. Its social services included: interest-
free loans, reciprocal help, social interchange and advice, assistance in
overcoming crises caused by immigration, or during illness and *shiva* (a
seven-day period of formal mourning observed after the funeral of a
close relative), and other valuable forms of support. Its religious activities comprised the operation of small synagogues, worship and study,
religious education for children and Passover supplies. The *hevras* had
their own patriarchal leaders and functioned in the Old World residential pattern.

The *hevras* were established in the East End, indigenously providing
a more gradual and viable adjustment to the new conditions of life in
England. They were characterized by more personal egalitarian
contacts; they were more 'democratic' and less hierarchic than the organizations of the élite. The hevras included strong elements of *Gemilut
Chasadim* (acts of loving kindness), personal charity which always
existed alongside communal (public) charities. *Gemilut Chasadim*
involves personal activities such as visiting the sick, helping during the
shiva, and acts of charity that cannot be reciprocated, for example,
burying the dead.

Some of the *hevras* were named after East European towns. There were some fifteen to twenty *hevras* that functioned in the 1870s in London. The services they offered negated those of the élite as they were not made conditional on modification of sociocultural behaviour and not based on deterrence and formal stipulations. The relief of the *hevras* was based on, or was closer to, the precept of traditional Jewish charity being also more discreet. Some of the *hevras* came under the influence of contemporary Friendly Societies and adopted secularized elements of compensatory insurance with some redistribution variants (in case of illness, burial and *shiva*). The *hevras* were an integral part of the working-class milieu.

The Fabian, Beatrice Webb (neé Potter), who had visited the East End in 1889, had been impressed by the tendency to clannishness of the newly arrived immigrants from Poland and their social obligations for the maintenance of the 'family and charitable relief of co-religionists' (Potter 1902: 171, 191–2).

The very existence of the *hevras* was evidence that the Board did not respond sufficiently to the needs and pressures of the Jewish population in the East End – providing assistance in an autocratic and despotic way. The élite felt that nothing should be done by the poor themselves for their collective needs. The *hevras* indicated that the estranged assistance of the Board was largely resented.

Because of the help offered by the *hevras*, together with the reciprocal assistance within the family and neighbourhood in the East End, the policies of the Board to limit immigration met only with partial success. The *hevras*, together with the Jewish trade unions, and Zionist and anarchist groups, functioned outside the institutional network of the élite, threatening its security.

The functions of the *hevras* had been ignored and denied by the élite. The establishment regarded them as a serious obstacle to a proper Anglicization of the immigrants. The *Jewish Chronicle* had suggested that the *hevras* should be eradicated (*Jewish Chronicle*, 5 December 1884). They were described by the Jewish élite as 'makeshift' *hevras* or 'bedroom' *hevras* (*Jewish Chronicle*, 3 April 1896), and were accused of duplicating services and distributing indiscriminate charity. Moreover, the *hevras* were regarded as manifesting the ingratitude of the poor. However, the *hevras* were supported by the somewhat more independent group of arrivistes within the élite headed by Samuel Montague.

In its opposition to the *hevras*, the élite was joined by the religious establishment which criticized them for undermining the Anglo-Jewish religious discipline and wasting their financial resources. The establishment attempted to suppress the *hevras* collectively and possibly individually. Williams, writing about the Manchester Board, points out that on 'at least one occasion, relief was refused to an applicant on the grounds that he was an official of a "clandestine society", a *hevra'* (Manchester Board of Guardians Minutes Book, 6 January 1875, quoted in Williams 1976: 286, 418).

The *hevras* provided social prestige to working and middle-class donors and organizers. Their leadership reflected a process of differentiation and gradual embourgeoisement in the Jewish East End, and in the working class as such. Some of the supporters of the *hevras* belonged to the middle class. Relatively few of the middle-class people joined the élite. They gained status and power in the *hevras* and other organizations created for the immigrants. They did not belong to the upwardly mobile who detached themselves from the cause of the East End working class. The financial supporters of the *hevras* were also less assimilated and many of them remained in the East End and were aware of the fundamental realities of the immigrants and their poverty. Other supporters were owners of workshops who, according to Pollins (1981), were 'at no great economic advantage over their employees' (1981: 4). Other owners of workshops, however, had exploited the labour of the newcomers or 'greeners', in other ways and, as such, were opposed to the workers' demands for better working conditions.

In their opposition to the Jewish radicals, the middle-class donors had identified themselves with the élite. The very rich members of this class were eventually accepted into the élite. Williams (1990), relating to the counterpart of this class in Manchester, styles its members *'alrightniks'* in American Yiddish slang (1990: 23, 26).

The demise of many of the *hevras* can be explained by the difficulties of the East End communities to maintain financially the numerous charities. Nor were the resources of the East-Enders sufficient to create alternative larger philanthropic institutions of their own, independent of those of the élite. However, in spite of their limited resources they permitted the working class and the poor to cling to their own institutional experiences and associations.

The decline of the *hevras* after a relatively short period of time can be explained by their shortcomings deriving from the dilemmas of voluntary social action and the emergence of more universal, collective and compulsory arrangements.

Marxism argues that the ability of the working class to realize better how the social structure influenced their lives and how to bring about change, lay generally in large workplaces. Most of the Jewish workers were employed in small sweatshops in the Jewish area of the East End.

The continued irregularities of employment deriving from the seasonal nature of the needle trade industry caused difficulties in finding a common voice to express forcefully their identities and grievances. The same irregularities made the working class continually dependent on the temporary and intermittent assistance expanded by the Board and other Jewish philanthropies.

In turn, these institutions

> were ancillary to economic arrangements, their chief function was to regulate labour . . . to absorb and control enough of the unemployed to restore order; then as turbulence subsides, the relief system contracts. (Piven and Cloward, 1971: 2)

The most popular radicals among the Jewish working class were those who recognized the need for 'immediate and tangible ameliorations in their daily life' (Kershen 1990: 43). Countering the accepted view that the poor immigrant Jews were 'pariah *Ostjuden* capitalists' (Cuddihy 1976 edn: 139–40), lacking in class consciousness and therefore harder to organize, Kershen emphasizes their class orientation. She claims that 'some sixty five per cent of the organized tailoring workforce in London was Jewish, though in total it represented only thirty per cent of the whole' (Kershen 1988: 4). In 1901, 20,000 tailors in the United Kingdom were Jewish, most of them living in London and Leeds and working in sweatshops in the Jewish areas. However, according to Finestein (1993) 'this evil was neither introduced by nor limited to Jewish employers' (1993: 189).

The City of London Jewish Tailors' Society was established already in 1867. From 1874 to 1940, about forty Jewish trade unions were set up; however, only a dozen were active for more than one year. In the context of this study, it can be assumed that the applicants to the Board were not passive receivers of the harsh policies and procedures of the Board, but that their contacts with the latter was imprinted with tensions derived from class antagonism.

Immigrants' aspirations to social mobility is regarded in some historical studies as 'false consciousness', however, whether or not it existed, such consciousness could not last too long in the light of the harsh realities of the life of immigrants in England. Therefore, except for some immigrant arrivistes, the permanence of their membership in the working class consisted of a significant number of persons over a considerable period of time.

The increasing heterogeneity and upward social mobility in the East

End decreased the opposition to the philanthropic institutions of the élite. While in the 1800s there was no real Jewish middle class in London and the majority of Jews could be regarded as poor or paupers (Green 1991: 33–4), by the 1880s, the middle class consisted of half of the community (Liebman 1975: 151, 155). The middle class adopted a emancipationist ideology of laissez-faire liberalism and individual success. The communal positions to which the middle class aspired were under the tutelage of the élite.

The intelligentsia, as a group within the larger middle class, was closed to the opinions of the domineering classes on which it had depended economically many times and, consequently, was ready to fulfil its expectations. There were some tensions between the intelligentsia and the middle classes but they manifested themselves as family quarrels, rather than class conflict. The tendency of the intelligentsia towards secularization and coordination of the synagogal social facilities was compatible with those of the leaders of the Board, to achieve overall control of the poor.

Many of the members of the Jewish middle classes, including the immigrant parvenus, created congregations west of the City and accepted the authority of the élite to gain a sense of 'free rider' comfort, but also from admiration for the élite's achievements, with a willingness to imitate its attitudes (Endelman 1980: 7).

JEWISH PHILANTHROPY AT THE TURN OF THE CENTURY: INCREMENTALISM AND SURVIVAL

The discussion now focuses on the incremental approach adopted by the Jewish élite in order to accommodate some limited demands of the growing working class in the East End.

Bermant refers to the Cousinhood as a member of that 'compact union of exclusive brethren with blood and money flowing in a small circle' (1971: 1). This group formed an oligarchic regime in the sense that it exercised its political control through a substantially close group of individuals. However, not all members of the élite were deeply or even moderately involved in philanthropic activities. Some limited themselves to the holding of honorific positions, accompanied by giving relatively large donations.

Financially and socially secure and enjoying the aura of being 'big givers' and committed philanthropists, increasingly members of the élite in the late nineteenth and early twentieth centuries lost interest in

Jewish affairs or began to consider them as marginal. They increasingly found scope in political and social activities of the host society and were caught up in the general culture of West End indifference. This process became evident to the more sensitive members of the Jewish middle class by the mid-century. A contributor to the *Jewish Chronicle*, Hertz Ben Pinhas, stressed the need for supporting elementary adult education as more important to the community 'than that so many esquires race in their chariots' (*Jewish Chronicle*, 27 March 1850).

Leopold de Rothschild (1845–1917), partner in N. M. Rothschild and Sons, bankers, Nathaniel's youngest brother, was the honorary treasurer of the Board from 1879 until his death. While he headed some important Jewish institutions, his passions were the owning and breeding of race horses, and motoring. Leopald considered the greatest moments of his life to be his election to the Jockey Club in 1891, and breaking the contemporary speed limit by six miles per hour in 1902. He initiated the formation of the Royal Automobile Club. These achievements coincided with the crisis caused by severe persecution of the Russian and Romanian Jews culminating with the Kishinev, Bessarabia pogrom. Those events in Eastern Europe were the impetus for large waves of immigrants to England. In 1881, Albert Edward (the future Edward VII) struggled through a snow storm to attend the Central Synagogue where the wedding of Leopald was officiated – the first time that a member of the English Royal family had attended a synagogal service (Black 1988: 9).

The other Rothschild brother, Alfred (1842–1918), concentrated his expenditure on eighteenth-century French art and furniture, which he collected in the country house he built at Halton. Alfred was interested in British foreign affairs, disregarding important diplomatic interventions on behalf of the outraged Jewish population in Eastern Europe that largely attracted the Gentile attention in England at this period. Alfred was not a member of the Jewish Board of Guardians nor did he gain any reputation for significant donations. Like other Rothschilds, he socialized primarily with non-Jews and figured in the circle of King Edward VII (Endelman 1990: 17–76). T. H. S. Escott reported in 1886, that the West End Jews were habitually to be seen in the drawing and dining rooms of society 'including the very *crème de la crème*, the possessors of the bluest of blue blood available' (Endelman 1990: 17–76). With such competing interests for more members of the élite, the control of the Jewish working class and the poor through paternalistic philanthropy lost much of its attractiveness in favour of national affairs.

However, as a whole, the Cousinhood represented its fundamental interests and enjoyed a virtual monopoly of power by keeping decisive control over significant community divisions throughout a network of interlocking relationships. It headed the communal institutions, philanthropic and religious, averting the challenges of the working and lower middle classes. Inside the decision-making processes, however, the Rothschilds were able to exercise control of their own, adding an additional autocratic variant to the oligarchy. The oligarchy remained self-selective and stood in an autocratic relationship to the remainder of the community. Sometimes the élite was responsive to the more vociferous demands of the poor working and middle classes in order to retain its power.

Contrary to the accepted view of a cohesive élite, Gutwein, in his book, *The Divided Elite: 1882–1917, Economics Politics and Anglo-Jewry* (1992), maintains that there were conflicting economic interests amongst the members of the élite, reflected in ideological divisions and approaches to communal issues. Gutwein, using a pluralist approach, relates primarily to the dispute between Nathaniel Rothschild and Samuel Montague. It seems that the divisions he suggests were predominantly caused by divergent views as to the strategies and tactics, through which the élite was to maintain the status quo, rather than by substantive ideological differences.

Indeed those divergences were aggravated by personal ambitions to advance careers using the conservative tendencies of the élite; they were not related to changes in the policy implementations of its institutions, such as the Board.

Gutwein (1992) does not provide evidence to prove an intrinsic divergence of interests. The elitist conflicts were ultimately resolved by cooperation and reciprocal favours, leaving out the basic interests of the immigrant poor and the working class. Moreover, the power of the élite, as a whole, was not democratized by the dispute over the domination of the élite in the East End. To the extent that compromises were reached by the conflicting members of the élite they proved profitable to the élite itself, although some marginal concessions were made to the demands of the working class and the poor. Those concessions were related to the continuation of an independent administration of their institutions, and some projects of the élite such as housing, social and cultural activities in the East End.

The Cousinhood included amongst others, the sons of the houses of Rothschild, Cohen, Samuel, Montefiore and Goldsmid. The time dedicated to philanthropic policy making and management by many important members of the élite was important in establishing a tradition of institutional control and its continuation. The regime of the Anglo-Jewish élite was a continuation of the plutocratic and oligarchic dominance prevalent in the autonomous Jewish population in the feudal countries of Europe. The rise of the élite in England coincided with the increasing religious and ethnic toleration of the Victorian age. The emancipation of the wealthy Jewish class in England and its increased acceptance into the non-Jewish society, generally weakened their contact with the community. Consequently, the ability of the community to support the poor decreased considerably, at the same time augmenting the power of those members of the élite who continued to assume leading roles in the establishment of communal institutions. The tremendous increase in the financial power of the élite and the continuous arrival of penniless immigrants widened its social differentiation.

From the 1880s, the class conflict in the East End was increasingly manifest, even though the encounter between the classes was not accompanied by a more direct and violent attempt of the working poor to actualize their power. This change was caused mainly by the mass immigration of the pauperized proletariat heavily concentrated in the East End Jewish 'ghetto'. The social and economic structure of the East European working class in the East End was the basis of a few ideological movements. The common denominator, however, was their opposition to the domineering features of the élite's supremacy. Concomitantly, during the latter part of the nineteenth century the more independent and discontented middle class, including the professional intelligentsia, started to undermine the élite's prerogatives and controls by a more gradualist strategy rather than through radical changes in the services rendered to the poor. The issue relating to the immigration policy created controversy between the élite and some parts of the middle class.

After more than half a century during which the Jewish élite persistently dominated all other Anglo-Jewish classes, especially the poor, it started to encounter more manifest opposition. The conflicting but quiescent strained relationships developed into open class struggle. Some of the public figures that dared to protest vociferously on behalf of the poor and the immigrants were the Romanian born Sephardi Chief Rabbi, Moses Gaster, and the Zionist leader, Leopold Greenberg. They did so despite political repercussions and the xenophobia caused by the mass immigration.

This immigration that the élite could not prevent, became, in the last decade of the nineteenth century and the first of the twentieth century, an important and urgent public issue, such as the Reports of the Board of Trade and the Royal Commission on Aliens. The opposition to the élite within the community and the exposure of its activities to the scrutiny of the non-Jewish nativism forced it to expand and intensify some of its social services. Efforts were made by the élite, to better some of the most abhorrent and appalling conditions of the immigrants in addition to a more intensified Anglicization. By doing this, the Jewish élite had succeeded in maintaining its control and continued to represent the community to the host society in the light of its interests.

On the larger political scene, the majority of the Jewish élite shifted its allegiance from the Liberals to the Unionist and Conservative parties, mirroring a similar trend within the non-Jewish bourgeoisie.

Samuel Montague, First Baron Swaythling (1902), was an MP for Whitechapel between 1885 and 1900, a member of the Board of Guardians (1865–83) and Chairman of the Loans Committee (1873–82). As a member of the Visiting Committee, he introduced systematic visitation. He was a relative of the Cohens and Rothschilds by marriage.

During the last part of the nineteenth century, Montague and Landau were accepted more by the Jewish population and, as such, were able to compete successfully in the East End with the prestigious position of Rothschild – although his electoral achievements were maintained at great pains. Montague's popularity can be attributed also to his political style and fluency in Yiddish. Black comments: 'he walked amongst them (the poor) better than other princes of the community who stood however benevolently at a distance, embarrassed, if not outraged, by their vulgarity' (Black 1988: 18). Allowing for his populism, it seems that his large and consistent donations to the more independent religious and social institutions in the East End contributed more to his status than his style. Through these donations Montague was able to control the small institutions created by the population in the East End.

Montague accepted communalism as a means of social control which would aid in the gradual absorption of the immigrants. Under his own supervision, he was prepared to give the East-Enders an interest in directing their small synagogues and *hevras*. Montague was orthodox and hardly an ignoramus in religious matters; he made visible his appreciation for Jewish ethics and religious values. He largely supported institutions established in the East End, including the semi-independent Jews' Temporary Shelter, in this way strengthening his parliamentary status. Through his intensive intervention, one representative of the Federation of Minor Synagogues was accepted to sit at the Board's meetings.

The opposition of the Board to the representation of the non-wealthy and non-contributory members and its reluctant readiness for very limited compromise in this respect, is reflected in the description of the meeting of the Executive Committee on the representation of the Minor Synagogues at the Board; the minutes of this meeting are worth quoting at length:

> The Executive Committee were favoured at their Meeting with the presence, as Delegates from the Federation, of Messrs. Samuel Montague, M.P., H. Landau, and I. Webber, who stated that the request to be represented at the Board, was made as much in the interest of the Board as in that of the Federation. It was contended that the proposed representation would afford the Board an increased influence over the members of the Minor Synagogues, particularly in the work of the Sanitary Committee, and also in the direction of obtaining financial support. It was also urged that the Federation of the Minor Synagogues were entitled to Representation at the Board, in the same way as the United Synagogue, and the Berkeley Street Congregation now possessed it; and that a nominal sum should be fixed to be paid by the Federation annually to the Funds of the Board.
>
> The delegates further expressed their opinion that the Federation could, through its representative, render valuable assistance in the administration of the relief given by the Board.
>
> The Executive Committee desire to impress on the Board, that the admission of a Representative from the Federation, would mark a distinctly new departure, since the Board from its foundation has been constituted entirely on the basis of representation of contributors, and not of recipients of relief; and the Committee would further state their confident belief that the latter class have never in any way suffered from any want of knowledge by the Board, of their claims and requirements.
>
> The Executive committee, however, recommend that one gentleman should be admitted to a seat at the Board, as a Representative of the Federation, and this they advise in the expectation that some greater means may be thereby afforded for influencing the poor in sanitary and other matters, and also in the hope, held out by the Delegates of the Federation, that some considerable financial support would be thus obtained from a class which at present gives very little, but which, they are led to believe, could contribute in small amounts a substantial sum to the funds of the Board. (Board of Guardians Minutes Book, 1 March 1882: 514)

The annual contribution of this Federation to the Board was regarded as a symbolic relinquishment of the stigma of dependency attached to the East-Enders. This contribution was intended to prove that the East-Enders were no longer objects of relief and control.

Montague regarded the Federation as an important mechanism for improving the conditions of the Jewish working class in the East End. With his tacit acceptance and possible encouragement, the Board was blamed for not supporting the liberation of the working class from charity by the reform of the communal policy.

Montague severely criticized both the rabbinical authorities and the West Ends' upper-middle classes for seeing the East-Enders as 'uneducated, charity cases'. In 1889 he demanded that a new synagogue proposed for the East End by Nathaniel Rothschild (in the framework of the Rothschilds' East End Scheme) should be part of a larger complex of social services, including the local unit of the Jewish Board of Guardians on which the indigenous inhabitants would be represented. In an article, published in the fiftieth anniversary issue of the *Jewish Chronicle*, entitled 'The Jewish Charitable Administration', the Board of Guardians was criticized by Montague who suggested establishing an alternative to the Board in the form of a Federation of Autonomously Operating Agencies, supervised by a central Charity Board composed of the representatives of all the independent social services. The implementation of this proposal could weaken the élite by reducing the domination exercised by the Board of Guardians in the field of philanthropy.

The publication of this critique and proposal is evidence of some democratization and politicization regarding the aims and functions of the Board in the institutional structure of the community controlled by the élite and headed by Rothschild. Notwithstanding his criticism, Montague shared the basic beliefs of the élite which meant he was not motivated to a more complete and radical politicization of the Board. Indeed, Black writes:

> these banking Titans [N. Rothschild and S. Montague] however, always set aside their struggle for pride of place within the Anglo-Jewry when great issues arose . . . the two worked harmoniously on the thorny political and organizational issues of alien immigration. They agreed on which poor and immigrant Jews should be socialised. They differed on how those things were to be accomplished. (Black 1988: 18)

At the same time, however, Black complains that Montague's monumental work among the East End poor is written 'down or off and described as a cynical manipulation' (p. 18).

Montague described himself as a 'self-made man' while, in fact, he originated from a rich Liverpool middle-class family. He believed in a laissez-faire doctrine and regarded the collectivistic trend as debilitating and enervating. He 'had little sympathy with the men who failed to get on' as his daughter wrote of him (L. H. Montague 1912: 31). Montague represented the élite's use of social Darwinism to rationalize views about their own superiority over the immigrants. By implication, the élite concluded 'logically' that capitalistically developed England was evolutionarily superior to Eastern Europe's less-developed economies. Some current historical reports describe Montague as an oppressive capitalist concealing authoritarianism behind the façade of religiosity.

Montague belonged to a parvenu group within the élite. The whole group can be regarded as representative members of a somewhat more moderate and enlightened capitalism. More sympathetic to the unmet needs of the Jewish working class in the East End, he recognized the importance of some reforms to the policies of philanthropic institutions. However, this was for the sake of the stability of the contemporary socioeconomic regime and its need for a healthier workforce.

The major quarrels between Montague and Nathaniel Rothschild ended in some 'rapprochements'. Ultimately, Montague identified himself with the general aims of the élite led by Rothschild; for instance, Montague offered Rothschild the presidency of the Federation of Minor Synagogues in the East End and accepted serving under him as vice-president. In this way Montague could share his financial responsibility to the Federation with Rothschild. Montague knew that despite the hard feelings of the East-Enders towards the establishment and its institutions, Rothschild's benevolence was highly appreciated in the East End, consequently Montague preferred to criticize the establishment rather than Rothschild personally.

Both Montague and Rothschild feared the appeal of radical doctrines for a part of the Jewish proletariat and were keen to undermine such influences. In Montague's opinion the neglect of the working class by the establishment was the cause of the rising socialism and anarchism in the East End. The Jewish radicals, on the other hand, criticized both orthodoxy and philanthropic paternalism.

Indeed, it was difficult to rival Nathaniel Rothschild, the 'Financial Lord', as he frequently acted behind the scenes, making his intentions clear only to a few close friends. In his autocratic way, Rothschild indicated to the important members of the élite what causes were to be supported, preventing them from giving to the 'unworthy' and 'impractical' ones – known as 'Rothschild's diktats'. Older members of the

Cousinhood acknowledged Rothschild as their supreme leader and his preferences were comparable to the laws. He was known to donate the largest amounts of money and was regarded in some sections as the leader of the world's Jewry.

Rothschild was consistently interested in the management of the Board and maintained his strong connections with it through his close allies, the Cohens, the presidents of the Board. Regarding philanthropies, Rothschild emphasized efficient, uniform and economical administration and avoidance of multiplication of institutions with similar aims. Rothschild wanted the poor Jews to be dealt with according to the laws of the land through the adoption of hard-hearted laissez-faire philosophy, rather than traditional sectarianism. The Chief Rabbi, Dr Nathan Adler, accepted without question the principles and practices of the Board, acting in harmonious cooperation with the Rothschilds and Cohens.

Rothschild had feared, along with other members of the élite, that highlighting differences between Jews and Gentiles could be interpreted as separatism, which he conceived to be an alien disloyal spirit, contradictory to the supreme aim of Anglicizing the Jewish poor. However, it can be argued that giving more leeway to the immigrants and allowing for a more natural process of absorption, could have forestalled much suffering by the poor.

In England, in the nineteenth century, no legislation or official policy enforced Jews to give up some of their heritage, rather such pressures were applied voluntarily on the poor by the Jewish élite in a tacit consensus between the leading English classes and the Anglo-Jewish patriciate.

It can also be argued that the large subscriptions of the Rothschilds to their preferred causes somewhat slackened the involvement of the Jewish middle classes and other subscribers, and strengthened the dependence of all the community on the richest members of the élite, preventing the establishment of more flexible institutions. The large donations increased centralized control and reduced the moral worth of many small contributors. In spite of the opposition of the East-Enders, supported by Montague and his group, and the fear of the élite that its authority was being eroded by the rising tide of poor immigrants, Rothschild's ability to control the community had remained unshaken. Rothschild had derived his power from his tremendous wealth and status as the chief spokesman for big business in Britain. In 1885 he became a peer of the realm. However, later on during the nineteenth century and at the beginning of the twentieth century, the controlling power of the Jewish élite was affected by the weakening of its economic power, based mainly on financial and commercial capital. It was also connected with the decline of family partnerships and the City of London, the decrease in the rate of industrial profits and wealth of the rich classes. This process was accompanied by the failing dogmatic thinking of the unregulated capitalistic economy.

The right to vote was an additional source of political power which became available to the working class. The constituency of Whitechapel was created in 1884 following Gladstone's Reform Bill. It was made possible by some increase in the electoral power of the naturalized Jewish voters in Whitechapel, mostly Yiddish speaking, almost all of whom worked for Jewish employers, orthodox by religious affiliation and concerned with issues of Jewish charity. By the end of the nineteenth century half of the Jews in Whitechapel had the right to vote comprising a quarter of all the Jews in London, and in 1885 Montague became the Liberal MP for Whitechapel. In the general election of 1900 the Rothschilds supported at Whitechapel the restrictionist, David Hope Kyd, who belonged to a group of Conservative MPs who made the mostly Jewish immigration the predominant issue of their campaigns (Alderman 1989: 39).

Despite his basic subordination to the policy of the élite as dominated by Rothschild, Montague represented a somewhat divergent ideological current within the élite. He proposed a more decentralized social and religious policies of the community and more progressive taxation. During the period that followed the mass immigration until his death, Montague was considered the champion of the Jewish working and poor classes and their small synagogues in the East End. He was the foremost opponent to the extreme conservativism represented by Nathaniel Rothschild and his ally and brother-in-law, Lionel Louis Cohen who, from 1869 until his death in 1887 was the president of the Board and of the United Synagogue.

Montague was blamed by Rothschild and other members of the élite for causing intra-communal class antagonism in order to gain undeserved popularity. He supported some of the moderate demands of the Jewish working class for improved working conditions while, at the same time, placating their more radical ones. The strategy of Montague was to obtain some compromises between the Jewish workers and their employers. The election of Montague, as the MP for Whitechapel, politicized the issue connected with the organization of Jewish institutions dominated by the élite, including the Board of Guardians. In 1882, Montague advocated a more sensitive and humane policy, regarding the Board as responsible for all the poor Jews in London, that is, according to the original definition of its purpose by the synagogues. However, the Board insisted on being responsible only towards those who belonged already to the community. In the light of the consensus between Montague and the élite to a significantly reduced immigration, the controversy about the scope of the Board regarding new immigrants, lost much of its meaning.

The institutions established by the élite and those initiated by the poor were characterised by reciprocal suspicions and fears. The absence of a more personal contact between the élite and the poor permitted the emergence of the intermediary upper-middle-class group headed by Montague. The advent of this group prevented a complete split and further polarization of the community. This intermediate group consisted of persons who served in secondary positions on the Jewish Board of Guardians for a considerable period of time before attaining social acceptance by the élite and the first generation immigrant, Herman Landau.

The instrumental contacts of this group with the poor, and their organizational ability in providing communal and welfare services, as well as financing them, were motivated by the basic interests of the wealthy class. So, in spite of being more sensitive to the social needs of the immigrant poor in comparison with the élite, this group did not encourage the development of the working class as a political force which could replace the institutional structure.

Such a different framework could solve the most pressing problems connected with the status and welfare of the immigrant poor. As such, the emerging upper-middle-class intermediate group acted as a conservative force restraining the resentment and discontent in the East End and enabling the Board of Guardians to continue its restrictionist policy undisturbed.

Concomitantly, the intermediary group enabled the élite to make the institutional changes needed to accommodate the alternative institutions established in the East End and, in this way, to avoid the complete realignment of the separated social formations. Those institutional changes occurred through an incremental process which included the expansion of the services offered to the poor immigrants by the Board, and some concessions to the initiative of the middle classes and the poor themselves.

The other factor that supported the incremental processes rather than a basic realignment was the motivation of the élite to placate the resentment against the Board's functions, especially with regard to the immigrants, so as to prevent the expansion of radical and leftist activities in the East End.

It was this intermediary middle-class group of second and third generation natives that, although sometimes critical of community services dominated by the élite, had supported institutional complementarity rather than the competition of a divisive process. This deliberate and conscious choice of the intermediary group had been dictated by the overlapping interests with the élite. The criticism by the intermediary group of the élite, combined with the availability of models of expanded social concerns on the contemporary national scene, increased its flexibility and enabled it to maintain the long-established and enduring mechanism of control.

The survival of the Jewish Board of Guardians at the end of the nineteenth century and beyond it, can therefore, be explained also by its readiness to adopt deliberately a general policy of gradualism, in order to retain the existing institutional structure.

The pragmatic approach of the élite towards the poor and its readiness to accept the intermediary intervention of the upper middle class has been analysed, showing that this approach enabled the Board and the Jewish élite to survive this stormy period of mass immigration.

Conclusions

In Victorian Britain, one of the most wealthy and powerful empires that has ever existed, the Jewish élite accumulated tremendous wealth. Social and religious tolerance permitted it to translate its economic influence into Jewish political power. The confluence of this power external to the Jewish community, with significant internal influence and the symbiotic relationship between them, created an unprecedented mechanism of quasi-official controls over the poor. In its known non-interventionist outlook, the British government issued no charter to legalize the Jewish communal organizations. The Jewish community remained a voluntary corporate body, comparable to the other religious groups which were not members of the established Church. Up until the Jewish mass immigration in the 1880s, the manifest interest of the British government in Jewish affairs was minimal. Nor were national or local authorities interested to establish collective responsibility for Jewish vagrancy, delinquency and poverty, as initiated by the scheme of Colquhoun and van Oven at the very beginning of the nineteenth century. This scheme proposed to give the Jewish élite legal power over the poor – a privilege granted by the old regimes in Europe.

Whereas it was a decree issued by Napoleon I which placed Jewish notables in positions of responsibility for the French Jewry as an instrument of state control, the power of the Anglo-Jewish élite, seized within the Jewish community, permitted it to fulfil 'voluntarily' the controlling functions. The liberty that the Jewish élite enjoyed in Britain was clearly differentiated from the establishment of Napoleon's consistory system in France, with its manifest tendency of productivization of the French Jewry and the obligatory regulation of religious and communal methods under the state's supervision.

The Jewish élites on the Continent had exercised authority and power in the internal life of their communities, such as the nexus of welfare and charitable institutions (Katz 1993: 90). Philanthropy was regarded as commendable and highly desirable, because the fulfilment of the basic needs of the poor was regarded by the *hallachah* as a matter of rights.

In reality, however, the deterioration of the communal arrangements based on mandatory elements and their substitution by voluntaristic arrangements, aggravated the inadequacy of the relief given to the poor. Other socioeconomic and political factors contributing to the widespread poverty amongst the Jewish population, increased the importance of optionality, contingency, generosity or mere charity, which permitted Jewish individuals and groups to shirk their mandatory duties and the use of their surplus wealth for philanthropic purposes. This change considerably increased the discretionary power of the wealthy class over the way their money was distributed, resulting in a more preferential assistance to protégés and impoverished previous middle-class members. This tradition was continued in London.

The division of the community along such lines had crystallized before the beginning of the nineteenth century. During the nineteenth century the élite gradually achieved great wealth and considerable influence. As such, it came to share many of the economic and political interests of the wealthy classes in Britain.

The élite's economic and political interests were interrelated with its philanthropic involvements. The main interest of the élite was expanding business and profits, undisturbed by the impact of economic and social problems related to Jewish poverty and immigration; that is, they feared Jewish poverty could bring about negative reactions from the host community, detrimental to its own position. However, a significant outburst of anti-Jewish feeling did not occur until the mass immigration of the 1880s, and the Jewish élite continued to prosper financially in spite of the anti-alien movement created at that time.

The Jewish élite had continuously claimed and attempted to convince the other elements of the community that it represented the whole Anglo-Jewry. This view was accepted prima facie and amplified by the middle classes in the host society.

The Jewish wealthy and middle classes had adopted extravagant ways of life and distanced themselves from the concentration of the Jewish working class in the East End. While the Jewish élite was strongly influenced by the approaches to the poor generally prevalent in British society, the Jewish poor classes were continually 'strengthened' by the import of traditional approaches to charity brought over by the waves of immigrants and, as such, were less influenced by the parallel English classes.

The élite showed eagerness to adopt individualistic and laissez-faire concepts which were compatible with its economic interests. The whole ideological climate was used by the élite to justify its long-term policy towards the poor. However, the élite also claimed that it continued to apply universal and Judaic principles of morality and charity. In this way, the élite had lost sight of the collectivistic aspects of traditional charity, *tzedakah*. To the extent that some awareness existed of the significance of such aspects, the élite preferred to omit them and did not display the flexibility needed to synthesize Jewish tradition and contemporary social philosophy. Rather, the Jewish élite swallowed 'ready made' philosophy whole. Sometimes, the members of the Jewish élite selected, from the context of the tradition of Jewish charities, some parts that corresponded with their interests as evidence of their continued fidelity to Jewish tradition. Beyond this level, no consideration or analysis was thought necessary. After the separation from the synagogues' relief funds, with the establishment of the Board, there was no question whether the work of Jewish charity should be exercised according to Judaic principles. It was assumed that no contradictions existed between the *hallachah* and contemporary philosophy and that they were syntonic and interchangeable in all aspects. By equating loyalty to the philanthropic organization with loyalty to Judaism, each institution claimed legitimacy as a continuation of historical Judaic tradition.

The Jewish élite had also been attracted to an optimistic view of a liberal and progressive society which was basically individualistic (especially under the influence of the Jewish Enlightenment). As far as the relief of the poor was concerned, the class interests of the élite overrode ethnic solidarity.

However, the threatening result of the disorganization of Jewish charity during the first half of the nineteenth century, caused by institutional fragmentation, had moved the Jewish Ashkenazic élite (belonging to three separate synagogues) to consider joint action. Several times such considerations waned when the anxieties of the élite over impending calamities subsided temporarily.

Institutional arrangements for comprehensive control had been proposed by members of the élite, in the form of different schemes which did not come into fruition until the establishment of the Board.

From the beginning of the nineteenth century and until the founding of the Board in 1859, the schemes proposed were to be financed mainly by special taxes on Jews. However, the Jewish élite was not ready to accept such an additional obligatory burden. Moreover, the élite feared that such mandatory arrangements might 'invite' the interference of the state or local government in its affairs. The tendency of the Jewish élite to remain independent was characteristic also of non-Jewish voluntary associations. An additional factor that can explain the failure of the schemes was the fear of the élite that, if successful, they could attract even greater numbers of immigrants.

The disorganization of the Jewish charities, reflected in the lack of a competent and permanent mechanism able to assess and relieve the needs of the poor, acted intermittently, at least, as a deterrent to immigration. The less organized the institutions were, the weaker was their appeal to potential immigrants and transmigrants from the Continent. At the beginning of the century, such factors were underestimated by Colquhoun, a police official and follower of Bentham.

The élite had been interested in controlling the Jewish poor and immigrants on a voluntary basis, assuming, however, a quasi-official status with respect to the host authorities. Benzion Dinur claims that attempts by the Jewish wealthy class to pre-empt the prerogatives of Jewish autonomy were a long-standing tradition.

By the late 1850s, the Jewish élite could no longer evade the results of disorganization. Moreover, its increasing political emancipation implied a fulfilment of the expectations of the host society to uphold social order, that is, the solution of the severe social problems of the Jewish poor. The activities of the Board were supposed to replace the haphazard synagogal arrangements which had operated formerly. Instead, the poor, and especially the 'foreign' poor, were to be subordinated to the secular (but not secularist) Board.

The Board generally reflected the views of élite members, who financed its activities and assumed leadership positions within its hierarchy. Over more than half a century, the Board drew its power from a number of such members of the élite who were continuously recruited and integrated into its activities. The ability of the Board to coordinate the responses of its wealthy members can help explain its endurance.

The watchwords of the élite's conservatism were control and efficiency. Both these tendencies combined to maintain the Board's monopolistic status in dominating communal philanthropy and, generally, receiving unquestioning deference until the 1880s. To the extent that immigration continued, it forced the Board to confront unlimited need that required corresponding acts of succour. From its foundation the Board negated the positive rights of the newly arrived immigrants by refusing to be the primary and immediate respondent to their needs. It did so by a rule instituted at the establishment of the Board. The newly arrived immigrants were refused any assistance for a period of six months, which meant that the interventions of the Board excluded extreme distress in the cases of new immigrants, who were often in urgent need of assistance.

Regarding to immigration, which was the main issue, the Board had been faced with two extreme alternatives: the first was to accept the positive duties derived from the needs of the immigrants according to the *hallachah* and to significantly increase its burden; the second extreme was the laissez-faire approach, that is, complete indifference. The 'middle way' that the Board chose, by imposing the Six Months Rule on newly arrived immigrants, reflected that it was less than willing to give the immigrants the initial help that they needed. Excluding new immigrants from relief for a period of six months in order to make them 'malleable' and easy to repatriate or transmigrate and for deterring potential immigrants abroad, was a sort of control by inaction. However, the lack of a more immediate and comprehensive control over the newly arrived immigrants, encouraged the expansion of the institutions created by the lower and middle classes as alternatives to those of the élite.

While the Board had insisted on its continuous responsibility for all the Metropolitan Jewish poor, it was, in fact, structured to take action only in a relatively small number of cases. The others were regarded as suitable to be handed over to the workhouses and assisted periodically in cases of emergency. The latter category included those that the Board was unable to transmigrate or repatriate.

At the beginning of the nineteenth century, the Jewish élite had preferred to maintain its own poor, seldom allowing them to apply for parochial relief, although, as ratepayers, they were entitled to claim it. The Anglo-Jewish leaders had felt that such applications would cause serious antagonistic reactions from the British public. Moreover, dietary laws had prevented the Jewish élite from placing the poor in the workhouses. Throughout its existence, the Board continued to be alert to the contemporary definitions of the problems relating to poverty and proposed solutions in an attempt to maintain 'a good place' on the British philanthropic scene. In this process, however, the Board had been selective, opting to follow the conservative trends of this philanthropy.

Since its establishment, the Board was characterized by a tendency to take on the organizational characteristics of its host environment, including the Poor Law arrangements. From the middle of the nineteenth century, members of the Jewish middle class had gained experience as Poor Law Guardians, elected as individuals in their parishes of domicile (Alderman 1989: 3). From the early 1830s, the Jewish élite had been increasingly interested to make use of the Poor Law arrangements, partly as a means through which the Jewish poor could be deterred and controlled. The voluntary charities, working along the lines of the statutory Jewish élite, had been strongly influenced by the strict principles of the New Poor Law.

In 1869, with the establishment of the Charity Organization Society and the publication of the Gochen Minutes, the Board joined the English sectors, re-emphasizing the need for deterrence, especially for those considered 'undeserving'. Feeling much more secure, the Jewish élite had gradually renounced the principle of 'Jews take care of their own'. The élite continued to support the poor from its own resources, however, at the same time, it increasingly attempted to harness the central and local authorities, shifting a considerable part of the burden onto them.

In the twenty-year-old struggle, although only partly successful, the Jewish élite recruited the most politically influential and able persons to follow the developments of statutory provision and to obtain as many concessions as possible from the Poor Law authorities. This strife reflected the importance that the Board attributed to the use of the unions' policies and arrangements to deter those considered paupers, 'unwanted' immigrants, and those that the Board regarded as recalcitrant or otherwise to be isolated or penalized.

In this struggle, the Board used its quasi-official status to bring about significant legal changes affecting the lives of the poor. In fact, the fears of the Poor Law authorities that they might attract immigrants and have to assume increasing responsibilities for them instead of the Board, was the main obstacle to making extended use of the workhouses.

It can also be assumed that the alternative Jewish Workhouse – an old-age home, established by a member of the middle class in direct opposition to the policy of the Board – had some restraining effect on the Board in this matter. The relatively small number of Jewish poor in the workhouses is evidence of their independence and self-sufficiency. Their ability to immigrate can be seen as a sign of the power that they possessed as a group that had uprooted itself in order to escape danger and to improve its social or material situation. The reciprocal help between Jews, and the small institutions that they established, had been the main oppositional element *vis-à-vis* the Board.

The ability of the immigrants to receive help from such institutions as *hevras* and other sources, had made the Board's Six Month Rule partly unworkable. Their power was reflected also in their ability to stand aloof or to be minimally involved with the mechanism designed by the élite, paying lip service to the élite's notions and its attempts to conceal aspects of the social realities of the poor.

By providing for the education of the children of the poor, the élite facilitated a continuation of their religious and ethnic life as well as a preparation for integration into the host society. The implementation of the Board's policy in the field of education had manifested paternalistic social planning. In their formative years, the children of the poor were considered to be more malleable, and as such capable of being influenced by the precepts of the élite. According to this concept, the parents were less educable than their children and, as such, beyond this kind of help. Together with educational institutions, the Board had attempted to impart discipline, obedience, punctuality, cleanliness, thrift and gratefulness. The conservative programme of Anglicization meant that the Jewish working class was to be imbued with the values of English citizens who knew their correct place in the hierarchical order.

Ambitious and rapid Anglicization meant that immigrants were expected to give up their culture and language. Elimination of the original culture as a means of adaptation left the immigrants with few resources of their own and caused unnecessary alienation from both themselves as well as from the dominant élite. Under the influence of the élite through the contemporary Jewish media, the deficiencies attributed to the poor, sometimes described in subhuman terms, became a matter of middle and upper-class consensus, and therefore, a 'truism' permitting unrestricted generalization and accusation. The emphasis of the institutions of the élite had been on searching for personal defects and imposters rather than identifying the underlying conditions that generated poverty or were an obstacle in the adjustment of the new immigrants. This tendency largely continued until the end of the century and in some respects, beyond it.

Founded for the relief of the 'strange' poor only and for the purpose of eradicating mendicity, the Board had engaged in continuous efforts to prove its ability to assist the native and long-settled poor, including the stipendiary poor of the three city synagogues. The Board presented a systematic and more humane approach to the 'better classes' of the poor. Such an approach was characteristic of other philanthropic societies before the establishment of the Board, and reflected contemporary developments in the field.

In the distribution of its resources, the Board evidenced clear continuous preferential treatment for the better classes of the poor, amongst them impoverished members of the middle class. This preferential treatment largely contradicted the other claims of equity with regard to the criteria for the relief of the poor.

The elements of the Board's planning that can be discerned, give evidence of preferential provision and services for members of select small groups, especially children of poor, previously middle-class people, promising healthy young unburdened by family responsibilities. This planning was the alternative offered as an immediate solution for the contemporary acute and chronic poverty of the Jewish masses. Consequently, the criteria for eligibility were based mainly on the future potential of the applicants rather than the intensity of their present distress. This withdrawing policy allotted very limited resources to the sick, the handicapped and the widespread multi-children families.

The reluctance of the Jewish élite to relate to the needs of the major categories of Jewish poor and to use the relatively tranquil years before the 1880s for realistic preparation based on a consistent, well-articulated policy, caused severe suffering to the immigrants and an anti-alien movement with anti-Semitic overtones. It is argued that those two developments could have been avoided and that the élite had the financial resources to do so.

The élite attributed the prevention of a more severe anti-Semitic outbreak to its restrictionist policy, implemented by large-scale continuous transmigration and repatriation, that is, exporting the problem, as well as to other measures of preventing immigration, such as the Six Months Rule. However, the outbreak could have been avoided by more constructive and humane means.

In addition to the regular subsidies received from the synagogues, the Board recruited additional resources, mainly from the wealthiest members of the élite, in this way strengthening their control over the Board's policy. Those resources, however, were far from being sufficient for a fairer redistribution of resources. The major shortcoming of the Board was not that it was too generous but that it was too restrictive in its expenditure and was dominated by an exaggerated prudence. The Board often expressed its fear of becoming the victim of its own generosity, encouraging pauperism and immigration. However, the Board recognized that most of the immigrants fitted the Smilesian prototype and became economically independent within a relatively short period of time after their arrival in Britain.

In instituting a policy of under-provision from its foundation, the Board found justification in the ideas derived from the classical economists and laissez-faire economics. According to those philosophies, relief interfered with the supply and demand in the labour market, pushing down production and profits. In this context the Board regarded human misery as aggravated by an unwise liberality, consequently, the meagre assistance provided to the poor was considered the root of all the problems.

The most controversial issue that faced the Board was the influx of immigrants and the relief of those that settled in London in spite of all the measures taken by the Board and its allied organizations. The immigration to Britain was an integral part of a west-bound movement that comprised millions of people and was caused by expanding economics and their consequent exigencies. As far as Jewish immigration was concerned, those general circumstances were aggravated by additional political discrimination and economic exploitation. Obviously, the restrictionist policies of the Board could not have any serious impact on such forces; the Board was unable to stop immigration in spite of all its efforts in this direction. Moreover, in the final analysis, the lack of statutory measures which could prevent immigration expressed the interests of the ruling industrial class (of which the Jewish élite was an integral part) in a continuous stream of cheap labour, lowering prices and motivating people to work even harder for minimal wages.

The dilemma of the Board and other Jewish charities managed by the élite was also how to provide the minimal necessities of life to the poor immigrants without creating, by this very relief, the slightest incentive for them to remain in England; how to encourage transmigration rather than integration. Still another dilemma that faced the Board and other Jewish institutions was with regard to the use of the legal power of the state to prohibit immigration of Jewish poor, as opposed to the continuation of the limitations instituted by the Board in its quasi-official capacity.

In this context, to the extent that the Board accepted responsibilities for aiding the immigrants, it did so in spite of finding them distasteful and unwanted. Rather than adapting itself to the growing needs and demands caused by the immigration, the Board attempted to maintain a status quo, hampering as much as it could the initiatives of the other classes to create their own alternative institutions. The conservatism of the Board was also evident in its reluctance to relate to the collective problems of the poor. The crises of immigration were not individual ones and, as such, they required large-scale interventions to correct the institutional structure that generated or exacerbated the situation of the poor; for example, only towards the end of the nineteenth century was the first model housing project erected by Rothschild.

The institutions established by the élite and those initiated by the poor were characterized by reciprocal suspicions and fears. From the beginning of the nineteenth century and even before, the Jewish élite was afraid of the large number of Jewish poor demanding and pressing for relief en masse, resenting their power, despite the fact that they did not belong to any formal organization. On the other hand, the élite regarded with apprehension the significant number of poor who did not apply to the Board and the other institutions.

The confrontation between the élite and the poor was to a large extent muted, sometimes latent, however always real. After the 1880s, the large waves of immigrants added, in part, to the conflict leading to the establishment of social and religious institutions of the immigrants in the East End, creating some redistribution of power in the community. The tenacity of the élite in defending its position can be explained by its ability to avert a deeper conflict with the working and lower-middle class in the East End. This was done by keeping their institutions from becoming completely independent and more antagonistic to those of the establishment. Using flexible tactics, the élite was able to incorporate some of those institutions, albeit allowing them some independence. Some of them became mechanisms of control of the élite itself when the latter succeeded in bringing them into its orbit by financing their expenditure.

Within certain limits, such institutions were allowed to express class protests publicly (such as those headed by Samuel Montague). When confronted with opposition, the Board was ready to compromise on partial or temporary control, such as in the case of the Jews' Temporary Shelter, and to limit itself to the control of some aspects of the functions of the institutions, tactically waiting in its typical pragmatic way for opportunities to expand its control. According to Lukes, actual conflict is not necessary; 'the most effective and insidious use of power is to prevent such conflict existing' (Steven Lukes 1973: 23).

The élite was not able to eliminate the conditions that created independent organizations in the East End but had forestalled larger and deeper immigrant conflict and possibly another order of social arrangement. This process by which the élite maintained its institution was possibly through the extensive financial resources that the members of the élite and especially Rothschild, consented to donate for different social, educational and religious projects in the East End.

Sustaining its power, the élite was able to do '"the defining", to determine what was considered a social problem, to shape legislation, etc.' (George and Wilding 1976: 2). In this process, the Board served the interests of the élite in the most crucial issues of immigration, transmigration and repatriation, by determining policies and carrying them out through its mechanisms. The Board was instrumental in maintaining the political stability of the élite by ameliorating some of the most severe and aggravating situations of the poor in the East End.

The absence of a more open and direct contact between the élite and the poor had permitted the emergence of the intermediary upper-middle-class group headed by Montague. The advent of this group prevented a complete split and further polarization of the community. This intermediary group consisted of persons who served in secondary positions on the Jewish Board of Guardians for a considerable period of time before attaining social acceptance by the élite and the first generation immigrant, Herman Landau. The instrumental contacts of this group with the poor and their organizational ability in providing communal and welfare services, as well as financing them, had been motivated by the basic interests of the wealthy class. So, in spite of being more sensitive to the social needs of the immigrant poor in comparison with the élite, this group did not encourage the development of the working class as a political force which could replace the institutional structure. Such a different framework could solve the most pressing problems connected with the status and welfare of the immigrant poor. As such, the emerging upper-middle-class intermediary group had acted as a conservative force, restraining the resentment and discontent in the East End and enabling the Board of Guardians to continue its restrictionist policy undisturbed.

Concomitantly, the intermediary group enabled the élite to make the institutional changes needed to accommodate the alternative institutions established in the East End and, in this way, to avoid the complete realignment of the separated social formations. Those institutional changes occurred through an incremental process which included the expansion of the services offered to the poor immigrants by the Board, and some concessions to the initiative of the middle classes and the poor themselves.

The other factor that had supported the incremental processes, rather than a basic realignment, was the motivation of the élite to placate the resentment against the Board's functions, especially with regard to the immigrants, in order to prevent the expansion of the radical and leftist activities in the East End.

It was this intermediary middle-class group of second- and third-generation natives that, although sometimes critical of the community services predominated by the élite, had supported institutional complementarity rather than the competition of a divisive process. This deliberate conscious choice of the intermediary group had been dictated by the overlapping interests with the élite. The criticism by the intermediary group of the élite, combined with the availability of models of expanded social concerns on the contemporary national scene. The increasing demands for restricting aggressive economic behaviour, introducing collective social morality by state interference for mitigating severe social distress, had flexed the position of the élite and made it possible to maintain the long established and enduring mechanism of control. The survival of the Jewish Board of Guardians at the end of the nineteenth century, and beyond it, can therefore be explained also by its readiness to deliberately adopt a general policy of gradualism in order to retain the existing institutional structure.

The lower middle class and the working class did not possess sufficient resources and political experience to act by itself or in collaboration with the middle class to create an independent alternative to the Board. The establishment of such alternative services could have activated the latent potential for the polarization of the community.

Despite the general decline of the élite because of the decrease in its financial power, the oligarchic regime of the community continued. Between 1900 and 1947, three of the presidents of the Board were descendants of Levi Barnet Cohen (1740–1808), and no one served less than seven years. The same family had controlled the Board since its foundation.

As discussed in the Introduction, philanthropy has been treated in this book as a collective action of a group or a class, reflecting its main interests. The main argument is that the philanthropic activities of the Anglo-Jewish élite and its principal mechanism was aimed at controlling and regulating the Jewish poor.

The evidence shows that under the influence of contemporary individualistic ideologies, the Jewish philanthropic élite was at once limited and punitive. The ability of the Jewish philanthropy to absorb external influences was potentially a progressive feature to the extent that it proved conducive to improving the situation of the Jewish poor.

The Anglo-Jewish philanthropists of the nineteenth century were part of a wider society, the predominant ideology of which contributed to the individualism of their approach, further aggravated by the perceived threat presented by immigration and its concomitant problems. In other circumstances, the more collective strands of Jewish tradition might have been more in evidence.

Appendix I: Excerpts from Laws Concerning Gifts for the Poor – Mishneh Torah by Rabbi Moshe ben Maimon (Maimonides, 1135–1204)

Book Seven – The Book of Agriculture
Chapters: VII, IX, X
[Including The Eight Degrees of Charity]
Translated from the Hebrew by
Isaac Klein
(copyright Yale University Press, New Haven and London, 1979)
(All emphases are in the original translation)

CHAPTER VII

1. It is a positive commandment to give alms to the poor of Israel, according to what is fitting for them, if the giver can afford it, as it is said, *Thou shalt surely open thy hand unto him* (Deut. 15:8), and again, *Then thou shalt uphold him; as a stranger and a settler shall he live with thee . . . that thy brother may live with thee* (Lev. 25:35–36).

2. He who seeing a poor man begging turns his eyes away from him and fails to give him alms, transgresses a negative commandment, as it is said, *Thou shalt not harden thy heart, nor shut thy hand from thy needy brother* (Deut. 15:7).

3. You are commanded to give the poor man according to what he lacks. If he has no clothing, he should be clothed. If he has no house furnishings, they should be bought for him. If he has no wife, he should be helped to marry. If it is a woman, she should be given in marriage. Even if it had been his wont to ride a horse, with a manservant running in front of him, and he has now become poor and has lost his possessions, one must buy him a horse to ride and a

manservant to run before him, as it is said, *Sufficient for his need in that which he wanteth* (Deut. 15:8). You are thus obligated to fill his want; you are not, however, obligated to restore his wealth.

4. If an orphan is about to be wed, one must first rent a house for him, spread a bed for him, and provide all his furnishings, and only then have him marry a wife.

5. If the poor man comes forth and asks for enough to satisfy his want, and if the giver is unable to afford it, the latter may give him as much as he can afford. How much is that? In choice performance of this religious duty, up to one-fifth of his possessions; in middling performance, up to one-tenth of his possessions; less than this brands him as a person of evil eye. At all times one should not permit himself to give less than one-third of a shekel per year. He who gives less than this has not fulfilled this commandment at all. Even a poor man who lives entirely on alms must himself give alms to another poor man.

6. If a poor man unknown to anyone comes forth and says, "I am hungry; give me something to eat," he should not be examined as to whether he might be an impostor – he should be fed immediately. If, however, he is naked and says, "Clothe me," he should be examined as to possible fraud. If he is known, he should be clothed immediately according to his dignity, without any further inquiry.

7. One must feed and clothe the heathen poor together with the Israélite poor, for the sake of the ways of peace. In the case of a poor man who goes from door to door, one is not obligated to give him a large gift, but only a small one. It is forbidden, however, to let a poor man who asks for alms to go empty-handed, just so you give him at least one dry fig, as it is said, *O let not the oppressed turn back in confusion* (Ps. 74:21).

8. A poor man traveling from one place to another must be given not less than one loaf of bread that sells for a pondion when the price of wheat is one sela' per four se'ah. We have already explained the value of all measures. If he lodges for the night, he must be given a mattress to sleep on and a pillow to put under his head, as well as oil and pulse for his repast. If he stays over the Sabbath, he must be provided with food for three meals as well as oil, pulse, fish, and vegetables. If he is known, he must be supplied according to his dignity.

9. If a poor man refuses to accept alms, one should get around him by making him accept them as a present or a loan. If, on the other hand, a wealthy man starves himself because he is so niggardly with his money that he would not spend of it on food and drink, no attention need be paid to him.

10. He who refuses to give alms, or gives less than is proper for him, must be compelled by the court to comply, and must be flogged for disobedience until he gives as much as the court estimates he should give. The court may even seize his property in his presence and take from him what is proper for him to give. One may indeed pawn things in order to give alms, even on the eve of the Sabbath.

11. A munificent person who gives alms beyond what he can afford, or denies himself in order to give to the collector of alms so that he would not be put to shame, should not be asked for contributions to alms. Any alms collector who humiliates him by demanding alms from him will surely be called to account for it, as it is said, *I will punish all that oppress them* (Jer. 30:20).

13. A poor man who is one's relative has priority over all others, the poor of one's own household have priority over the other poor of his city, and the poor of his city have priority over the poor of another city, as it is said, *Unto thy poor and needy brother, in thy land* (Deut. 15:11).

CHAPTER IX

1. In every city inhabited by Israélites, it is their duty to appoint from among themselves well-known and trustworthy persons to act as alms collectors, to go around collecting from the people every Friday. They should demand from each person what is proper for him to give and what he has been assessed for, and should distribute the money every Friday, giving each poor man sustenance sufficient for seven days. This is what is called "alms fund."

2. They must similarly appoint other collectors to gather every day, from each courtyard, bread and other eatables, fruits, or money from anyone who is willing to make a free-will offering at that time. They should distribute these toward that same evening among the poor, giving therefrom to each poor man his sustenance for the day. This is what is called "alms tray."

3. We have never seen nor heard of an Israélite community that does not have an alms fund. As for an alms tray, there are some localities where it is customary to have it, and some where it is not. The custom widespread today is for the collectors of the alms fund to go around every day, and to distribute the proceeds every Friday.

4. On fast days food should be distributed to the poor. If on any fast day the people eat all through the night without distributing alms to the poor, they are accounted the same as if they had shed blood, and it is they who are referred to in the verse in the Prophets, *Righteousness lodged in her, but now murderers* (Isa. 1:21).

When does this apply? When the poor are not given bread and such fruit as is eaten with bread, for example, dates and grapes. If, however, the alms collectors merely delay the distribution of money or wheat, they are not accounted shedders of blood.

5. Contributions to the alms fund must be collected jointly by two persons, because a demand for money may not be addressed to the community by less than two collectors. The money collected may, however, be entrusted for safe-keeping to one person. It must be distributed by three persons, because it is analogous to money involved in a civil action, inasmuch as they must give to each poor man enough for his needs over the week. The alms tray, on the other hand, must be collected by three collectors, since the contribution to it is not set, and must be distributed likewise by three distributors.

6. Contributions to the alms tray are to be collected every day, those for the alms fund each Friday. The alms tray is to provide for the poor of the whole world, while the alms fund is to provide for the poor of the town alone.

7. The residents of the town may use alms fund moneys for the alms tray, or vice versa, or divert them to any other public purpose that they may choose, even if they had not so stipulated when they collected them . . .

8. Alms collectors are not permitted to separate one from the other in the market place, except as one turns to enter a gate while the other turns to enter a shop, in order to collect contributions.

12. One who has resided in the city for thirty days may be compelled to contribute to the alms fund, together with the other residents of the city. If he has resided there for three months, he may be compelled to contribute to the alms tray. If he has resided there for six months, he may be compelled to contribute to the clothing given to the poor of the city. If he has resided there for nine months, he may be compelled to contribute to the burial of the poor and to the other expenses connected therewith.

13. He who has food sufficient for two meals is forbidden to partake of the alms tray. If he has food sufficient for fourteen meals, he may not partake of the alms fund. He who has two hundred zuz, even if he does not use them to engage in trade, or he who has fifty zuz and uses them in trade, may not take of the gleanings, the forgotten sheaf, the corner crop, or the poor man's tithe. If he has two hundred denar less one, he may partake of all of these, even if a thousand persons give them to him at the same time. If he has money in his hand, but owes it as a debt or has it mortgaged against his wife's ketubbah, he is still permitted to take of these gifts to the poor.

14. In the case of a needy poor man who has his own courtyard and home furnishings, even if these include utensils of silver and gold, he may not be compelled to sell his house and his furnishings; rather he is permitted to accept alms, and it is a religious duty to give him alms. To what furnishings does this apply? To eating and drinking vessels, clothing, mattresses, and the like. If, however, he has other silver and gold utensils, such as a strigil, a pestle, and the like, he should first sell them and buy less expensive ones. When does this apply? Before he comes to ask for public assistance. If he has already asked for it, he must be compelled to sell his vessels and buy less expensive ones and only then may he be given alms.

15. If a householder traveling from town to town runs out of funds while still on the road and finds himself with nothing to eat, he is allowed to partake of the gleanings, the forgotten sheaf, the corner crop, and the poor man's tithe, as well as to benefit from alms, and when he reaches his home he is not obligated to repay, since at that particular time he was in fact a poor man. To what can this be compared? To a poor man who has become wealthy, and who is not obligated to repay past assistance.

16. A person who owns houses, fields, and vineyards, which, if sold during the rainy season would fetch a low price, but if held back until the summer would fetch a fair price, may not be compelled to sell them, and should be maintained out of the poor man's tithe up to half the worth of these properties. He should not feel pressed to sell at the wrong time.

17. If at the time when other people are buying such properties at a high price, he cannot find anyone to buy his property except at a low price, seeing that he is hard pressed to sell, he may not be compelled to sell, but is rather allowed to continue eating out of the poor man's tithe until he can sell at a fair price, with everyone aware that he is not pressed to sell.

18. If the amount collected for a poor man to provide adequately for his wants exceeds his needs, the surplus belongs to him. The rule is as follows: The surplus of what was collected for the poor must be used for other poor; the surplus of what was collected for the ransoming of captives must be used to ransom other captives; . . .

19. If a poor man contributes a perutah to the alms tray or to the alms fund, it should be accepted. If he does not, he may not be constrained to do so. If when given new garments he returns to the distributors his worn-out ones, they too should be accepted, and if he does not return them, he may not be constrained to do so.

CHAPTER X

1. It is our duty to be more careful in the performance of the commandment of almsgiving than in that of any other positive commandment, for almsgiving is the mark of the righteous man who is of the seed of our father Abraham, as it is said, *For I have known him, to the end that he may command his children, etc., to do righteousness* (Gen. 18:19). The throne of Israel cannot be established, nor true faith made to stand up, except through charity, as it is said, *In righteousness shalt thou be established* (Isa. 54:14); nor will Israel be redeemed, except through the practice of charity, as it is said, *Zion shall be redeemed with justice, and they that return of her with righteousness* (Isa. 1:27).

2. No man is ever impoverished by almsgiving, nor does evil or harm befall anyone by reason of it, as it is said, *And the work of righteousness shall be peace* (Isa. 32:17).

He who has compassion upon others, others will have compassion upon him, as it is said, *That the Lord may . . . show thee mercy, and have compassion upon thee* (Deut. 13:18).

Whosoever is cruel and merciless lays himself open to suspicion as to his descent, for cruelty is found only among the heathens, as it is said, *They are cruel, and have no compassion* (Jer. 50:42). All Israélites and those that have attached themselves to them are to each other like brothers, as it is said, *Ye are the children of the Lord your God* (Deut. 14:1). If brother will show no compassion to brother, who will? And unto whom shall the poor of Israel raise their eyes? Unto the heathens, who hate them and persecute them? Their eyes are therefore hanging solely upon their brethren.

3. He who turns his eyes away from charity is called a base fellow, just as is he who worships idols. Concerning the worship of idols Scripture says, *Certain base fellows are gone out* (Deut. 13: 14), and concerning him who turns his eyes away from charity it says, *Beware that there be not a base thought in thy heart* (Deut. 15:9). Such a man is also called wicked, as it is said, *The tender mercies of the wicked are cruel* (Prov. 12:10). He is also called a sinner, as it is said, *And he cry unto the Lord against thee, and it be sin in thee* (Deut. 15:10). The Holy One, blessed be He, stands nigh unto the cry of the poor, as it is said, *Thou hearest the cry of the poor.* One should therefore be careful about their cry, for a covenant has been made with them, as it is said, *And it shall come to pass, when he crieth unto Me, that I will hear, for I am gracious* (Exod. 22:26).

4. He who gives alms to a poor man with a hostile countenance and with his face averted to the ground, loses his merit and forfeits it, even if he gives as much as a thousand gold coins. He should rather give with a friendly countenance and joyfully. He should commiserate with the recipient in his distress, as it is said, *If I have not wept for him that was in trouble, and if my soul grieved not for the needy?*

232

(Job 30:25). He should also speak to him prayerful and comforting words, as it is said, *And I caused the widow's heart to sing for joy* (Job 29:13).

5. If a poor man asks you for alms and you have nothing to give him, comfort him with words. It is forbidden to rebuke a poor man or to raise one's voice in a shout at him, seeing that his heart is broken and crushed, and Scripture says, *A broken and contrite heart, O God, Thou wilt not despise* (Ps. 51:19), and again, *To revive the spirit of the humble, and to revive the heart of the contrite ones* (Isa. 57:15). Woe unto him who shames the poor! Woe unto him! One should rather be unto the poor as a father, with both compassion and words, as it is said, *I was a father to the needy* (Job 29:16).

6. He who presses others to give alms and moves them to act thus, his reward is greater than the reward of him who gives alms himself, as it is said, *And the work of righteousness shall be peace* (Isa. 32:17). Concerning alms collectors and their like Scripture says, *And they that turn the many to righteousness (shall shine) as the stars* (Dan. 12:3).

[THE EIGHT DEGREES OF CHARITY]

7. There are eight degrees of almsgiving, each one superior to the other. The highest degree, than which there is none higher, is one who upholds the hand of an Israélite reduced to poverty by handing him a gift or a loan, or entering into a partnership with him, or finding work for him, in order to strengthen his hand, so that he would have no need to beg from other people. Concerning such a one Scripture says, *Thou shalt uphold him; as a stranger and a settler shall he live with thee* (Lev. 25:35), meaning uphold him, so that he would not lapse into want.

8. Below this is he who gives alms to the poor in such a way that he does not know to whom he has given, nor does the poor man know from whom he has received. This constitutes the fulfilling of a religious duty for its own sake, and for such there was a Chamber of Secrets in the Temple, whereunto the righteous would contribute secretly, and wherefrom the poor of good families would draw their sustenance in equal secrecy. Close to such a person is he who contributes directly to the alms fund.

One should not, however, contribute directly to the alms fund unless he knows that the person in charge of it is trustworthy, is a Sage, and knows how to manage it properly, as was the case of Rabbi Hananiah ben Teradion.

9. Below this is he who knows to whom he is giving, while the poor man does not know from whom he is receiving. He is thus like the great among the Sages who were wont to set out secretly and throw the money down at the doors of the poor. This is a proper way of doing it, and a preferable one if those in charge of alms are not conducting themselves as they should.

10. Below this is the case where the poor man knows from whom he is receiving, but himself remains unknown to the giver. He is thus like the great among the Sages who used to place the money in the fold of a linen sheet which they would throw over their shoulder, whereupon the poor would come behind them and take the money without being exposed to humiliation.

11. Below this is he who hands the alms to the poor man before being asked for them.

12. Below this is he who hands the alms to the poor man after the latter has asked for them.

13. Below this is he who gives the poor man less than what is proper, but with a friendly countenance.

14. Below this is he who gives alms with a frowning countenance.

15. The great among the Sages used to hand a perutah to a poor man before praying, and then proceeded to pray, as it is said, *As for me, I shall behold Thy face in righteousness* (Ps. 17:15).

16. ... Whosoever serves food and drink to poor men and orphans at his table, will, when he calls to God, receive an answer and find delight in it, as it is said, *Then shalt thou call, and the Lord will answer* (Isa. 58:9).

17. The Sages have commanded that one should have poor men and orphans as members of his household rather than bondsmen, for it is better for him to employ the former, so that children of Abraham, Isaac, and Jacob might benefit from his possessions rather than children of Ham, seeing that he who multiplies bondsmen multiplies sin and iniquity every day in the world, whereas if poor people are members of his household, he adds to merits and fulfillment of commandments every hour.

18. One should always restrain himself and submit to privation rather than be dependent upon other people or cast himself upon public charity, for thus have the Sages commanded us, saying, "Make the Sabbath a weekday rather than be dependent upon other people." Even if one is a Sage held in honor, once he becomes impoverished, he should engage in a trade, be it even a loathsome trade, rather than be dependent upon other people. It is better to strip hides off animal carcasses than to say to other people, "I am a great Sage, I am a priest, provide me therefore with maintenance." So did the Sages command us. Among the great Sages there were hewers of wood, carriers of beams, drawers of water to irrigate gardens, and workers in iron and charcoal. They did not ask for public assistance, nor did they accept it when offered to them.

19. Whosoever is in no need of alms but deceives the public and does accept them, will not die of old age until he indeed becomes dependent upon other people. He is included among those of whom Scripture says, *Cursed is the man that trusteth in man* (Jer. 17:5). On the other hand, whosoever is in need of alms and cannot survive unless he accepts them, such as a person who is of advanced age, or ill, or afflicted with sore trials, but is too proud and refuses to accept them, is the same as a shedder of blood and is held to account for his own soul, and by his suffering he gains nothing but sin and guilt.

Whosoever is in need of alms but denies himself, postpones the hour, and lives a life of want in order not to be a burden upon the public, will not die of old age until he shall have provided maintenance for others out of his own wealth. Of him and of those like him it is said, *Blessed is the man that trusteth in the Lord* (Jer. 17:7).

Appendix II: Selective Chronology – Developments of English* and Jewish Social Policy and Philanthropy

---

1656   Official resettlement of the Jews in England after expulsion in 1290.

1690   The Ashkenazic Great Synagogue established in Dukes Place, City of London. The management of the synagogues was lay rather than ecclesiastical and controlled by small self-perpetuating oligarchies. Newly prosperous more recent arrivals founded new congregations, which in turn attempted to exclude the new generation of nouveaux riches.

1701   Bevis Marks Sephardic Synagogue erected in the City of London.

1707   Hambro's Synagogue, Ashkenazic breakaway congregation in the City of London.

1744   Persecution of Jews on the Continent.

1745–   Continued persecution motivates emigration.

1761   Ashkenazic New Synagogue erected in the City of London.

1771   Robbery in Chelsea by Jewish criminals, led to outbreak of anti-Jewish feeling. Memorandum submitted by representative of the Great Synagogue in London according to which limitations were imposed on Jewish poor immigrants from Holland. Deportation of Jewish peddlers arrested by police in an extensive round-up throughout England. Lord Suffolk offered thanks by a delegation of the Great Synagogue. Stern attitude of both Sephardic and Ashkenazic élites towards the immigrant poor.

1772   **Opinion given by Attorney General (Thurlow) 'The poor of whatever nation must be maintained by the officers of the parish where they are found. No other person is compellable to relieve them.'**

1779   The establishment of Bread, Meat and Coal Society *'Meshebat Nephesh'*

*Shown by bold print.

(Heb. literally 'restoring the soul') by Louis Cohen.

1800   Patrick Colquhoun's sixth edition of *Police of the Metropolis* emphasized the great extent of Jewish delinquency and proposed, together
with Joshua van Oven – philanthropic adviser to Abraham Goldsmid,
Jewish magnate – the establishment of a system for 'the entire management of the poor' to be financed by the poor rate and an additional
statutory rate on all Jews in London. The scheme included a Jewish
workhouse.

1801   **First census.**

1802   **Health and Morals of Apprentices Act.**

1802   Failure of the Colquhoun–van Oven Scheme, mainly due to the opposition of members of the élite to the mandatory tax proposed.

1806   Jews' Hospital, a children's home founded in Mile End, East End of
London, with money collected by A. Goldsmid for the
Colquhoun–van Oven Scheme.

1807   Jews' Free School established.

1808   **National Vaccine established.**

1815   Untenable treaty between the Three City Synagogues, regarding relief
of the 'foreign poor' who had no claim on them.

1820   Richer Jewish families moved to the west-central and then to the West
End of London.

1827   According to the regulations of the Great Synagogue, claims for relief
could be established by proving membership's connections (similar to
the establishment of parochial settlement under the Old Poor Law).

1828   **Madhouse Act, first asylum inspector appointed.**

1830   **Oastler's letters on 'Yorkshire Slavery'.**

1830–   Struggle for Jewish political emancipation initiated by the most
1858   prominent members of the élite who succeeded in abolishing the
exclusion of Jews from municipal corporations and Parliament.

1831   **Central Board of Health (cholera).**

1831   Following the great cholera epidemic, Jews' Orphan Asylum founded
by Abraham Green (a street vendor of Dutch pickled cucumbers), with
the money collected from the poor and the lower middle class in the
East End.

1834   **Old Poor Law reformed: Poor Law (Amendment) Act.**

1834   East End Unions, where most of the Jews lived, were faced with low
resources and great demands.

1834 on   Jewish élite generally pretended to prevent Jews from having to turn
to the Poor Law, except as a deterrent for 'incorrigible cases' or to
supplement Jewish communal assistance.

1834   The Jewish Board of Deputies suggested to Lord Althrop an amendment to enable Jewish poor to receive relief without violation of their
religious principles.

1835–   The 1834 treaty between the Three City Synagogues (the 'Conjoint

1839	Synagogues') modified through the special efforts of N. M. Rothschild.
1836	The restrictions on immigration, imposed in 1793, abolished.
1836	Registration of Aliens Act. Imperfect system by which all masters of arriving vessels were obliged to provide a list of aliens to customs officials.
1837	**Civil registration begun.**
1839	**Committee of the Council for Education established.**
1840	**Free vaccination instituted.**
1842	Publication of the **Chadwick Report.**
1844	**Factory Act, Health of Towns Commission.**
1844	Henry Faudel's Scheme – comprehensive plan for the amalgamation and centralization of Jewish charities.
1848	**Lunacy Act.**
1853	**Compulsory vaccination instituted.**
1856	Collective action of Jewish cigar-makers in industrial dispute against Jewish employers.
1857–1858	Abraham Benisch, editor of the *Jewish Chronicle* in a series of editorials proposed the establishment of a 'coordinating body' in poor relief to act as Board of Guardians 'for want of a better name'.
1858	Baron Lionel de Rothschild, became first Jewish MP.
1859	The Board of Guardians for relief of the 'strange poor' established. The Relief Committee of the Board started to consider twice weekly applications previously investigated by a paid officer.
1859	Restricted Jewish life in the German States, and aftermath of 1848 rising on the Continent were factors motivating immigration to England. While Jewish élite was advocating restrictions on immigration, Britain was indifferent or pro-immigrant. In London, Jews were concentrated in the eastern part of the City (Whitechapel, Mile End Road, Brick Lane, Spitalfields and adjacent areas). Most of the Anglo-Jewry was native born. The situation of the Jewish poor aggravated as a result of the geographical distance between the rich, who moved westward, and the poor.
1859	The publication of Ephraim Alex's pamphlet, *A Scheme for a Board of Guardians to be formed for the relief of the necessitous foreign poor*. The London Jewish Board of Guardians established by the Three City Synagogues. Ephraim Alex, Overseer of the Poor of the Great Synagogue, was nominated President. Lionel Louis Cohen was the Honorary Secretary, and from 1869 to 1887 was President. L. L. Cohen was a foreign banker and member of the Stock Exchange, later Conservative MP.
1861	Visiting and Work (named Industrial since 1983) Committees of the Board formed. The Board made arrangements by which sewing machines and tools could be hired and/or purchased on easy terms.

1862   Medical Committee of the Board formed.

1862   **Certified Schools Act authorized Poor Law Unions to send work-house children to schools of their own denomination at the expense of the union concerned.** The Board made intensive use of this arrangement.

1866   Loan Committee of the Board formed to help the setting up of small businesses.

1866   **Sanitary Act.** A Sanitary Inspector was appointed by the Board from the middle of the century intermittently and from 1884 was on a more permanent basis.

1867   **Metropolitan Poor Act.**

1867   Investigating Committee of the Board formed.

1868   Poor Law Sub-committee of the Board conducted negotiations with the statutory authorities.

1868   The Jewish electorate in the East End not large enough to be influential in the election campaign.

1869   Statutory Committee of the Board established.

1869   **Charity Organizations Society.** F. D. Mocatta, important supporter and active member of the Board, became the Vice-President of the C.O.S.

1869   **Poor Law Amendment Act empowered unions to put the poor of any one denomination together in a particular workhouse.** Section 17 inserted in the Commons on the motion of Sir David Solomons related specifically to Jews to whom outdoor relief may have been afforded by the Metropolitan Union. Opposition from those parishes where Jews were to be located – fearing that paupers from other parishes and even from abroad would become a charge on their rates.

1869   **'Goshen Minute' suggesting cooperation between the Poor Law statutory authorities and voluntary organizations.**

1869–   The Jewish Board of Guardians under the presidency of
1947   members of the Cohen family (except for the period 1920 to 1930).

1870   Committee for Legislative and Parochial Affairs established to protect the interests of the Board in relation to the wider community.

1870   **Forster's Education Act.**

1870   Jewish voluntary day school regarded as appropriate for immigrant Jewish poor only and no longer open to the natives who increasingly used the School Board system. Jewish day schools which submitted themselves to Government inspection succeeded in receiving grants (as did other denominational schools). Those arrangements further reduced the financial burden of the Jewish élite.

1870   United Synagogue founded by Lionel Louis Cohen, the President of the Board.

1870s   Rapid economic success of the members of the Jewish élite.

1870s   Significant services of the Board were partially financed by the

	Government, while it preserved its organizational independence.
1870– 1914	Jewish Trade Union founded.
1871	Sir George Jessel became the first Jewish member of Government (Solicitor General).
1871	Significant numbers of East European immigrants expelled from Russian border areas. Rumanian Jews fled persecution.
1871	The Jewish Workhouse established in the East End by Solomon (Sholey) Green with extensive lower middle-class financial and moral support. It survived for three years in spite of the fierce opposition of the Board. Its purpose was to absorb Jewish inmates from parish workhouses.
1872	**Public Health Act.**
1873	Canvassing Committee of the Board was established.
1874	Short lived organization of Jewish tailors from Lithuania founded in East London.
1875– 1876	Russo-Turkish War.
1875	**Artisans Dwelling Act.**
1876	First Jewish socialist worker organization 'The Hebrew Socialist Society'.
1876	Aaron Libermann, Jewish socialist leader, departed to America (returned 1879–1880). In his absence, there was a lack of proper leadership for those Jewish workers who were conscious of their difficult conditions and willing to organize themselves.
1876 on	Different Jewish clubs established in the East End inspired by the Settlement Movement.
1879	Emigration Committee of the Board established.
1881 on	Serious discriminations and restrictions on the economic and social life of the Jews in Russia and eastern Europe. Atrocious pogroms.
1881– 1906	Debates on immigration generally misinformed with regard to demographic data. Suspicion existed with regard to the returns of Jewish organizations. Restrictive legislation regarded by some members of the Jewish élite as a violation of the free trade principles.
1881– 1914	The Board used vague and ambiguous system of classification of immigrant, influenced by the Social Darwinism of the period. An application for relief before the end of the 'six month qualifying period' regarded as a proof of failure in the struggle for adaptation to the life in England.
1881– 1914	Fifty-four thousand Jewish immigrants repatriated by the Jewish Board of Guardians. In addition, an unknown number repatriated by other Jewish agencies, sometimes in cooperation with the Board.
1882	Promulgation of the 'Temporary orders concerning the Jews' ('May Laws') in Russia. Savage persecution continued until the 1917

Revolution.

1882   The Russo-Jewish Committee established with the help of Mansion House funds to assist persecuted Russian Jews.

1883–   The Socialist movement in Britain condemned the restrictive
1914   legislation (with few exceptions).

1884   **Toynbee Hall founded.**

1884   *The Lancet* published a special report on 'The Polish Colony of Jew Tailors' emphasizing the poor sanitation in the East End.

1884   The Socialist Jewish Centre established in the East End. Taken over by the Jewish anarchist group in 1892.

1884–   *Polishe Yidel* (Little Polish Jew) began publication. The first
1889   Socialist paper in Yiddish, it became *Die Zukunft* (The Future). *Arbeter Fraint* (Workers' Friend) also began publication. It was the organ of the left wing Jewish Socialists.

1885 on   More successful attempts to organize the Jewish proletariat.

1885   The Jewish Temporary Shelter was founded by Hermann Landau, a nouveau riche immigrant, in spite of the strong resistance of the Jewish élite. The Shelter provided immediate assistance, something that the Board did not. However, Laundau agreed to cooperate with the Board by promising to discourage 'the helpless, the sick, the worthless and the drones' (JC 15, 29 May 1885.) The inmates of the Shelter that could not find employment after fourteen days in England, and sometimes even before that, were turned over to the Board for repatriation.

1885   **Royal Commission on the Housing of the Working Classes, Housing of the Working Classes Act.**

1885   The Four Per Cent Industrial Dwellings Company was established by the Lord Rothschild, S. Montague (Liberal MP for Whitechapel) and N. S. Joseph, in cooperation with the Board and the United Synagogue.

1887   Effort made by the élite to expedite assimilation of the established immigrants 'to Anglicize, humanize and civilize them'. Festive sermon at New West Synagogue by Rabbi Hermann Adler (Chief Rabbi from 1891).

1887   The Federation of Minor Synagogues was founded by S. Montague (later the First Lord Swaything) to group the congregations formed by recent immigrants.

1888   **The House of Lords Committee on the Sweating System.**

1888   **House of Commons Select Committee on Immigration.** Neither committee saw the need for immediate action to restrict immigration.

1890s   **Tightening of the system established by the 1836 Registration of Alien Act.**

1892   The Trades Union Congress passed a protectionist ('fair trade') resolution against alien immigration (repeated in 1894).

1892   N. S. Joseph, an active member of the Board, became Chairman of the

	Executive of the Russo-Jewish Committee and the Conjoint Committee of the Russo-Jewish Committee and the Board, working from the Board's offices.
1893	The Russo-Jewish Committee began repatriation, despite lacking the mandate to do so.
1900	The Anti-Alien Movement became an important factor in the East End and Parliament. Increased Anglo-Jewish élite fears of anti-alienism.
1900	Public demonstrations and letters of protest to newspapers etc., by relatively large groups of young Rumanian Jews who reached London and were 'offered' repatriation in lieu of relief or assistance to emigrate to Canada.
1900	The resolution against repatriation, advanced before the Federation of Synagogues, failed due to the opposition of Sir Samuel Montague and Hermann Landeau, who were generally considered to be more sympathetic to the immigrants.
1900 on	Repatriation opposed by the Zionist Movement.
1902	**Royal Commission on Alien Immigration.** Lord Rothschild, Conservative MP, concurred with the Royal Commission's minority report opposing legalization of restrictive measures against immigration.
1902	**Balfour's Education Act.**
1900–1905	Anti-Semitic outbreaks, were most probably prevented by the voluntary immigration control instituted by the Jewish élite.
1904	The repatriation continued after a brief stop, due to severe pogroms in Russia such as the Kishinev outrage. Many were repatriated promptly upon their arrival. The aim of the élite was to make the parliamentary legislation superfluous.
1904	Strong anti-alien movement. Anti-alien legislation was introduced before Parliament.
1904	Annual Meeting of the Board – the President, Lionel Cohen, justified continuous repatriation by claiming that the repatriated 'had provided themselves failures'. The Board was accused by Leopold Greenberg: 'Jewish charities were supposed to help the Jewish poor; the Board was not created for the convenience of the Jewish rich'.
1904–1905	The Russo-Jewish Committee repatriated over one thousand individuals. Controversial repatriation of highly visible Jewish military deserters from the Tsar's army, who had received sympathetic publicity in the British press.
1905	**Unemployed Workmen's Act**.
1906	**The Aliens Act** aimed at Jewish paupers was passed. This Act laid the basis for future legal control over immigration in Britain. (The Jewish charities could repatriate only those who applied for relief). The Act proved highly effective in keeping immigrants out of England.
1906	Report received, according to which some of the Jewish deserters sent

back to Russia had been shot by the Tsar's firing squads.

1909   **Majority and Minority Poor Laws Reports.**

1911   **National Insurance Act, (incorporated: sickness, disablement, medical treatment, medicine, experimental scheme of unemployment).**

1914   First World War interrupted immigration from the Continent.

Glossary

The following terms are transliterations from Hebrew in Sephardic pronunciation, except where a word is widely used in Ashkenazic form. Other non-English terms not included in the Glossary are explained in the text.

Aliya	*pl. aliyot, lit. ascent.* being called to the Torah (q.v.); an honour bestowed on a worshipper.
Arbayters	workers *(German).*
Arev	*pl. arevim,* guarantor.
Ascamot	*lit. agreements,* regulations or communal statutes of the Sephardic congregations.
Ashkenazi	*pl. Ashkenazim,* a central or eastern European Jew, generally Yiddish-speaking.
Aufklaerer	enlightener; maskil (q.v.) *(German).*
Betteljuden	Jews who were forced to leave their original communities and moved continuously from a Jewish community to another, seeking charity *(German).*
Beytler	beggar *(Yiddish).*
Chutzpa	brazenness, gall.
Evion	*pl. evionim,* poor.
Gabbai Tzedakah	charity treasurer, collector and distributor of charity.
Gemilut Chassadim	deeds of loving kindness, sometimes combined with material help made through personal involvement; not confined to the poor.
Gvir	*pl. gvirim,* a wealthy and influential person.
Hallacha	the legal part of the Talmudic literature (q.v.); an interpretation of the laws of Scriptures.
Haskala	the westernising enlightenment Jewish movement.
Hevra	*pl. hevrot; hevras,* a society or fraternity, generally formed for social and religious purposes, often forming the congregation of a small synagogue; also spelt chevra *(Yiddish).*
Kasher or	usually used in connection with food prepared in accordance

Kosher	with Jewish dietary laws; ritually pure or fit.
Kehilla	*pl. kehillot*, a self-governing community, typically with its own social and religious institutions.
Koved	honour (*Yiddish*).
Landsleit	a fellow Jew who comes from the same district or town, especially in eastern Europe (*Yiddish*).
Landsmanschaft	*pl. landsmanschaften*, organisation or fraternity of persons originating from a particular town or district (*German*).
Lefi Kyodo	according to his status.
Maskil	*pl. maskilim*, adherent of haskala (q.v.).
Minyan	quorum of ten adult males required for divine public service; a prayer-group.
Mitzva	*pl. mitzvot*, a religious obligation, a worthy deed.
Nedava	*pl. nedavot*, alms given to a beggar.
Orchim	visitors, guests; worshippers in the synagogue who do not pay a membership fee to the congregation. The term was used to indicate 'foreign' poor.
Ostjuden	Jews of eastern Europe (*German*).
Parnas	chairman or president of a congregation, community or synagogue warden.
Rachmunes	profound feelings for the misfortune of others and a desire to help them; compassion.
Schlemiel	habitual bungler; dolt (*Yiddish*).
Schlimazel	extremely unlucky person, habitual failure (*Yiddish*).
Schnorrer	beggar, scrounger, one who takes advantage of the generosity of others; parasitic (*Yiddish and Hebrew*).
Sephardi	*pl. Sephardim*, Jews of Spanish or Portuguese descent.
Sepher Torah	scrolls of parchment containing the Pentateuch, read in a synagogue during services.
Shammash	synagogue sexton; beadle.
Shivah	seven-day period of confined formal mourning after the funeral of a close relative.
Shiva Tuve Ha'ir	*lit. seven good citizens*, executive of a local community.
Shtetl	small Jewish community in eastern Europe (*Yiddish*).
Talmud	collection of ancient rabbinic writings consisting of the Mishna and the Gemara, constituting the basis of religious authority for traditional Judaism.
Torah	entire body of Jewish religious law and learning,

including tradition.

Toshav   *pl. toshavim,* *lit. inhabitant,* person who pays a membership fee for a seat in the synagogue.

Tzedakah   charity and social justice, the latter implying assistance as a right and social equality.

Tzedakah Beseter   secret charity that spared the beneficiary the shame of public knowledge, sometimes even not knowing himself who had helped him.

Yikhus   family with respect to wealth and learning *(Yiddish).*

Yiddishkeit   Jewishness *(Yiddish).*

Select Bibliography

Adler, H. (1884). 'Remember the Poor, In Memory of the Baroness Charlotte de Rothschild' in H. Adler (ed.) *Anglo Jewish Memoirs and Other Sermons*, 1909, London: George Routledge & Sons.

Adler, M. N. (1927). 'Memoir of the Late Benjamin Gompertz, etc.', *The Assurance Magazine and Journal of the Institute of Actuaries*, XIII: 1–20.

Alderman, G. (1989). *London Jewry and London Politics, 1889–1986*, London: Routledge.

—— (1983). *The Jews in British Politics*, London: Clarendon.

—— (1992). *Modern British Jewry*, Oxford: Clarendon.

Alexander, L. (1802). *Answer to Mr. Joshua Van Oven's Letters on the Present State of the Jewish Poor with a Word to P. Colquhoun Esq., and Substances for Clauses to Frame a Bill to be Brought into Parliament for the Better Providing for the Poor of the German Jews*, London: Printed by the Author.

—— (1808). *The Axe Laid to the Root: or Ignorance and Superstition Evident in the Character of the Rev. Solomon Hirschell, Major Rabbi, etc.*, London: Printed by the Author.

—— [and Lemoine, H.] (1808). *Memoir of the Life and Commercial Connections of Benjamin Goldsmid of Roehampton*, London.

Arendt, H. (1968). 'On Humanity in Dark Times: Thoughts about Lessing', *Men in Dark Times*, trans. C. and R. Winston, New York: Harcourt, Brace & World.

Aris, S. (1970). *But There Are No Jews in England*, New York: Stein and Day.

Arkin, M. (1975). *Aspects of Jewish Economic History*, Philadelphia: The Jewish Publication Society of America.

Ascamot: *Laws and Regulations of the Congregation of Spanish and Portuguese Jews, The Gates of Heaven, (El Libro De Los Acuerdos)*, revised and amended 1906, London: Wertheimer, Lea & Co.

Ayerst, W. (1848). *The Jews of the Nineteenth Century: A Collection of Essays, Reviews and Historical Notices*, London: The London Society's House.

Bailey, R. and Brake, M. (eds) (1975). *Radical Social Work*, New York: Pantheon Books.

Bentham, J. (1778). *A View of the Hard-Labour Bill, etc.*, London.

—— *Tracts on Poor Laws and Pauper Management*, in J. Bowring, *The Works of Jeremy Bentham*, 1962 edn, 8: 367.

Bergman, Y. (1942). *Ha Tzedakah Be Yisrael* (Heb.), Jerusalem: Tarshish.

Bermant, Ch. (1969). *Troubled Eden*, London: Vallentine, Mitchell.

—— (1971). *The Cousinhood*, New York: Eyre and Spottiswoode.

Binenstock, T. (1951). 'Antiauthoritarian Attitudes in the Eastern European

Shtetel Community', *The American Journal of Sociology*, LVII, 2: 238–55.

Black, E. C. (1988). *The Social Politics of Anglo-Jewry, 1880–1920*, Oxford: Basil Blackwell.

Blizard, W. (1785). *Desultory Reflections on Police, with an Essay on Preventing Crimes and Amending Criminals*, London.

Booth, C. (1889). *The Life and Labour of the People in London (East London)*, London.

—— (1902). *The Life and Labour of the People in London: Series on Poverty, Industry and Religious Influences*, London.

Bottomore, T. (1983). *A Dictionary of Marxist Thought*, London: Blackwell.

—— (1993). *Élites and Society*, rev. and enlarged 2nd edn, New York: Routledge.

Bowring, J. (1962). *The Works of Jeremy Bentham*. First published 1838–1843, 1962 edn.

Brown, M. (1984). 'Anglo-Jewish Houses from the Resettlement to 1800', *TJHSE*, XXVIII.

—— (1989). 'The Jews of Hackney before 1840', *Jewish Historical Studies*, XXX: 81.

Buckman, J. (1983). *Immigrants and the Class Struggle: The Jewish Immigrant in Leeds, 1880–1940*, Manchester: Manchester University Press.

Carlebach, J. (1878). *Karl Marx and the Radical Critique of Judaism*, London: Routledge & Kegan Paul.

Cassell, C. E. (1957). 'The West Metropolitan Jewish School 1845–1897', *TJHSE*, XIX: 115–28.

Cesarani, D. (1990–92). 'The Importance of being Editor: The Jewish Chronicle, 1841–1991', *JHS*, XXXII: 261–2.

Chambers' Biographical Dictionary of Eminent Scotsmen (1853). Glasgow: Blackie and Son [Bibliographical entry of Patrick Colquhoun].

'The Charities and the Poor of London' (1855). *The Quarterly Review*, XCVII: 408–50.

Clark, C.L. and Asquith S. (1985). *Social Work and Social Philosophy*, London: Routledge and Kegan Paul.

A Citizen of London But no Magistrate (1800). *Observations on a Late Publication Intituled A Treatise on the Police of the Metropolis by P. Colquhoun*, London: H. D. Symonds.

Clarke, H. (1859–1860). 'Memoir of Sir Isaac Goldsmid, Bart., Baron Goldsmid and Da Palmeira', *Bankers Magazine*, June 1859: 375–82; July 1859: 449–57; April 1860: 220–4.

Cobbett, W. (1967). *Rural Rides*, G. Woodcock (ed.), Baltimore.

Cohen, A. (1943). *An Anglo-Jewish Scrapbook, 1600–1840: The Jew Through English Eyes*, London.

Cohen, H. F. (1937). *Changing Faces: A Memoir of Louisa Lady Cohen by her Daughter*, London: Martin Hopkinson.

Cohen, L. (1919). *Arthur Cohen – A Memoir by His Daughter for His Descendants*, London: Bickers and Son.

Cohen, L. (1935). *Lady de Rothschild and her Daughters, 1821–1931*, London: John Murray.

Cohen, S. J. (1815). *Shorshei Emunah [Elements of Faith for the Use of Jewish Youth]*, trans. J. van Oven, London.

Cole, G. (1938). *Persons and Periods*, London: Macmillan.

Collard, D. (1978). *Altruism and Economy: A study of Non Selfish Economics*,

Oxford: Oxford University Press.

Collini, S. (1976). 'Hobhouse, Bosanquet and the State: Philosophical Idealism and Political Argument in England 1880–1918', *Past and Present*, 72: 87–111.

[Colquhoun, P.] (1796). *A Treatise on the Police of the Metropolis by a Magistrate*, 3rd edn, revised and enlarged, London: H. Fry.

Colquhoun, P. (1799). *The State of Indigence and the Situation of the Casual Poor in the Metropolis, Explained, etc.*, London: H. Baldwin.

—— (1800). *A Treatise on the Commerce and Police of the River Thames*, London.

—— (1806). *A New and Appropriate System of Education for the Labouring People*, London: J. Hatchard.

—— (1806). *Treatise of Indigence*.

—— (1812). 'Proposition for Ameliorating the Conditions of the Poor', *Quarterly Review*.

—— (1818). *Considerations on the Means of Affording Profitable Employment to the Redundant Population of Great Britain*, London.

The Commercial Habits of the Jews (1809), London.

Critchley, T. A. (1967). *A History of Police in England and Wales, 1900–66*, London: Constable.

Crosland, C. A. R. (1963). *The Future of Socialism*, New York: Schoken Books.

Cuddihy, J. M. (1976). *The Ordeal of Civility*, 2nd edn, New York: A Delta Book.

Danzig, A. (1810). *Chayyei Adam*, Vilna.

A Daughter of Israel [pseud.] (1818) *The Jewish Preceptress, or, Elementary Lessons Written Chiefly for the Use of the Female Children Educated at the Jews Hospital*, London.

Domb, C. (ed.) (1980). *Maaser Kesafim – Giving a Tenth to Charity*, Jerusalem: Feldheim.

Durkheim, E. (1964). *The Division of Labour in Society*, London: The Free Press of Glencoe.

Eden, F. M. (1797). *The State of the Poor: Or A History of the Labouring Classes in England from the Conquest to the Present Period, with Parochial Reports*, 1928 edn, 3 vols, London: George Routledge & Sons.

Emanuel, C. H. L. (1910). *A Century and a Half of Jewish History*, London.

Emden, P. H. (1943). *Jews of Britain, A Series of Biographies*, London: Sampson Low, Marston and Co.

Endelman, T. M. (1979). *The Jews of Georgian England 1714–1830: Tradition and Change in a Liberal Society*, Philadelphia: Jewish Publication Society of America.

—— (1980). 'Liberalism, Laissez-Faire, and Anglo-Jewry, 1700–1905', *Contemporary Jewry*, 5, 2.

—— (1983). 'Native Jews and Foreign Jews in London, 1870–1914' in D. Berger (ed.) *The Legacy of Jewish Migration 1881 and its Impact*, New York: Brooklyn College Press.

—— (1990). *Radical Assimilation in English Jewish History, 1656–1945*, Indianapolis: Indiana University Press.

—— (1991). 'English Jewish History', *Modern Judaism* II, 1: 91–109.

—— (1992). 'Jewish Communal Structure in Britain from the Resettlement to the Present', *Studien zur judischen Geschichte und Soziologie – Festschrift Julius Carlebach*, Heidelberg: Carl Winter Universitätsverlag.

—— (1981). 'L'Activité Économique Des Juifs Anglais', *XVIIIᵉ Siècle*: 113–26.

Ensor, G. (1811). *On National Education*, London, Longman.

Entzinger, H. B. (1987). 'Race, Class and the Shaping of a Policy for Immigrants: The Case of the Netherlands', *International Immigration* XXV, 1: 5.

[Faudel, H.] (1844). *Suggestions to the Jews for Improvement on Reference to Their Charities, Education and Government, by a Jew*: London.

Faudel, H. (1844). *A Brief Investigation into the System of the Jews' Hospital*, London.

—— (1848). *A Few Words on the Jewish Disabilities addressed to Sir Robert Harry Inglis, Bart., M.P., etc.*, London: James Ridgway.

Feldman, D. (1994). *Englishmen and Jews*, London and New Haven: Yale University Press.

Fido, J. (1977). 'The Charity Organisations Society and Social Casework in London, 1869–1900' in A. P. Donajgrodzki (ed.) *Social Control in Nineteenth Century Britain*, Totowa, N.J.: Rowman and Littlefield.

Finestein, I. (1992). 'Jewish Emancipationists in Victorian England', in J. Frankel and S .J. Zipperstein (eds), *Assimilation and Community: The Jews in Nineteenth Century Europe*, Cambridge: Cambridge University Press, 52.

—— (1957). *A Short History of Anglo-Jewry*, London: Lincolns-Prager.

—— (1993). *Jewish Society in Victorian England: Collected Essays*, London: Valentine Mitchell.

Fishman, W. (1975). *East End Jewish Radicals, 1875–1914*, London: Duckworth.

Frankel, J. (1987). 'The Russian-Jewish Question and the Board of Deputies', *Transition and Change, Essays in Jewish History Presented in Honor of Shmuel Ettinger*, Jerusalem: The Historical Society of Israel.

Fraser, D. (1973). *The Evolution of the British Welfare State*, London: The Macmillan Press.

Frey, J. S. (1813). *Narrative of Joseph Samuel C .F. Frey with An Address to Christians of all Denominations*, London: Gale, Curtis and Fenner.

Frish, E. (1924). *An Historical Survey of Jewish Philanthropy*, New York: Macmillan.

Gainer, B. (1972). *The Alien Invasion, The Origin of the Aliens' Act of 1905*, London: Heinemann.

Garrard, J. A. (1971). *The English and Immigration, 1880–1910*, London: Oxford University Press.

Gartner, L. P. (1960). *The Jewish Immigrant in England, 1870–1914*, 2nd rev. edn 1973, London: George Allen & Unwin.

'George Ensor On National Education', Review in *The Quarterly Review* (1811).

George, V. (1968). *Social Security: Beveridge and After*, London: Routledge and Kegan Paul.

—— (1973). *Social Security and Society*, London: Routledge and Kegan Paul.

George, V. and Wilding, P. (1976). *Ideology and Social Welfare*, London: Routledge and Kegan Paul.

—— (1994). *Welfare and Ideology*, New York, Harvester, Wheatsheaf.

Ginsburg, N. (1979). *Class, Capital and Social Policy*, London: Macmillan.

Goldsmid, F. H. (1830). *Two Letters, in Answer to the Objections Urged Against Mr Grant's Bill for the Relief of the Jews*, London: W.J. Ruffy.

Gough, I. (1979). *The Political Economy of the Welfare State*, London: Macmillan.

Green, J. (1991). *A Social History of the Jewish East End in London, 1914–1939*, New York: The Edwin Mellen Press.

Gutwein, D. (1992). *The Divided Élite: Economics, Politics and Anglo-Jewry*,

1882–1917, Leiden: E.J. Brill.

Hart, J. (1977). 'Religion and Social Control in the Mid-Nineteenth Century' in A. P. Donajgrodzki (ed.) *Social Control in Nineteenth Century Britain*, Totowa, N.Y.: Rowman and Littlefield.

Heertje, A. (1970–73). *On David Ricardo (1772–1823)*, *TJHSE*, XXIV.

Henriques, H. (1974). *The Jews and the English Law*, Clifton, New Jersey: A.M. Kelley.

Highmore, A. (1810). *Pietas Londinensis*, London.

—— (1822). *Philanthropia Metropolitana: A View of the Charitable Institutions Established in and near London, Chiefly during the Last Twelve Years*, London.

Hochberg, S. A. (1988/92). 'The Repatriation of Eastern European Jews from Great Britain, 1881–1914', *Jewish Social Studies*, L, 1–2: 51.

Holmes, C. (1988). *John Bull's Island Immigration and British Society, 1871–1971*, London: Macmillan Education.

Howe, D. (1987). *An Introduction to Social Work Theory*, Aldershot, Hants: Wildwood House.

Huxley, T. H. (1888). 'The Struggle for Existence: A Programme', *Nineteenth Century*.

Hyamson, A. M. (1908). *A History of the Jews in England*, London: Methuen.

—— (1951). *The Sephardim of England. A History of the Spanish and Portuguese Jewish Community, 1491–1951*, London.

Jacobs, J. (1891). *Studies in Jewish Statistics, Social, Vital and Anthropometric*, London: D. Nutt.

Jacobs, J. and Wolf, L. (1888). *Bibliotheca Anglo-Judaica: A Bibliographical Guide to Anglo-Jewish History*, London.

Jewish Board of Guardians [London] Reprint of the Book of Remembrance 1859–1929, 1929.

Johnson, P. and Lesser, E. D. (1984). 'The Birmingham Hebrew Philanthropic Society' in Z. Josephs ed. *Birmingham Jewry II: More Aspects, 1740–1930*, Birmingham: The Birmingham Jewish History Research Group.

Jones, C. (1977). *Immigration and Social Policy in Britain*, London: Tavistock.

'On Juvenile Delinquency in the Metropolis' (1816). *The Philanthropist*, VI: 199–210.

Kaplan, M. (1972). *Judaism as a Civilisation*, 2nd edn, NewYork: Schocken.

Kant, I. (1964). *The Doctrine of Virtue*, trans. M. J. Gregor, New York: Harper and Row.

Katz, J. (1972). *Emancipation and Assimilation: Studies In Modern Jewish History*, Westmead, Farnborough.

—— (1993). 'On Jewish Social History: Epochal and Supra-Epochal Historiography', *Jewish History*, VII, 1: 90, Haifa University Press.

Kershen, A. J. (1988). *Trade Unionism amongst the Jewish Tailoring Workers of London, 1872–1915*, Research Papers of the London Museum of Jewish Life, Department of History of the University of Leicester.

—— (1990). 'Trade Unionism amongst the Jewish Tailoring Workers of London and Leeds, 1872–1915' in D. Cesaran (ed.) *The Making of Modern Anglo-Jewry*, Oxford: Basil Blackwell.

Kingsley, C. (1850). *Alton Locke*, London.

—— (1877). *Cheap Clothes and Nasty* in *Alton Locke*, 1877 edn.

Kokosalakis, N. (1982). *Ethnic Identity and Religion: Tradition and Change in*

Liverpool Jewry, Washington, D.C.: University Press of America.

Kropotkin, P. (1972). *Mutual Aid: A Factor of Evolution*, Avrich P. (ed.), London: Allen Lane.

Kutzik, A. (1959). *Social Work and Jewish Values: Basic Area of Consonance and Conflict*, Washington, D.C.: Public Affairs Press.

Laws and Regulations of the "Gates of Hope" Incorporated Charity Schools for Educating, Clothing, and Apprenticing, etc. (1844) London: L. Thompson.

Laws and Regulations of the Society called "Meshebat Naphesh" [Restoring the Soul] for the Relief of the Poor (1797). London: L. Alexander.

Lehmann, R. P. (1961). *Nova Bibliotheca Anglo-Judaica: A Bibliographical Guide to Anglo-Jewish History, 1937–1960*, London.

—— (1973). *Anglo-Jewish Bibliography, 1937–1970*.

Lemoine, H. (1810). Letter, 'On the present State of the Jews', *Gentleman's Magazine*, June: 514–16.

'Letter' *Monthly Magazine*, 26, September 1806: 108–12.

Levin, M. (1975). *The Idea of Professional Modernization in the Ideology of the Haskalah Movement* [Heb.], Jerusalem: Bialik Institute.

Levin, S. S. (1957). 'The Origins of the Jews' Free School', *TJHSE*, XIX: 1–18.

Liberles, R. (1987). 'The Jews and Their Bill: Jewish Motivations in the Controversy of 1753', *Jewish History* 2, 2: 29–36.

Liebman, A. (1979). *Jews and the Left*, New York: John Wiley.

Lindo, E. H. (1838). *A Jewish Calendar [with a list of Religious and Charitable Institutions of the Jews in London with the Date of Their Foundation]*, London: L. Thompson.

Lipman, V. D. (1954). *Social History of the Jews in England*, London: Watts.

—— (1959). *A Century of Social Service, 1859–1959*, London: Routledge and Kegan Paul.

—— (1975). 'The Anglo-Jewish Community in Victorian Society' in D. Noy and I. Ben-Ami (eds) *Studies in the Cultural Life of the Jews in England*, Jerusalem: The Magnes Press.

—— (1990). *A History of the Jews in Britain since 1858*, Leicester: Leicester University Press.

Lissack, J. M. (1851). *Jewish Perseverance or the Jew, at Home and Abroad: An Autobiography*, London: Adams.

Low, S. Jnr. (1850). *The Charities of London, Comprehending the Benevolent and Religious Institutions, their Origin and Design, Progress and present Position*, London: Printed by the author.

Magnus, L. (1909). *The Jewish Board of Guardians and the Men Who Made It*, London: The Jewish Board of Guardians.

Mahler, R. (1946). 'The Social and Political Aspects of the Haskalah in Galicia', *YIVO Annual of Jewish Social Science*.

Maimon, R. Moshe ben, [Maimonides – 1135–1204]). *Gifts for the Poor, The Book of Agriculture, Mishneh Torah*, I. Klein trans. (1979), New Haven: Yale University Press.

—— (1950). 'Progress and Reaction in the Development of Jewish Culture', *Yevul* (Heb.), Merhavia, Ha-Shomer Ha-Tzair.

—— (1952). *Divre Yeme Yisrael: Dorot Ahronim, 1780–1815, 1815–1848 [A History of Modern Jewry: Last Generations]*, Maanit, Israel.

Malthus, T. R. (1817). *Essay on Population*, 1878 edn, London.

Mandler, P. (1987). 'The Making of the New Poor Law Redivivus', *Past and Present*, 117: 131–57.

Marcus, J. R. (1974). 'Shed a Tear for a Transport: The Sad Fate of Feibel, the son of Joseph Jacob of Jever', *Raphael Mahler Jubilee Volume*, Tel Aviv.

Margoliouth, M. (1851). *History of the Jews in Great Britain*, 3 vols, London: Richard Bentley.

Marks, D. W. (1854). 'Never Miss an Opportunity for Doing Good', *Sermons*, II, 1862, London: Barnet.

Marks, D. and Loewy, A. (eds) (1882). *Memoir of Sir Francis Henry Goldsmid, Bart. M.P.*, London.

Marshall, T. H. (1965). *Social Policy*, London: Hutchinson University Library.

—— (1968). *The Old Poor Law, 1795–1834*.

Marx, K. (1975). *Marx and Engels: Collected Works*, London: Lawrence and Wishart.

Maunder, S. (1847). *The Treasury of Knowledge*, London.

Mayhew, H. (1851). *London Labour and the London Poor*, 1967 edn, 4 vols, London: Frank Cass.

Mazlish, B. (1968). 'James Mill and the Utilitarians', *Daedalus*, 97, 3.

'Memoir of the Late Abraham Goldsmid' (1810), *Gentleman's Magazine*, LXIII, Part 2nd.

Mendelsohn, E. (1970). *Class Struggle in the Pale: The Formative Years of the Jewish Workers' Movement in Tsarist Russia*, Cambridge: Cambridge University Press.

"Meshebat Naphesh" [Restoring the Soul] Early History and Anecdotes, 5540–5640 (1879), London.

Merrington, W. (1976). *University College Hospital and Its Medical School*, London: Heinemann.

Midwinter, E. (1994). *The Development of Social Welfare in Britain*, Buckingham: Open University Press.

Mill, J. S. (1859). *On Liberty*, London.

Mills, J. (1853). *The British Jews*, London.

Mishkinsky, M. (1973). 'The Jewish Labour Movement and European Socialism' in H. H. Ben-Sasson, and S. Ettinger (eds) *Jewish Society Through the Ages*, New York: Schocken Books.

Misrahi, R. (1977). *Marx et la question Juive*, Paris: Gallimand.

Mizruchi, E. (1983). *Regulating Society: – Marginality and Social Control in Historical Perspective*, New York: The Free Press.

Mocatta, A. (1969–70). 'Frederic David Mocatta, 1828–1905', *TJHSE*, XXIII.

Montague, L. H. (1913). *Samuel Montague: First Baron Swaythling*, London.

'The Necessity of Erecting an Hospital for Jews of the German and Polish Communities in London', Letter, *Hebrew Review and Magazine of Rabbinical Literature*, Vol III, 11.9.1835.

Morton, F. (1962). *The Rothschilds* [Hebrew translation] Tel Aviv, Or.

Newman A. (1976). *The United Synagogue*, London: Routledge and Kegan Paul.

—— (1981). *The Jewish East End, 1840–1939: Proceedings of the Conference held on 22 October 1980*, London: JHSE.

—— (1985). 'A Note on Recent Research on the Jewish East End of London', *JJS*, 27, 2: 135–8.

Nusbaum, D. (1978). *Social Justice and Social Policy in the Jewish Tradition: The Satisfaction of Basic Human Needs in Poznan in the Seventeeth and Eighteenth*

Centuries, Unpublished Ph.D. dissertation, The Florence Heller Graduate School for Advanced Social Work, Brandeis University, USA.

Owen, D. (1965). *English Philanthropy 1660–1960*, London: Oxford University Press.

Panitz, E. L. (1963–4). 'The Polarity of American Jewish Attitudes towards Immigration', *American Jewish Historical Quarterly*, LIII, 1–4: 111, 120.

Pellatt, A. (1829). *Brief Memoir of the Jews in Relation to their Civil and Municipal Disabilities*, London: Hatchard.

Peretz, I. L. (1947). 'Four Generations – Four Wills', *Peretz*, S. Liptzin trans and ed., New York: Yiddish Scientific Institute.

Philo Judaeis [pseud.] (1802). *A Letter to Abraham Goldsmid, Esq. Containing Strictures on Mr. Joshua van Oven's Letters on the Present State of the Jewish Poor Pointing out the Impracticability of Ameliorating their Condition through the Medium of Taxation and Coercion, etc.*, London: Blacks and Parry.

Piccioto, J. (1956). *Sketches of Anglo-Jewish History*, I. Finestein (ed.), London.

Pieris, R. (1954). 'The Contributions of Patrick Colquhoun to Social Theory and Social Philosophy', *University of Ceylon Review*, XII, 3: 129–60.

Pinker, R. (1971). *Social Theory and Social Policy*, London: Heinemman Educational Books.

—— (1979). *The Idea of Welfare*, London: Heinemann.

Piven, F. F. and Cloward, R. A. (1971). *Regulating the Poor: The Functions of Public Welfare*, New York: Vintage Books.

Pollins, H. (1981). *A History of the Jewish Working Men's Club and Institute, 1874–1912*, Oxford: Ruskin College Library.

—— (1982). *Economic History of the Jews in England*, Rutherford Associated University Presses.

Popper, K. R. (1957). *The Open Society and its Enemies*, London: Routledge & Kegan Paul.

Potter, B. (1888). 'East London Labour', *The Nineteenth Century* XXIV: 138.

—— (1902). 'The Jews of London' in C. Booth (ed.), *Life and Labour of the People in London, 1890–1900*, 1st ser. iv., London.

Poulantzas, N. (1979). *Political Power in Social Classes*, London: Verso Edition.

Poynter, J. R. (1969). *Society and Pauperism*, London: Routledge & Kegan Paul.

'Proposals of Mr. Rothschild, to the Committee of the Great Synagogue', *The Hebrew Intelligencer*, 1 January 1823.

Radzinowicz, L. (1956). *A History of English Criminal Law and Its Administration*, London: Stevens and Sons.

Raynor, P. (1985). *Social Work, Justice and Control*, Oxford: Basil Blackwell.

Reeves, F. (1983). *British Racial Discourse, A Study of British Political Discourse about Race and Race-related matters*, Cambridge: Cambridge University Press.

Rose, E. J. B. (1969). *Colour and Citizenship: A Report on British Race Relations*, London: Oxford University Press.

Rose, M. (1972). *The Relief of Poverty, 1834–1914*, London: The Economic History Society.

Rosenfeld, Ch. W. (1890). *Torat Ha'adam, Teaching of Humanity: A Treatise Throwing some Light on Certain Movements of the Day*, M.M., trans, London.

Ross, E. A. (1922). *Social Control: A Survey of the Foundations of Order*, London: MacMillan.

Roth, C. (1937). *Magna Bibliotheca Anglo-Judaica: A Bibliographical Guide to*

Anglo-Jewish History, new edn, London.

—— (1938). *Anglo-Jewish Letters, 1158–1917*, London: The Sucino.

—— (1943). *History of the Jewish People*, London.

—— (1949). *History of the Jews in England*, 2nd edn, London.

—— (1950). *History of the Great Synagogue*, London.

—— (1962). 'The Court Jews in Edwardian England', *Essays and Portraits in Anglo-Jewish History*, Philadelphia.

Rubens, K. D. (1980). *The Four Per Cent Industrial Dwellings Company Limited Its Formation and Its East End Developments, 1885–1901*, Submitted to a Symposium on London's East End, London.

Rubinstein, W. C. (1982). *The Left, The Right and The Jews*, London: Croom Helm.

Rules and Regulations for the Management of the Jews' Hospital, Mile End Called Neveh Tzedek, [Abode of the Righteous] (1808), London: J. Daniel.

Rumney, J. (1933) *The Economic and Social Development of the Jews in England, 1730–1860*. Ph.D. diss., University of London.

Russell, C. and Lewis, H. S. (1900). *The Jews in London: A Study of Racial Character and Present Day Conditions: Being Two Essays Prepared For the Toynbee Trustees*, London: T. Fischer Unwin.

Salaman, G. and Thompson K. (1980). *Control and Ideology in Organizations*, Milton Keynes: The Open University Press.

Salbstein, M. N. (1982). *The Emancipation of the Jews in Britain: The Question of the Admission of the Jews to Parliament, 1828–1860*, London: Fairleigh Dickinson University Press.

Saville, J. (1957–8). 'The Welfare State: An Historical Approach', *New Reasoner*, 3.

Schappes, M. U. (1950). *A Documentary History of the Jews in the United States*, New York: The Citadel Press.

Schweinitz, K. de (1961). *England's Road to Social Security*, New York: Perpetua Edition, A. S. Barnes.

Shalom Aleichem [pseud.] (1955). *The Great Fair, Scenes From My Childhood*, trans T. Kahana, New York: The Noonday Press.

Shapiro, E. S. (1987). 'Jews with Money', *Judaism*, 36, 1: 7–16.

Simey, M. (1951). *Charitable Effort in Liverpool in the 19th Century*, Liverpool.

Smith, R. M. (1981). 'The London Jews' Society and Patterns of Jewish Conversion in England, 1801–1859', *JSS*, XLIII, 3–4: 275–90.

Smollett, T. G. (1790). *History of England*, London.

Southey, R. [Don Manuel Alvarez Espriella] (1960). 'Letters from England' in E. Rosenberg (ed.) *From Shylock to Svengali: Jewish Stereotypes in English Fiction*, Stanford: Stanford University Press.

Sraffa, P. (1951–5 and 1973). *The Works and Correspondence of David Ricardo*, I–XI, Cambridge.

Stallard, J. H. (1867). *London Pauperism Amongst Jews and Christians: An Inquiry into the Principles and Practice of Outdoor Relief, etc.*, London: Saunders & Otley.

Stedman-Jones, G. (1971). *Outcast London*, Oxford: Clarendon Press.

Stein, S. (1964). 'Some Ashkenazi Charities in London at the End of the Eighteenth and the Beginning of the Nineteenth Centuries', *TJHSE*, XX: 63–81.

Susser, B. (1993). *The Jews of South-West England: The Rise and Decline of their Medieval and Modern Communities*, Exeter, Devon: University of Exeter Press.

de Swaan, A. (1988). *In Care of the State*, Cambridge: Polity Press.

Titmus, R. M. (1968). *Commitment to Welfare*, London: Allen and Unwin.
—— (1970). *The Gift Relationship*, London: Pelican.
Trevelyan, G. M. (1944). *English Social History*, 1946 edn, London: Longman.
Tucker, J. (1753). *A Letter to a Friend Concerning Naturalizations*, London.
Van Oven, J. (1802). *Letters on the Present Station of the Jewish Poor in the Metropolis with Propositions for Ameliorating Their Condition, etc.*, London: W. J. and J. Richardson.
Veblen, T. (1899). *The Theory of Leisure Class*, 1953 edn, New York: The New American Library.
Walker, H. and Beaumont, B. (1981). *Probation Work: Critical Theory and Socialist Practice*, Oxford: Basil Blackwell.
Wendeborn, F. A. (1791). *A View of England Towards the Close of the Eighteenth Century* trans from German by the author, II, London.
White, J. (1981). *Rothschild's Buildings*, London.
Widroff, J. (1987). *Medieval Jewish Social Welfare Institutions*, Unpublished Doctor of Social Welfare Dissertation, Yeshiva University, Wurzweiler School of Social Work, USA.
Wilensky, H. L. and Lebeaux, C.H. (1958). *Industrial Society and Social Welfare*, 1968 edn, New York: The Free Press.
Williams, B. (1976). *The Making of Manchester Jewry, 1740–1875*, Manchester: Manchester University Press.
—— (1990). '"East and West": Class and Community in Manchester Jewry, 1850–1914' in D. Cesarani (ed.) *The Making of Modern Anglo-Jewry*, Oxford: Basil Blackwell.
Woodroofe, K. (1966). *From Charity to Social Work in England and the United States*, London: Routledge & Kegan Paul.
Wolf, L. (1934). 'Early Ashkenazi Charities', in C. Roth (ed.) *Essays in Jewish History*, London: JHSE.
Young, A. F. and Ashton, E. T. (1956). *British Social Work in the Nineteenth Century*, London: Routledge & Kegan Paul.
Zborowski, M. and Herzog, E. (1952). *Life Is With People: The Culture of the Shtetl*, 1962 edn, New York: Schocken Books.
Zunz, O. (1985). 'Reflections on American Social History' in O. Zunz (ed.) *Reliving the Past*, Chapel Hill: The University of North Carolina Press.

Printed Materials – Newspapers and Journals (London)

Arbeter Fraint
Bankers' Magazine
Commons Journal
The Gentleman's Magazine
Hebrew Review and Magazine of Rabbinical Literature
The Jewish Chronicle
Monthly Magazine
Polishe Yidel – Die Zukunft
The Philanthropist
The Quarterly Review
The Voice of Jacob

Index